D1265130

THE TRADITIONS OF ELEAZAR BEN AZARIAH

BROWN UNIVERSITY
BROWN JUDAIC STUDIES

Number 2

THE TRADITIONS OF ELEAZAR BEN AZARIAH

by Tzvee Zahavy

SCHOLARS PRESS
Missoula, Montana

THE TRADITIONS OF ELEAZAR BEN AZARIAH

by

Tzvee Zahavy

Published by
SCHOLARS PRESS
for
Brown University

Distributed by

SCHOLARS PRESS
University of Montana
Missoula, Montana 59812

THE TRADITIONS OF ELEAZAR BEN AZARIAH

by

Tzvee Zahavy

Library of Congress Cataloging in Publication Data

Zahavy, Tzvee.
The traditions of Eleazar ben Azariah.

(Brown Judaic studies; no. 2)
Bibliography: p.
Includes indexes.
1. Eleazar ben Azariah. 2. Talmud—Criticism, interpretation, etc. I. Title. II. Series.
BM502.3.E38Z33 296.1'23'06 76-46373
ISBN 0-89130-095-3

Printed in the United States of America
1 2 3 4 5
Printing Department
University of Montana
Missoula, Montana 59812

To

My Father and Mother

Zev and Edith Zahavy

CONTENTS

Page

PREFACE

This study sets forth the definitive limits of our knowledge about Eleazar b. Azariah, a rabbinic authority of the second century C.E. It is an analytical historical investigation of the extant evidence about the master, not a narrative biography of the man. Essentially all of the facts and conclusions reached in the pages which follow are based upon intensive literary-critical analysis of rabbinic texts. I first learned of the value of the critical examination of rabbinic literature for historical purposes from the work of my teacher, Professor Jacob Neusner. In his *Eliezer Ben Hyrcanus: The Tradition and the Man* (Leiden, 1973) he crystallizes the enterprise of analytical biography of rabbinic masters. This study continues and expands upon the agendum set down there. From Professor Neusner's more recent studies in the multi-volumed *A History of the Mishnaic Law of Purities* (Leiden, 1974-77) I have learned further that rabbinic editors often significantly reshaped our sources. Thus the literary and substantive context of each pericope must be taken into consideration. In the chapters which follow I add this new dimension to the study of the sources pertaining to a single master. Most notably I consider the formal context of pericopae in Mishnah in Chapter V (section vi. b), and the substantive context of the legal rulings in Mishnah-Tosefta in Chapter VII.

Clearly Professor Neusner has provided the scholarly underpinnings for this study. Throughout my three years at Brown he has also supported this undertaking in a personal way by reading and offering critical insights on each page. During that time I presented most of the material that follows in his dissertation seminar. I can in no way adequately express my gratitude for the time and effort he invested in overseeing my research.

I also recognize my debt to Professors Ernest F. Frerichs and Horst R. Moehring who served as readers for the dissertation. Through their courses at Brown I was able to perceive many of the ideals of critical scholarship. Friends and fellow students at Brown shared as well in the progress of this work. From among them I single out Professor William Scott Green of the University of Rochester. He helped me through my first semester at Brown and continues to offer stimulation and advice. Professors Baruch Bokser of the University of California at Berkeley, Charles Primus of Notre Dame University, Jack Lightstone of Concordia University, Richard Sarason of Brown University, Rabbi Shammai Kanter, Joel Gereboff, Irving Mandelbaum, Michael Rosen and Spencer Ackerman all offered helpful insights and criticism on various portions of the work. Though many may be thanked, the responsibility for shortcomings in the study remains solely my own.

Rav Joseph B. Soloveitchik, my *rebbe*, encouraged me to undertake further graduate studies after my ordination. I thank him for his guidance and continued concern. The Memorial Foundation for Jewish Culture and the National Foundation for Jewish Culture provided grants which helped support this project. I also gratefully acknowledge the generous assistance towards the publication of this volume from the Max Richter Foundation and from Mr. Howard L. Apothaker in memory of Esther Eisenberg.

My wife Bernice and my son Yitzhak Eliyahu serve as my inspiration and support. Without them and their love I could not have so greatly enjoyed this enterprise. My parents encouraged me throughout twenty-two years of schooling and provide me with the ideals to live up to. It is to them that I dedicate this book with the greatest of affection.

T.Z.
Minneapolis, Minnesota

ABBREVIATIONS

A.Z.	'Abodah Zarah
Arak.	'Arakhin
ARN	'Abot deRabbi Nathan
b.	Babli, Babylonian Talmud
B.B.	Baba' Batra'
Bekh.	Bekhorot
Ber.	Berakhot
Bert.	Obadiah di Rossi, commentary of, in M. ed. Romm, Vilna, 1887.
Beṣ.	Beṣah
Bik.	Bikkurim
B.M.	Baba' Mesi'a'
B.Q.	Baba' Qamma'
B.R.	Bereshit Rabbah
Chron.	Chronicles
Dan.	Daniel
Deut.	Deuteronomy
E	Erfurt MSS of T.
Ed.	'Eduyyot
EJ	*Encyclopedia Judaica*, Jerusalem, 1971.
Epstein, *Tan.*	Jacob N. Epstein, *Introduction to Tannaitic Literature*, Jerusalem, 1962.
Erub.	'Erubin
Ex.	Exodus
Ez.	Ezekiel
G	Abraham I. Katsh, *Ginze Mishnah*, 159 Fragments from The Cairo Genizah in the Saltykov-Schedrin Library in Leningrad, Jerusalem, 1970.
Gen.	Genesis
Giṭ.	Giṭṭin
Goodblatt	David Goodblatt, *Rabbinic Instruction in Sassanian Babylonia*, Leiden, 1975.

GRA	Elijah b. Solomon Zalman (1720-1797), commentary of, from M. ed. Romm.
H	Hamburg MSS of b.
Ḥag.	Ḥaggigah
Ḥal.	Ḥallah
HD	*Ḥasde David*; David Pardo, *Sefer Ḥasde David*, part iv, Jerusalem, 1970.
Ḥul.	Ḥullin
Jastrow	Marcus Jastrow, *A Dictionary of the Targumim, The Talmud Babli and Yerushalmi and Midrashic Literature*, reprint, New York, 1971.
Jer.	Jeremiah
K	Georg Beer, ed., *Faksimile-Ausgabe des Mischna Codex Kaufman A50*, Jerusalem, 1968.
Kal.	Kallah
Kel.	Kelim
Ket.	Ketubot
Kil.	Kil'ayim
L	W. H. Loew, *HaMishnah 'al pi Ketav-Yad Cambridge*, Jerusalem, 1967.
Lev.	Leviticus
M.	Mishnah
MA	*Mishnah 'Aḥaronah*; Ephraim Isaac of Premsyla, commentary of, from M. ed. Romm.
Maas.	Ma'aserot
Mak.	Makkot
Meg.	Megillah
Mekh.	Mekhilta
Men.	Menaḥot
Miq.	Miqva'ot
M.Q.	Mo'ed Qaṭan
M.S.	Ma'aser Sheni
MS	*Melekhet Shlomo*, Shlomo bar Joshua Adeni (1567-1625), commentary of, in M. ed. Romm.

Mu.	*Babylonian Talmud: Codex Munich*, repr. Jerusalem, 1971.
N	*Mishnah 'im Perush HaRambam: Defus Rishon Napoli*, [5]252, Jerusalem, 1970.
Naz.	Nazir
Ned.	Nedarim
Neg.	Nega'im
Neh.	Nehemiah
Neusner, *Development*	Jacob Neusner, *Development of a Legend*, Leiden, 1970.
Neusner, *Eliezer*	Jacob Neusner, *Eliezer b. Hyrcanus: The Tradition and the Man*, Leiden, 1973.
Neusner, *HJB*	Jacob Neusner, *A History of the Jews in Babylonia*, Leiden, 1965-70.
Neusner, *HMLP*	Jacob Neusner, *A History of the Mishnaic Law of Purities*, Leiden, 1974-77.
Neusner, *Pharisees*	Jacob Neusner, *Rabbinic Traditions About the Pharisees Before 70*, Leiden, 1971.
Nid.	Niddah
Num.	Numbers
O	Oxford MSS of b.
Ohal.	'Ohalot
P	*Shishah Sidre Mishnah. Ketav-Yad Parma De Rossi 138*, Jerusalem, 1970.
Par.	Parah
Par.	*Parašah*
PB	*Mishnah Codex Parma "B" De Rossi*, intro., M. Bar Asher, Jerusalem, 1971.
Pes.	Pesaḥim
Pis.	Pisḥa
Prov.	Proverbs
Ps.	Psalms
Qid.	Qiddushin
Qoh.	Qohelet
R., Rab.	Rabbah, Rabbati

R.H.	Rosh HaShanah
Rosh	Asher b. Yehiel (1250-1327), commentary of, in M. ed. Romm.
Sam.	Samuel
San.	Sanhedrin
Sens	Samson ben Abraham of Sens (1150-1230), commentary of.
Shab.	Shabbat
Sheb.	Shebi'it
Sof.	Soferim
Song	Song of Songs
Soṭ.	Soṭah
Suk.	Sukkah
T., Tos.	Tosefta
Taan.	Ta'anit
Tam.	Tamid
Tanḥ.	Tanḥuma
Ter.	Terumot
Ṭoh.	Ṭoharot
TYB	*Tiferet Yisrael Boaz*, see TYY
TYT	*Tosafot Yom Tob*, Yom Tob Lipman Heller (1579-1654), in M. ed. Romm.
TYY	*Tiferet Yisrael Yakhin*, Israel ben Gedaliah Lipschutz (1782-1860) with supercommentary of Barukh Isaac Lipschutz (TYB), in M. ed. Romm.
Uqṣ.	'Uqṣin
y.	Yerushalmi, Palestinian Talmud
Yad.	Yadayim
Yeb.	Yebamot
Zeb.	Zebaḥim

TRANSLITERATIONS

	א	=	'
	ב	=	*b*
	ג	=	*g*
	ד	=	*d*
	ה	=	*h*
	ו	=	*w*
	ז	=	*z*
	ח	=	*ḥ*
	ט	=	*ṭ*
	י	=	*y*
ך	כ	=	*k*
	ל	=	*l*
ם	מ	=	*m*
ן	נ	=	*n*
	ס	=	*s*
	ע	=	ʿ
ף	פ	=	*p*
ץ	צ	=	*ṣ*
	ק	=	*q*
	ר	=	*r*
	שׁ	=	*š*
	שׂ	=	*ś*
	ת	=	*t*

CHAPTER ONE

INTRODUCTION

According to rabbinic tradition Eleazar b. Azariah was a major figure at Yavneh. Rabbinic literature mentions Eleazar in a minimum of two hundred pericopae. One tradition implies that he was an important political figure at Yavneh and alleges that he played a role in the events surrounding the deposition of Gamaliel II from the patriarchate.[1] Many other pericopae juxtapose his dicta with those of Aqiva, Eliezer, Joshua, and others to whom are attributed still more substantial corpora of traditions. For anyone concerned with the formative period of rabbinic Judaism, the study of Eleazar and his traditions, therefore, is naturally interesting. This is the first systematic investigation of all the materials in rabbinic literature pertaining to Eleazar.[2] Previous attempts to sketch the life of our master and to summarize his traditions suffer from three major flaws. First, they build their descriptions on incomplete evidence. Notably, most ignore the legal traditions entirely.[3] Second, they accept the data at face value and make no attempt to apply to the traditions critical methods of historical inquiry.[4] Third, they simply make incorrect statements of fact.[5] A critical study of the entire corpus of traditions is therefore called for.

I cannot offer a biography of Eleazar or produce any extended account of his life and thought. For, as I shall demonstrate, our data contain few facts about his life. Furthermore, the extant biographical information is limited, episodic, and sometimes cryptic. One might hope that this study could at least draw a coherent sketch of Eleazar's intellectual concerns. That is, from the individual sayings one perhaps could discern the major trends of Eleazar's thought. But the traditions attributed to him offer no sustained discussion of a circumscribed set of subjects either legal, theological, or exegetical. The diversity of the material thus makes intellectual biography impossible.

There is yet a positive potential usefulness for the traditions even though they tell us little about a historical personage. The materials attributed to a single man provide us with an opportunity to examine a sample body of rabbinic tradition, which gives us significant primary information about later rabbis' perceptions of the master. We can observe how the rabbis shaped, developed, and preserved the traditions about a single man, and fashion from the data a history of the formation and development of that tradition.

Several traits of the traditions, however, render our study difficult. The works containing our data were compiled over a long span of time. The earliest was redacted about 200 C.E., a century after Eleazar's lifetime. The latest compilations containing data about him were not edited until the middle ages. The traditions are widely dispersed throughout this literature. They are preserved as autonomous pericopae, individual units of tradition formulated independent of and incorporated into the various compilations. Some of these pericopae are themselves complex structures shaped through the combination of two or more of the most basic units of rabbinic tradition, independent lemmas. Both the simple and the more complex units of tradition have been preserved in highly formulaic language. Moreover, the materials may have been glossed or interpolated in the course of their formulation and transmission. The nature of the literature determines the methods we employ for the study of the data. It will not suffice merely to collect all the traditions. We must differentiate among the strata of the corpus. That is, we separately consider traditions which first appear in the earliest compilations and those in the latest documents. Moreover, we analyze the literary and formal characteristics of the material at each level of the tradition.

Through form-analysis and literary criticism, the basic tools of our exegesis, we break apart the pericopae to isolate and describe the component parts of the tradition. Only then do we go on to synthesize and summarize our results for the tradition as a whole: the formal, literary, and substantive traits of the corpus.

Let us now turn to the body of our study. In Chapters II (for the legal materials) and III (for the non-legal items), I arrange and comment upon the traditions. They are arranged according to the documents in which they first appear beginning with Mishnah-Tosefta. By so doing I distinguish between the strata of the tradition so that I may later describe the lines of its development. In the commentary I systematically raise a number of issues. First, I consider the literary form in which Eleazar's saying is preserved. I show, for instance, that few of his traditions are juxtaposed with those of other masters in carefully formulated, well-balanced disputes, which combine the lemmas of the unit in tight literary constructions. Second, I discuss the literary structure of the pericopae. Where more than one single unit can be discerned I ask whether the separate units of a pericope relate closely or address disparate issues or problems. Third, I note the context in which the tradition occurs. Fourth, I explain the subject matter of the pericope. For the most part I add little in this regard to the exegeses supplied by the standard rabbinic commentaries to the text. But in several instances my formal and literary analysis of a pericope provides an alternative explanation of the legal problem at issue. My fifth concern in the commentary is to discuss any distinct historical and biographical questions raised by the pericope. Finally, I note whether I can provide any further attestation for the tradition. That is, can I demonstrate a firmer *terminus ante quem* for a ruling by showing that a saying was known in substance before the time of the redaction of the compilation in which it now appears? In sum, in Chapters II and III

I raise a set of questions which allows me to isolate the most basic units of the form and substance of the pericopae and describe the significant traits of the individual items.

In Chapters IV through VIII I proceed to synthesize the results reached in my exegeses and make some generalizations about the tradition. Primary to a study of the history of a tradition is careful delineation of the various levels or strata of the tradition, as I have noted. Before undertaking any significant study of the formal or substantive traits of the tradition as a whole and their historical development, one must carefully show which items appear first in the earliest compilations and which appear only in later documents. In Chapter IV I thus summarize the most general traits of the tradition as a whole. I show for instance that in the earliest stratum of tradition, the materials in Mishnah-Tosefta, legal rulings predominate, while the latest level of the corpus has no interest in the law at all. I also collate one set of results out of the commentary in Chapters II and III. I show that more than 25% of the traditions in Mishnah-Tosefta may be attested to a period preceding the compilation of the document. Thus I set out the strata of the tradition: the attested materials in Mishnah-Tosefta; Mishnah-Tosefta-traditions; materials in the Tannaitic Midrashim; Tannaitic materials in the gemarot; other traditions in the gemarot; items appearing first in the later rabbinic compilations. From this schematization of the traditions in Chapter IV, I proceed to the study of the formal and substantive traits of the tradition as a whole.

In Chapter V I deal with the literary forms found in the tradition. First I organize the materials and assign each pericope to an appropriate category of form. I next ask whether there is anything distinctive about the literary forms used to present Eleazar's sayings. I show that for approximately one-third of his items in M., the forms of Eleazar's traditions are significantly at variance with those of the traditions attributed to other

Yavneans. May any conclusions be drawn about the history of the transmission and formulation of his tradition? In a few cases I assume that tradents were responsible for the distinctive forms of Eleazar's tradition. In most cases I show that redactors and not tradents are responsible for the present literary shape of the unusual items. I do this by considering the formal preferences of the contexts of each pericope in Mishnah. Presently we know that chapters of Mishnah have distinctive formal preferences.[6] I therefore can show that editors of Mishnah imposed these preferences on some of Eleazar's traditions by revising them.

I assume that the remaining traditions were cast in their present form by tradents. Who were the tradents of Eleazar's traditions? Specifically I wish to know whether the tradental processes which carried forward the traditions of Aqiva, Eliezer, Joshua, and others also stand behind the transmission of Eleazar's materials. Or, did they circulate separately from the traditions of other major figures, joined to sayings of other masters only at a later date? The evidence, as I shall show, strongly suggests that the latter is the case.

The fact that Eleazar's traditions stand outside of the tradental mainstream which transmitted the traditions of other major Yavneans leads me to consider the possibility that the substance of the sayings attributed to him may also diverge from the main concerns expressed in the corpora attributed to other masters. In Chapter VII I therefore ask whether Eleazar's rulings deal with issues common to the traditions of other Yavneans. I show that at a general level Eleazar's agendum of issues is strikingly similar to the agenda of the traditions attributed to the Houses, Eliezer, Joshua, and Ishmael. But I also note that at specific concerns, there are few points of detail which Eleazar's rulings share in common with traditions attributed to other masters. To illustrate this fact I note that I show for instance that about 20% of the rulings in each of the Yavnean corpora deal with agricultural taboos. But Eleazar's law deals with tithes in several cases, Eliezer and Joshua's with Heave-offering, Ishmael's with *demai*', etc. Rulings attributed to Eleazar do not focus on the same specific aspects of the law as those in the other corpora. It seems then that in substance, as well as in form, Eleazar's traditions were peripheral to the major Yavnean traditions. It is predominantly at the redactional stage that they become linked with materials of other Yavneans in the compilations of the literature.

What role do Eleazar's specific rulings play in the formation of those compilations? I limit my discussion to the substantive role that specific rulings play in Mishnah. It is now clear that Mishnah-editors often use traditions assigned to individual masters as the foundations in their construction of the legal structures of a chapter or tractate. A single ruling may express a thought or principle which generates some further law and perhaps even underlies the conception of an entire chapter.[7] In the course of my analysis of the legal traditions in Chapter VII, I thus ask two further questions. First, do Eleazar's laws play any consistent role in the development of the law of Mishnah? For instance, do they consistently generate further laws? Second, does any one of his dicta contain a legal principle which generates a chapter of Mishnah? Our results, mainly negative, further indicate the peripheral nature of the corpus.

In Chapter VII I also raise two further sets of issues regarding the legal rulings. First, is the tradition in any way coherent? Since our materials are attributed to a single man, one might have expected that they would address a limited set of problems in a sustained way. One should have found that the problems relate to one another. As I said at the outset the themes of Eleazar's pericopae are instead not only diverse but also disjointed. I demonstrate that the rulings are not based on a coherent set of principles. That is, I cannot discern a distinct legal philosophy underlying the substance of the rulings.

I finally ask if I can uncover within the legal sources any lines of the history and development of the tradition. In this regard I investigate whether legal rulings assigned to Eleazar in later sources expand or refine the themes attributed to him in earlier strata of the tradition. Or is there no continuity between early and late traditions? I raise the same two questions of continuity and coherence in Chapter VIII for the non-legal traditions. I demonstrate that the theological and exegetical traditions attributed to Eleazar at each level of the tradition show little coherence of either theme or method. I find also, with minor exceptions, no lines of continuous development from stratum to stratum, so too for the stories. In Chapter IX I summarize the results. I conclude that the traditions as a whole do not represent Eleazar as a central Yavnean figure. Instead his traditions are clearly peripheral to the central tradental processes and redactional concerns of the literature. Some may conclude that this is a powerful argument for their authenticity.

The translations of the sources which follow in the next two chapters are based on the following editions of the texts:

Mishnah: Unfortunately no critical edition of M. now exists, although one is currently being produced in Israel.[8] I use H. Albeck, *Shishah Sidre Mishnah*, Jerusalem-Tel Aviv, 1952-1959, as the basic text but check it against all manuscripts available to me. However, only those variants which significantly alter the meaning of a passage are noted in the translation.

Tosefta: I use the critical editions of S. Lieberman (ed.), *The Tosefta* and M. S. Zuckermandel (ed.), *Tosefta Based on the Erfurt and Vienna Codices*, Jerusalem, 1963.

Mekhilta de R. Ishmael: H. S. Horovitz, and I. A. Rabin (eds.), *Mekhilta d' R. Ishmael*, Jerusalem, 1960.

Mekhilta de R. Simeon bar Yohai: Y. N. Epstein and E. Z. Melamed, *Mekhilta d'Rabbi Simeon b. Yoḥai*, Jerusalem, 1955.

Sifré Deuteronomy: L. Finkelstein (ed.), *Sifré on Deuteronomy*, New York, 1956.

Sifré Numbers: H. S. Horovitz, *Sifré d'be Rab*, Jerusalem, 1966.

Sifra: I. H. Weiss, *Sifra d'be Rab or Sefer Torat Kohanim*, New York, 1947.

Yerushalmi: Venice edition along with B. Ratner, *Sefer Ahavat Zion VeYerushalayim*, I-X.

Babli: Vilna edition along with R. Rabbinovicz, *Variae Lectiones in Mischnam et in Talmud Babylonicum.*

Bereshit Rabbah: J. Theodor and Ch. Albeck, *Midrash Bereshit Rabbah*, Jerusalem, 1965.

Leviticus Rabbah: M. Margulies, *Midrash Wayyikra Rabbah*, Jerusalem, 1960.

Abot de R. Nathan: S. Schechter, *Abot de Rabbi Nathan*, New York, 1945.

Tanḥuma: S. Buber, *Midrasch Tanḥuma.*

Pesikta de R. Kahana: Mandelbaum, *Pesikta de R. Kahana*, Jerusalem.

Exodus Rabbah, Numbers Rabbah, Song of Songs Rabbah: H. Zundel, *Midrash Rabbah*, New York, 1957.

Kallah, Soferim, Kallah Rabbati, Abadim: ed. M. Higger (see bibliography).

Other MSS and editions consulted are listed in the bibliography.

In the translations which follow and the comments to each, I try to give only data which bears directly on Eleazar's tradition. Where a lemma appears in a lengthy pericope or unit, I often translate only the contextual material immediately pertinent to it. In the comment, I then summarize the larger context of the pericope. Legal materials are given in Chapter II following the order of their appearance in M.-T. Relevant parallels accompany each source. Legal items appearing first in the midrashim, b., and y. are inserted where they seem to fit most logically according to their subject matter. Accordingly, for instance, a pericope in b. dealing with the *shema'* liturgy follows the sources in M.-T. on the same subject (No. 5). The non-legal traditions in Chapter III are grouped by document and by theme. Thus, following the deposition story (No. 77), for example, I give all other items dealing with any element of the narrative. In the remaining chapters (IV through IX), I refer to the sources, either by giving the reference to an item's location (e.g., M. Ber. 1:5), or its number according to my system (e.g., No. 1), that is the arabic numeral which precedes the translation of each pericope in Chapters II and III.

Grounds for calling an attribution into question are noted in the comments. MSS evidence, parallels in other sources with contrary attributions, Eleazar's conjunction with Ushans instead of Yavneans are factors which merit discussion and evaluation on an individual basis in each case. Clearly confusion can arise in the course of transmission between Eleazar b. Azariah and Eleazar b. Arak, Eleazar the Modaite, Eleazar b. Shammua, Eliezer b. Jacob, or even Eliezer b. Hyrcanus. But where there is no warrant to question an attribution, we accept it. For further discussion of this issue, see Neusner, *Eliezer* I, pp. 1-3 and Y. N. Epstein, *Introduction to the Text of the Mishnah*, Vol. II, pp. 1162-1182.

I give translations of Aramaic phrases or passages in italics. Biblical verses are set off from the text by quotation marks. The RSV translation is used throughout. In the course of my translations I add words of explanation in brackets. Transliterations of some Hebrew or Aramaic phrases are provided in lower case italics. For the sake of convenience I have omitted all diacritical marks from names. Thus 'Ele'azar b. 'Azariah I give as Eleazar b. Azariah, 'Aqiva as Aqiva and so on.

NOTES

CHAPTER I

[1]y. Ber. 4:1, b. Ber. 27b-28a.

[2]Previous studies include S. Safrai, "Eleazar b. Azariah," *Encyclopedia Judaica*, Vol. VI, pp. 586-88, Jerusalem, 1971; W. Bacher in *Aggadot HaTannaim*, Vol. I, pt. i, ch. 10, Jaffa, 1920; S. Mendelsohn, "Eleazar b. Azariah," *Jewish Encyclopedia*, Vol. V, pp. 97-98, repr. N.Y., 1970; Y. Konovitz, *Ma'arekhet Tannaim*, Jerusalem, 1967, provides an incomplete list of the sources. M. Gorelik, *Legal Traditions of Eleazar b. Azaryah*, unpub. doc. diss., Brandeis University, 1973, does a primitive form-critical analysis of most of the legal traditions.

[3]Cf. Safrai, Mendelsohn and Bacher.

[4]Gorelik provides the only critical analysis of some of the sources.

[5]Safrai for instance says that Eleazar's aggadic materials are far more numerous than his legal traditions. We count 68 legal and 52 non-legal items in the corpus.

[6]On the formal preferences of chapters, see, e.g., Neusner, *HMLP*, III, Ch. 33; cf. esp. XXI, Chs. II and V.

[7]See, e.g., Neusner, *HMLP*, III, pp. 332ff. on Aqiva's varied role in the law; cf. also XXII.

[8]*Mishnah: The Six Orders of Mishnah with Variant Readings....* Vols. I and II: *Zera'im*, ed. R. Nissan Zaks, Jerusalem, 1972-73. Published by *Makhon HaTalmud HaYisraeli HaShalem*. Director: R. Joshua Hutner.

CHAPTER II

THE LEGAL TRADITIONS

i. *Zera'im*

1. A. We mention the exodus from Egypt at night.

B. Said R. Eleazar ben Azariah, "I am now like a seventy year old and was not worthy [of understanding] that the exodus from Egypt be said at night, until Ben Zoma expounded it:

C. "As it is stated: 'So that you may remember the day on which you left Egypt all the days of your life (Deut. 16:3).'

D. "'The days of your life' [would have implied only] the days. 'All the days of your life' [includes] the nights."

E. And the sages say, "'The days of your life' [would have included only] this world. 'All the days of your life' [includes] the days of the messiah."

M. Ber. 1:5; Sifré, ed. Finkelstein, p. 188; Tos. Zer., Lieberman, p. 4, ls. 40-46 (Mekhilta, Horowitz-Rabin, p. 60 omits attribution to Eleazar)

Comment: The *shema'* consists of three paragraphs to be recited in the morning and at night (M. Ber. 1:1, 2:1). The third paragraph mentions the exodus from Egypt. A is a simple declarative sentence (using the present participle verb) stating the law that the exodus be mentioned at night. In the context of the first chapter of M. Ber., it refers only to the third paragraph of the *shema'*. C-D provides exegetical support for A. E contradicts A. B tells us only that Eleazar did not know the law until Ben Zoma taught it. I do not know why B interrupts between A and C, unless it originally served as the introduction to the unit C-D and was left intact when the redactor appended the exegetical material to A. E disagrees with the law of A and of D and was appended to D to provide the exegetical basis for the view which opposes C-D and A.

We find a clear connection between B-E and the *shema*ʿ in Mishnah and Tosefta. In the Mekhilta and Sifré, however, B-E is linked to the idea of remembering the exodus at night, without specifically referring to the *shema*ʿ. Furthermore, in the Passover Haggadah, B-E is cited as a reference to the recitation of the Haggadah at night, and not to the *shema*ʿ. The redactor of our pericope interpreted B-E to be referring to the *shema*ʿ and cites the unit here to prove A.

The statement, "I am like a seventy year old" is puzzling. B. Beraḥot 28a offers the following explanation: Eleazar ascended to the patriarchate at an early age and his beard miraculously turned white as a sign of sagacity. He therefore looked like a seventy year old man. We will discuss below the tendency to read references of Eleazar's patriarchal service into previous material. The issue of the recitation of the *shema*ʿ at night may be related to the larger question of the establishment of the evening liturgy as a requirement, which was allegedly a major issue at Yavneh.

2. A. R. Eleazar ben Azariah says, "The additional service is only said with the congregation of the city (*ḥbr ʿyr*)."

B. And the sages say, "With the congregation of the city and not with the congregation of the city."

C. R. Judah says in his name, "Wherever there is a congregation of the city the individual is free from the additional service."

M. Ber. 4:7

Comment: The additional service is said in lieu of the additional sacrifice offered in the Temple on Saturdays, New Moons, and holidays. A-B are in dispute form. B depends on A for its referent. C is added to A-B and

Judah attests Eleazar but assigns to him a different opinion. [The phrase *ḥbr ʿyr* is ambiguous. It may mean one of three things: either 'official of the city,' or 'place of assembly of the city,' or 'congregation of the city.' See on this b. Megillah 27a, b. R.H. 34b, and b. Ḥullin 94a where the three possible alternatives are evident in *beraitot*.[1]] Judah introduces the issue of the individual's obligation to recite the additional service and makes it dependent on the existence of the *ḥbr ʿyr*. This strongly suggests that the phrase means 'congregation of the city,' the translation we have accepted. From A-B alone, however, we could not deduce the exact meaning of the phrase.

Now let us turn to the dispute. The sages and Eleazar disagree about whether the additional service is strictly a communal obligation or an individual obligation as well. Eleazar insists that outside the communal structure the additional service is not said. The sages allow it to be said exclusive of the congregation. Judah's opinion is a compromise. He says that where the communal structure includes a congregation, the individual does not say the additional service. This is in agreement with Eleazar. Where there is no congregation, the individual must say the additional service. The sages would certainly agree with this. Thus Judah modifies Eleazar's ruling and includes part of the sages' law in his compromise.

3. A. R. Judah said, "One time I was following R. Aqiva and R. Eleazar ben Azariah and the time for reciting the *shemaʿ* arrived. It seemed to me that they had given up hope of reciting [it],

B. "because they were busy with communal needs.

C. "I recited and studied, and afterwards they began [to recite] and the sun had already appeared on the mountaintops."

Tos. Ber. 1:2, Lieberman, p. 2, ls. 13-16

A. *tny*: R. Judah said, "*m'śh*: I was walking by the way behind R. Eleazar ben Azariah and behind R. Aqiva,

B. "and they were involved in [performing] commandments.

C. "And the time came for the recitation of the *shema'* and I thought that they had given up hope of reciting [it]. I recited and studied and afterwards they began [to recite] and the sun had already appeared on the mountaintops."

y. Ber. 3a

Comment: Judah serves as the source once again for material concerning Eleazar ben Azariah. According to both accounts he is clearly surprised that the other two sages allegedly said the *shema'* so late in the morning. He apparently followed the preceding opinion of Tos. Ber. 1:2, which says that the morning *shema'* may be said (after the time that it becomes light enough to see and recognize one's fellow at a distance of four *'amot*) until the sun rises. Judah either does not know or rejects the ruling given in M. Ber. 1:2 which says that the morning *shema'* may be said until the third hour.

The story seems to be a unitary anecdote which serves as a precedent and involves Eleazar and Aqiva. B in both sources looks very much like a gloss, inserted to justify the sages' neglect of their obligation to recite the morning *shema'* on time and thus disqualify the source as a precedent. The time for the recitation of the *shema'* is an issue also in M. Ber. 1:2 where Eleazar appears as well. On the question of Eleazar and Aqiva, see below, pp. 265ff.

4. A. *m'śh b*: R. Ishmael and R. Eleazar ben Azariah were staying in one place. R. Ishmael was reclining and R. Eleazar ben Azariah was sitting erect. When it came to the time to recite the *shema'*, R. Ishmael rose and R. Eleazar ben Azariah reclined.

B. Said to him R. Ishmael, "What is this, Eleazar?"

C. He said to him, "Ishmael my brother.

D. "They say to one, 'Why is your beard grown?' And he says to them, 'May it be against the destroyers (*mšḥytym*).'

E. "I who was sitting erect, reclined. And you, who were reclining, arose."

F. He [R. Ishmael] said to him, "You reclined to carry out the words of the House of Shammai, and I arose to carry out [the words of] the house of Hillel."

G. Another matter (*dbr 'ḥr*), "So that the students should not see and establish the law according to your words."

Tos. Ber. 1:4, ed. Lieberman,
p. 2, ls. 18-25

Comment: This pericope presents us with several difficulties. First, we do not know what the term 'destroyers' in D means. A more basic difficulty is that F attempts to link A-E to a dispute between the Houses. Let us first examine the contents of the pericope. Ishmael was reclining and Eleazar was sitting erect. When the time for reciting the *shema'* came, they switched positions. In B Ishmael asks Eleazar what he has done. C-D is Eleazar's puzzling response with his reference to the 'destroyers.' F is set in direct discourse between Ishmael and Eleazar and tries to connect the incident to the Houses-dispute concerning the correct posture which must be assumed for the recitation of the *shema'*.

All the commentators take for granted that the pericope illustrates M. Ber. 1:3:

> The House of Shammai say, "In the evening every man should recline and recite [the *shema'*], but in the morning he should stand up"...The House of Hillel say, "Every man recites in his own way."

I do not see any direct relationship between A-E and this Houses-dispute. Reclining in no way indicates that one is a Shammaite as F alleges. Even Hillelites may recline and recite the *shema*ʿ.

If we assume that A-E is the original pericope, then we have merely a story about two sages switching positions followed by an exchange between them, a discussion about people who do contrary things, such as growing their beards long. We cannot make a definitive statement about the meaning of D, because of the obscure term 'destroyers.' It is important to note that the redactor took the original pericope, A-E, and found in it an illustration of the above mentioned Houses-dispute. It is not uncommon for Yavnean sages to be represented as having also disputed issues which were argued by the Houses.

G of course notices that the neat equation of F between Eleazar and the House of Shammai and Ishmael and the House of Hillel is meaningless. Ishmael says, "I arose to carry out [the words of] the House of Hillel," but the House of Hillel never stipulates that an erect posture be assumed. The gloss G explains the intent of F. Ishmael arose to counterbalance Eleazar's reclining, lest the students get the wrong impression and assume that the law follows the House of Shammai. It is clear that the redactor of the pericope has attempted to work out the positions of the Houses by combining two sources. Ishmael does not commonly appear with Eleazar (see below, p. 269).

> A. And once (*wkbr*) R. Ishmael was reclining and expounding, and R. Eleazar b. Azariah was sitting erect. The time for the recitation of the *shema*ʿ arrived. R. Ishmael arose, and R. Eleazar b. Azariah reclined.
>
> B. R. Ishmael said to him, "What is this Eleazar?"
>
> C. He said to him, "Ishmael my brother.
>
> D. "They said to one, 'Why is your beard grown?' He said to them, 'May it be against the destroyers (*mšḥytym*).'"

E. He [R. Ishmael] said to him, "You reclined according to the words of the House of Shammai and I arose according to the words of the House of Hillel."

F. Another matter (*dbr 'ḥr*): So that the matter should not become a fixed requirement. For the House of Shammai say, "In the evening everyone should recline and recite. But in the morning [everyone] should stand up [and recite the *shema*']."

Sifré Deut., ed. Finkelstein,
34, pp. 62-63, ls. 8-13

Comment: Note the differences between this version and the Toseftan version. A begins with *wkbr*, omits the phrase "they were staying in one place," and states that Ishmael was "reclining and expounding." E of the Tosefta was omitted. F is much more explicit in its rejection of the Shammaite position than G was in the Tosefta.

A. *tny*: *m'śh b*: R. Eleazar ben Azariah and R. Ishmael were resting in one place and R. Eleazar ben Azariah was reclining and R. Ishmael was sitting erect. The time of the recitation of the *shema*' arrived. R. Eleazar ben Azariah arose and R. Ishmael reclined.

B. R. Eleazar said to R. Ishmael,

C. "He says to one in the market, 'Why is your beard grown'? And he says, 'May it be against the destroyers (*mšḥytym*).'

D. "I who was reclining arose, and you who was standing, reclined."

E. He [R. Ishmael] said to him, "You arose according to the words of the House of Shammai and I reclined according to the words of the House of Hillel."

F. Another matter, "[I did thus] so that the students should not observe [my actions] and fix the law according to the words of the House of Shammai."

y. Ber. 1:3

Comment: This account has the actions of the Rabbis reversed and preserves the general outline of the Toseftan-Sifré version. Other differences are as follows: Ishmael's question (Tos. B) is omitted. Eleazar's example is set in the marketplace. Eleazar is accused of rising to reflect the view of the Shammaites. It is this last point which forces most of the exegetes to suggest that the issue here is the morning *shema*ʿ rather than the evening *shema*ʿ. It would seem to me more likely that this version became confused in transmission and the names reversed.

A. *wmʿśh b*: R. Ishmael and R. Eleazar ben Azariah were sojourning (*mswbyn*) in one place and R. Ishmael was reclining and R. Eleazar ben Azariah was sitting erect. When the time for the recitation of the *shema*ʿ arrived, R. Eleazar ben Azariah reclined and R. Ishmael arose.

B. R. Eleazar ben Azariah said to R. Ishmael, "Ishmael my brother, I will tell you a parable: What is this analogous to? It is analogous to one, to whom they say, 'Your beard is grown.' He said to them, 'May it be against the destroyers (*mšḥytym*).'

C. "Likewise you [do the same thing]. All the time that I was sitting erect, you were reclining. Now that I have reclined, you have arisen."

D. He [R. Ishmael] said to him, "I did according to the words of the House of Hillel, and you did according to the words of the House of Shammai.

E. "And not only this but, [I acted thus] so that the students should not observe [my posture] and fix the law for the generations."

b. Ber. 11a

Comment: This version is a slightly emended and expanded account of the Toseftan-Sifré version. Ishmael's question is omitted. Eleazar's analogy is presented as a parable. C (E of the Tosefta) has been altered slightly, but preserves the sense in which we understood it. For a synoptic chart of the parallel versions of this pericope, see Gary Porten, *The Traditions of Rabbi Ishmael*, Leiden, 1976, pp. 19-21.

5. A. *dtnn*: R. Judah says in the name of R. Eleazar b. Azariah,

B. "One who recites the *shema*ʿ must hear his own words.

C. "As it is written, 'Hear, O Israel, the Lord our God, the Lord is one (Deut. 6:4).'"

D. *Said to him* R. Meir, "Behold it is written, 'And these words which I command you this day shall be upon your heart (Deut. 6:6)';

E. "[we] follow the intent of the heart [and audible recitation is not central].

F. "These, these are the words [which determine the proper fulfillment of the commandment] (*hn hn hdbrym*)."

b. Ber. 15a

Comment: The pericope gives two opinions on the issue of whether audible recitation of the *shema*ʿ is necessary for the fulfillment of the commandment. A-C is Judah's citation of Eleazar's ruling; D-F is Meir's view. Both are based on Scripture. The *beraita* editor added "said to him" in D which gives the pericope the appearance of a dispute.

Although it is prefaced by *dtnn*, Judah's citation of Eleazar's ruling does not appear in Mishnah. The *beraita* is cited in the discussion in b. of M. Ber. 2:3 which gives the following dispute:

A. One who recites the *shema*ʿ and does not hear his words fulfills [the commandment].

B. R. Yosé says, "He does not fulfill [the commandment]."

Eleazar's ruling agrees in effect with Yosé's in M. Meir's ruling in the *beraita* introduces the concept of intention as the determining factor.[2]

Judah appears frequently as a tradent of Eleazar. This pericope attests Eleazar's interest in delineating the procedure for the recitation of the *shema'* which is reflected in M. Ber. 1:5, Tos. Ber. 1:2 and 1:4.

6. A. Said R. Ilai, "I asked R. Joshua about which sheaves the House of Shammai disputed.

B. "He said to me, 'The teaching about which sheaves [concerns those which he left] near the stone fence or the stack or the cattle or the implements--and forgot it.'

C. "When I came and asked R. Liezer he said to me, 'They agree concerning those--they are not [in the category of] forgotten sheaves.

D. "Concerning what do they disagree? Concerning a sheaf which he [the harvester] took hold of to bring to the city and placed at the side of the gate--and forgot it [there].

E. "[Concerning] that, the House of Shammai says it is not a forgotten sheaf

El. "because he acquired it.

F. "And the house of Hillel says [it is a] forgotten sheaf.'

G. "When I came and recited before R. Eleazar b. Azariah, he said to me, 'These matters were spoken [to Moses] at Sinai (E; *htwrh 'ylw dbrym n'mrw msyny*--L).'"

Tos. Peah 3:2, Lieberman, p. 51, ls. 12-19

Comment: Sheaves which were left in the field during the harvest belong to the poor (Deut. 24:19). The pericope is a narrative containing a legal discussion about forgotten sheaves. Ilai asks Joshua and Eliezer about the details of the Houses-dispute concerning forgotten sheaves. A is truncated and should have read, "about which sheaves the House of Hillel and the House of Shammai disputed." Joshua replies with the law of Mishnah Peah 6:2: The House of Shammai rules that a sheaf left near a landmark is not in the category of forgotten sheaves (B). Eliezer answers Ilai with Mishnah Peah 6:3's statement that the House of Shammai holds that a sheaf which the harvester had intended to bring to the city but instead left next to the gate is not considered a forgotten sheaf (C-E).

Eleazar, in G, says that the matters are a tradition from Sinai. This statement in similar form is attributed to Eleazar in two places. Its meaning in context is unclear. Apparently he affirms Eliezer's answer as it is presented by Ilai.

The form of the pericope is unusual:

A-B: Ilai asks Joshua--Joshua answers.
C-F: Ilai asks Eliezer--Eliezer answers.
G: Ilai recites before Eleazar--Eleazar comments.

Eliezer follows Joshua, which is rare. The names of the masters are mentioned in this order so that Eleazar can affirm Eliezer's statement. We find the identical form in Tosefta Ḥallah 1:6.

Ilai is represented as reciting before Eleazar. This implies that he was Eleazar's student. His son, Judah, preserves several of Eleazar's traditions.

A. Said R. Ilai, "I asked R. Joshua about which sheaves the House of Shammai and the House of Hillel disputed.

B. "He said to me, '[They disputed] this teaching: [If he left] the sheaf near the stone fence or the stack or the cattle or the implements--and forgot it; The House of Shammai say [it is in the category of] forgotten sheaves and the House of Hillel say it is not [in the category of] forgotten sheaves.'

C. "When I came to R. Eliezer, he said to me, 'The House of Shammai and the House of Hillel did not disagree concerning the sheaf near the stone fence or the stack or the cattle or the implements. [They agree that] it is [in the category of] forgotten sheaves.

D. "Concerning what did they disagree? Concerning the sheaf which he took and put next to the stone fence, next to the stack, next to the cattle, next to the implements.

E. "[Concerning that] the House of Shammai say it is not forgotten sheaves because he acquired it.

F. "And the House of Hillel say [it is] a forgotten sheaf.'

G. "And when I came and recited before R. Eleazar b. Azariah he said to me, 'The covenant! These matters were spoken to Moses at Horeb.'"

y. Peah 6:2, 19b

Comment: In this version of Tosefta Peah 3:2, A and C include the House of Hillel and its ruling, respectively. B reverses the opinions of the Houses. D preserves the stipulation of Mishnah and Tosefta that the harvester had taken hold of the sheaf but omits the phrase "to bring to the city." It also substitutes "next to the stone fence, ...stack,...cattle,...implements" for Mishnah and Tosefta's "next to the gate." G is also a variant of Eleazar's lemma in Tosefta.

7. A. Until when can they be called saplings?

B. R. Eleazar ben Azariah says, "Until they become free for common use (*šyḥwlw*)."

C. R. Joshua says, "Seven years old."

D. R. Aqiva says, "'Sapling' as its name [implies]."

M. Sheb. 1:8

Comment: It is forbidden to work a field in the seventh year. In some instances it is even forbidden to plow a field in the latter part of the sixth year. If a tract of land is considered an orchard and not a field, however, it may be worked during the entire sixth year. The presence of either three trees or ten saplings in a *bet seah* of land (2500 square cubits) gives it the status of an orchard. The issue in our mishnah is: What is a sapling and what is a tree? Or, at what stage of development does a sapling become a tree?

A asks a direct question, 'Until when are they called saplings'? Eleazar answers the question directly, 'Until they become free for common use.' In the first three years after a tree has taken root, the fruit is considered *'orlah* and it is forbidden to eat it. In the fourth year the fruit may be redeemed (with money) and eaten. y. Sheb. suggests that Eleazar's ruling that the sapling acquires the status of *tree* as soon as the fruit becomes free for common use, may mean either in the fourth or the fifth year. In the fifth year the fruit becomes free immediately, but in the fourth year it may be redeemed and eaten.

A-B serve as the primary unit of the pericope. Both Joshua and Aqiva rule on the same issue and their rulings are redacted onto A-B. Neither one directly answers the question of A. Joshua, in C, says 'seven years old.' In order to have directly answered A he should have said, 'Until the eighth year.' Aqiva, similarly, should have answered, 'Until people call it a tree' and not, 'Sapling, as its name.' The redactor preserved the language of their rulings even though it meant that the text would be a bit awkward. The pericope is thus an example of material on the same subject from two different circles combined by the editor at a second stage of redaction. The language of the original sources has been carefully preserved.

8. A. "A man may set out in his field three dungheaps in every *seah's* space.

B. "More than this--he must set out circlewise (L, K, and P omit *mḥzyb*)."

C. The words of R. Simeon.

D. The sages prohibit [setting out more] unless he lowers [the additional heap] three [handbreadths] or raises it three [handbreadths from the surface].

E. One may store his dung together [in one large mound].

F. R. Meir prohibits [storing it together] unless he lowers it three or raises it three.

G. If he had a small amount [set out] he may continually add on to it.

H. R. Eleazar b. Azariah prohibits unless he lowers it three or raises it three

I. or unless he puts it on the rocks.

M. Sheb. 3:3

Comment: Cultivation of a field is prohibited in the seventh year. Fertilization is one of the stages of the process of preparing a field for cultivation. The issue here is how to permit someone to bring dung out to his field in the seventh year without violating any prohibitions. The preceding rulings in Chapter Three say that one may bring out dung to his fields in the seventh year and may place three heaps in every *seah's* space (2500 square cubits). Each heap may consist of ten baskets and each basket may contain one *lethek* (15 *seah*--90 *qabim*). One may increase the size of each heap by adding more baskets, but only three heaps are permitted. Simeon permits the addition of more heaps. Our mishnah opens with a repetition of Simeon's ruling (A-B). One may set out heaps in a field. If there are more than three in a *seah's* space, the heaps must be arranged in a circle (following the reading of N). Sages permit the addition of more heaps if the ground level beneath them is raised or lowered from the ground by three handbreadths (D). This will make it apparent to onlookers that the landowner is not fertilizing the field (Maimonides).

E is a separate ruling which permits the farmer to set out one large heap of thirty baskets instead of three heaps of ten each. Meir qualifies this ruling by adding that this large heap must be raised or lowered from the ground by three handbreadths. A-D and E-F are Ushan rulings.

G rules that dung may be brought out little by little during the seventh year. One need not bring out the ten baskets all at once even though it may appear to others as if he is fertilizing the field (Maimonides). In H Eleazar requires that the heap be raised or lowered or set out on rocky ground as a sign that it is not being used for fertilization.

The mishnah consists of three separate laws which deal with setting dung out on a field during the seventh year. They all contain a common qualification that the heap be raised or lowered three handbreadths from ground level. A-F as I said are two Ushan rulings on the matter:

A-D: More than three heaps (Simeon)--raise or lower (sages).
E-F: One large heap--raise or lower (Meir).

G-I is a Yavnean ruling:

Little by little--raise or lower or on the rocks (Eleazer).

Because of the common ruling that raising or lowering is a sufficient modification of normal procedure to allow dung to be set out in the field in the seventh year, the three laws were redacted together in one pericope.

Eleazar rules that placing the heap on rocky ground is a sufficient variation whereas the sages and Meir omit this qualification. We have only two rulings in Eleazar's name concerning laws of the seventh year. I can find no logical sequence to the rulings in this pericope which would imply that Eleazar's came first. We are therefore left with a pericope which places Eleazar after two Ushans and brings the accuracy of the attribution of his lemma into question.

9. A. If one uproots seedlings from his own [garden] and plants them in his own [garden], he is free [from the obligation to tithe them].

B. If one bought [produce] which was planted in the ground--he is free [from the obligation to tithe it].

C. [If] one gathered (*lqṭ*--K, L, N; P has *lqḥ*--bought) [produce] to send to his fellow--he is free.

D. R. Eleazar b. Azariah says, "If their kind were being sold in the market, they are liable."

M. Maas. 5:1

Comment: This pericope introduces a chapter which specifies when produce becomes liable to tithes. The obligation to take tithes begins when edible produce has been harvested for one's own use or when untithed edible or inedible produce is bought for use. However, if inedible produce is harvested it is excluded from liability to tithes. Thus seedlings uprooted for transplanting are free from liability (A). Furthermore unplucked produce that is bought is free from liability, and fruit gathered to be sent to someone else is not liable to tithes (B-C).

Eleazar proposes a different criterion for determining liability to tithes. Intention of the owner plays no role. Liability is determined by the marketability of the produce. If the fruit is sold in the marketplace, it is liable to tithes regardless of whether the owner intended to consume the food or not. His ruling subsumes much more produce to liability to tithes.

Maimonides explains that D qualifies C only. Eleazar's lemma may in fact be a general rule relating to all cases, as we have explained above.

10. A. R. Judah said in the name of R. Leazar b. Azariah, "One who sends his fellow seedlings and young herbs (*'ṭwnyn*; E has *'ṭynyn*) and flax stalks (*pštn*; Jastrow suggests *tltn*-fenugrec), he [the recipient] must tithe them [as he would tithe] untithed produce [*wdyy*].

B. "because most people are to be suspected concerning them [of sending untithed produce]."

C. And the sages say, "They are like all the fruits and [the recipient] need only tithe them [as he would tithe] *demai*."

Tos. Maas. 3:8, Lieberman, p. 239, ls. 21-23

Comment: Seedlings, young herbs and flax stalks are not commonly sold in the marketplace (Lieberman). The issue of Tos. is the same as the issue of D in Mishnah: Is produce which is not found in the market liable to tithes? Mishnah, however, focuses on the responsibility of the sender to remove tithes. C in M. rules that he need not. Eleazar's lemma qualifies that ruling. Judah, as we have seen previously (p. 15) often modifies or interprets Eleazar's rulings. Here in A he shifts the emphasis of Eleazar's law from the obligation of the sender to that of the recipient. Since produce not sold in the market is not liable to tithes, the recipient must remove tithes as he would remove them from any untithed food, since the sender did not.

Judah's interpretation suggests that Eleazar's law is not based on the statistical probability that people will not take tithes from the produce specified, but rather on the assumption that the sender is under no legal obligation to do so. The gloss, B, implies that the recipient's obligation is based on the statistical fact that most people do not tithe the produce, thereby muting the thrust of Judah's statement of the law. The sages in C remove the distinction between fruits sold in the market and those that are not. All must be tithed by the recipient as he would tithe *demai* (i.e., without removing Heave-offering and keeping the first tithes for himself).

It is likely that B-C was appended to A. Had A-C been in dispute form from the outset, it should have read:

"One who sends...Eleazar--tithe *wdyy*
sages --tithe *dm'y*."

A. *wtny*: Thus R. Judah said in the name of R. Eleazar b. Azariah, "Even (*'p*) one who sends young herbs, seedlings, and stalks of fenugrec to his fellow--he should not eat them until he takes tithes from them

B. "for it is the habit of people to send untithed produce to their fellows according to these words."

y. Maas. 5:1

Comment: The gloss B in y. explains that since the sender is under no legal obligation to take tithes from the produce under question, the recipient therefore, must separate the tithes. As we have seen, Tosefta has a variation of this gloss, which suggests that the obligation stems from the statistical probability that the sender has not removed the tithes. It is possible that y. preserves the original language of the gloss to Judah's statement of Eleazar's ruling and that Tosefta altered it when the opinion of the sages was appended.

11. A. [Concerning] one whose produce was far away, he must [orally] designate [some of] it [Heave-offering and tithes].

B. *m'śh b*: Rabban Gamaliel and the elders were travelling on a ship.

C. Said Rabban Gamaliel, "The tenth which I will measure out is hereby given to Joshua and its place is leased to him.

D. "The other tenth which I will measure out is given to Aqiva (N and L: 'b. Joseph') so that he may accept it on behalf of the poor, and its place is leased to him."

E. Said R. Joshua, "The tenth which I will measure out is given to Eleazar b. Azariah and its place is leased to him."

F. And they received from each other compensation.

M. M.S. 5:9 (b. Qid. 26b;
b. B.M. 11a)

Comment: The pericope deals with the process of removal. In the fourth and seventh years, on Passover, all stores of tithes had to be distributed. If one was a distance from his home, he had to orally assign part of his produce for Heave-offering and tithes. In the story (B-F) Gamaliel, Joshua, Aqiva, and Eleazar were on a ship when the time for removal arrived. Gamaliel gave his first tithe to Joshua, the levite, and his Poor-man's tithe to Aqiva for distribution to the poor. Joshua gave a tenth to Eleazar. Each transaction was legally effected through the leasing of the property on which it was stored.

If Joshua was a levite and Eleazar a priest we do not know why Joshua gave Eleazar tithes. Maimonides therefore explains that the tenth which he gave him was in reality Heave-offering of tithes. Albeck says that Joshua gave him tithe of the tithe which he received from Gamaliel. The simple meaning of E is that Joshua, the levite, gave tithe to Eleazar, the priest. This contravenes both Biblical and Mishnaic law (Numbers 18:21-32 and M. Giṭ. 3:7), which unequivocally state that Heave-offering belongs to the priest and first tithes go to the levite.

Moreover it is strange that Joshua, the levite, would actually have given tithe to Eleazar. It is likely therefore that tradents of Eleazar attached E onto the Gamaliel story B-D. The pericope then is in the following form:

A:	General rule
B-D (and F):	Gamaliel story
E:	Gloss of Joshua speaking of Eleazar.

The purpose of the gloss is to show Joshua's submission to Eleazar's ruling regarding tithes which is stated simply, but clearly in b. Yeb. 86a-b (with parallels in b. Ḥul. 131b, b. Ket. 26a, b. B.B. 81b and y. M.S. 5:5):

A. Heave-offering to the priests and first-tithes to levites, the words of R. Aqiva.
B. R. Eleazar b. Azariah says, "To the priest."

Yerushalmi M.S. 5:5 has the following version:

A. R. Joshua b. Hananiah said, "We do not give first tithes to the priesthood."

B. R. Leazar b. Azariah said, "We give first tithes to the priesthood."

Internal evidence in *babli* suggests that Aqiva was substituted for Joshua, who was the original disputant of Eleazar (see below).

The amoraic material just cited and E of our mishnah suggest that Eleazar was responsible for an important ruling concerning the practice of giving tithes, i.e., a tax law. As a priest it would have been to his advantage if tithes were given to the priesthood.[3] As patriarch perhaps he had it within his power to issue a dictum to that effect. The edict, however, contradicted scriptural law and the redactors of the Mishnah and Tosefta omit it. E in our pericope is not an explicit statement of the ruling, and therefore perhaps was left intact.

12. A. *tnw rbnn*: "Heave-offering to the priest and first-tithe to the levite." The words of R. Aqiva.

B. R. Eleazar b. Azariah says, "To the priest."

C. To the priest and not to the levite? *Say rather*: "Even to the priest."

D. *What is R. Aqiva's reason? For it is written*, "Speak to the levites and say to them (Num. 18: 26)." *Scripture refers to the levites.*

E. *And the other*? [Eleazar reasons] like that of R. Joshua b. Levi.

F. For said R. Joshua b. Levi, "In twenty-four places priests are called levites and this is one of them: 'And the priests, the levites, the sons of Zadok (Ez. 44:15).'"

G. *And* [what is the response of] *R. Aqiva? Here you may not say* [that levite means priest]. *For it is written*, "You shall eat [the tithe] in any place (Num. 18:31)." [This implies] one who is able to eat it in any place; a priest is excluded for he cannot eat it in a cemetery.

H. *And the other*? [Eleazar b. Azariah would explain it means] *any place that one desires, for it is not required* [that it be eaten within the confines of the] *wall* [of Jerusalem]; *or if* [someone] *in a state of uncleanness eats it, that person is not* [subject to] *lashes.*

I. [There was] *a certain garden from which R. Eleazar b. Azariah used to take first-tithe.*

J. *R. Aqiva went and moved the entrance* [of the garden] *to* [face] *a graveyard.*

K. *Said* [R. Eleazar b. Azariah], "*Aqiva with his pouch and I have to live* (*w'n' ḥyy*)."

b. Yeb. 86a-b

Comment: A-B gives the opinions of Aqiva and Eleazar in a variation of the dispute form. I-K is a story which illustrates the dispute. C-H is b.'s analysis for the scriptural basis of the views.

The issue of the pericope is of major importance as I pointed out above. Do tithes (i.e., taxes) belong to the priests or levites? The implications of the dispute are spelled out in the comment to M. M.S. 5:9 above. C dulls the point of the issue. Eleazar does not argue, according to C, that tithes are the exclusive property of the priests. Both the levites and the priests may take tithes. Aqiva restricts the rights of the priest.

I-K is given in an expanded form in the parallel in y. to which we now turn.

A. R. Abbahu said, "R. Joshua b. Hananiah and R. Leazar b. Azariah *disputed* [as follows]:

B. "R. Joshua b. Hananiah said, 'We do not give tithe to the priest.'

C. "And R. Leazar b. Azariah said, 'We do give tithe to the priest.'"

D. R. Joshua b. Hananiah *asked* R. Leazar b. Azariah, "It says 'You shall eat it in any place (Num. 18:31).' Come and eat it with him in the graveyard."

E. *He said to him*, "What does 'in any place' mean? Any place in the Temple courtyard."

F. *He said to him*, "It says 'you and your household.' May a woman enter into the Temple courtyard?"

G. R. Ba *would tell of this incident*:

H. R. Leazar b. Azariah *was wont to take tithe from a specific garden*. The garden had two entrances: one to a place of impurity [a graveyard] and one which opened to a place of purity.

I. R. Aqiva *went to him* (the owner). *He said to him*, "*Open this* [entrance] *and seal this* [one]. *If* [Eleazar] *comes, say to him 'come this way'* (through the graveyard)."

J. *He* (the owner) *agreed*.

K. "*If he sends his students* [to take the tithe] *tell him Scripture specifies that* 'you' *must come*."

L. R. Leazar b. Azariah heard [this and] said, "The awl of Aqiva b. Joseph has come here."

M. At that moment R. Leazar b. Azariah returned all the tithes he had taken.

y. M.S. 5:5 (56b-c)

Comment: Our pericope follows an extended discussion concerning tithes. The underlying assumption of the entire discussion in y. is that priests receive tithes. y. makes it clear that in the year of removal first-tithes are taken "from the unclean to the clean"--they are given to the priest. A-B gives the dispute. Here, however, Eleazar and Joshua are the parties. Aqiva enters only in the story at H. D-F repeats the argument given in G-H of b.'s version.

G-M has a version of the story found in b.'s pericope in I-K. The Aramaic sections of the story give a coherent account. The Hebrew sections add discrete details which develop the story. As in b.'s version, Aqiva outwits Eleazar. y. however adds the account of Eleazar's capitulation to Aqiva's view (L-M).[4]

13. A. Said R. Ilai, "I asked R. Joshua [concerning] cakes of a Thank-offering and wafers of a Nazirite--must Dough-offering be taken from them (*mh hn bḥlh*)?

B. "He said to me, 'They are free [from the obligation of Dough-offering].'

C. "When I came and asked R. Liezer he said to me, 'If he made them for his own use they are free [from the obligation]. [If he made them] to sell in the market, they are liable [to Dough-offering].'

D. "When I came and recited before R. Eleazar b. Azariah he said to me, 'The covenant! These matters were spoken from Mount Horeb.'"

Tos. Ḥal. 1:6, Lieberman,
p. 276, ls. 11-14

Comment: The pericope is a narrative containing a legal discussion. Its form is identical with Tosefta Peah 3:2.

Dough-offering must be removed from every loaf of bread. The issue here is whether the bread of a Thank-offering and those which accompany the offering of a Nazirite which he brings at the close of the period of his naziritship, are liable to Dough-offering. Mishnah Ḥallah 1:6 says, "Cakes of a Thank-offering and wafers of a Nazirite: If he prepared them for his own use--they are free [from the obligation of Dough-offering]. To sell in the market--they are liable [to Dough-offering]." Tosefta assigns this ruling to Joshua (C). If bread is to be used for an offering, it is not liable to Dough-offering. If one prepares them for sale in the market for use by someone else as an offering, they are liable to Dough-offering, since we fear that if he does not sell them he will eat them himself (Bartinoro).

Eleazar apparently confirms Eliezer's statement. His lemma is not wholly clear. (See the comment on Tos. Peah 3:2.)

A. *tny'*: Said R. Ilai, "I asked R. Eliezer (*mhw*) can one fulfill his obligation [of eating unleavened bread on Passover] with cakes of a Thank-offering or wafers of a Nazirite?

B. "He said to me, 'I have not heard [a teaching on this matter].'

C. "I came and asked R. Joshua. He said to me, 'Behold they said: Cakes of a Thank-offering and wafers of a Nazirite which he made for his own use--he cannot fulfill his obligation with them. [If he made them] to sell in the market--he may fulfill his obligation with them.'

D. "When I came and recited before R. Eliezer, he said to me, 'The covenant! These these are the matters which were spoken to Moses at Sinai.'"

E. *Another version*: "'The covenant! These these are the matters that were spoken to Moses at Sinai *and they do not require any substantiation* (*wl' t'm' b'y'*).'"

b. Pes. 38b

Comment: Neusner suggests that this pericope "in origin cannot be different from Tosefta Ḥallah 1:6 (Eliezer, I, p. 82)." In form it is identical, aside from the fact that Eliezer precedes Joshua here. The issue, however, is different. Here the question is whether one can fulfill his obligation of eating unleavened bread on Passover with the unleavened bread of a Thank-offering or of a Nazirite's offering. Eliezer rules that those which he made to sell in the market and had in mind to eat them himself if no one bought them, can be used for fulfilling the obligation to eat unleavened bread.

D reads Eliezer and not Eleazar. It is obviously an error. E is amoraic and explains the lemma of D: Eleazar affirms the ruling of C but gives no explanation, relying instead on the authority of tradition.

ii. *Mo'ed*

14. A. They may insulate [hot pots of food] with hides and move them about.

B. [They may insulate] with wool shearings [but] they may not move them about.

C. How does he act [when he wants to take the food out]? He takes the cover off [of the pot] and they [the wool shearings] fall away [by themselves].

D. R. Eleazar b. Azariah says, "He should tilt the basket on its side and take [the food out]

E. "lest he remove the pot [from the insulation] and not be able to replace it."

F. And the sages say, "He may remove [the basket] and replace it."

M. Shab. 4:2

Comment: It is permissible to insulate a pot before sundown on Friday in order to keep the food in it warm on the Sabbath. The insulation, however, cannot be moved around from place to place since it becomes *muqṣah* [i.e., any article whose use is prohibited on the Sabbath]. A states that hides may be used for insulation and may be moved off of the cover of the pot so that the food may be removed from the pot. The hides may be moved because they can be used also for carpets for sitting on and thus do not become *muqṣah*, since their use is permitted on the Sabbath. Wool shearings, however, are not usable forthwith, but only after they are spun and woven into cloth. B rules that although the shearings may not be moved about, they may still be used for insulation for pots. In order to remove the food from pots insulated with shearings, however, one may lift the cover of the pot and allow the shearings to fall away, since indirect movement of *muqṣah* is permitted.

In D, Eleazar rules on a related matter. The case involves a pot which was placed in a basket on the eve of the Sabbath. Insulation was stuffed between the outer wall of the pot and the inner wall of the basket. If the pot is removed the insulation may collapse, and prevent the replacement of the pot in the insulation (Bartinoro and b.). Eleazar rules, therefore, that one should tilt the entire basket on its side in order to remove the food from it. The sages rule that one may remove the pot from the basket and replace it, [if the cavity has not collapsed (Bartinoro and b.)].

Alternatively, D-F may have been the original dispute between Eleazar and the sages and E may be a gloss. If so, the dispute may be as follows. Eleazar regards replacing a pot in its insulation as identical to the act of insulating it on the Sabbath, which is prohibited. The sages hold that initial insulation is prohibited but subsequent insulation is permitted. The original form of the dispute would then be:

qwph mṭh ʿl ṣdh wnwṭl
R. Eleazar b. Azariah ʾwmr: ʾynw mḥzyr
wḥkmym ʾwmrym: mḥzyr.

15. [A. And with what may they not go out?...]

Rams may not go out with their wagon [under their fat tail] nor may ewes go out with the wood chip in their nose, nor may the calf go out with its rush-yoke, nor the cow with the hedgehog-skin [tied around its udder] nor with the strap between its horns.

B. R. Eleazar b. Azariah's cow used to go out with the strap between its horns

C. against the will of the sages.

M. Shab. 5:4 (cf. M. Beṣah 2:8 and M. Eduyyot 3:11)

Comment: Chapter Five lists the articles which may be worn by an animal on the Sabbath. Anything that does not serve as either clothing or protection for the animal is considered to be a burden. It is forbidden for one to place a burden on his animal on the Sabbath since both he and his animals are enjoined from labor on that day (Deut. 5:14).

A continues a list of articles which may not be placed on animals on the Sabbath. The wagon for the fat-tail protected that valuable part of the ram from damage. Its main purpose was to prevent the monetary value of the ram from decreasing and as such afforded little physical protection to the animal. The woodchip was a therapeutic device to protect against worms. The rush-yoke was used to accustom the young animal to the yoke. The thorny hedgehog-skin protected the cow's milk and prevented small animals from sucking at the cow's udders. Thus none of the articles mentioned in the list served as protection for the animal itself.

The purpose of the strap between the horns of the bull is not clear. b. suggests that it was used either as a decorative item or as a guide-strap with which one could lead the animal. B reports that Eleazar's cow used to go out on the Sabbath wearing a strap between its horns. Both this report and the law which precedes it are absent from Tosefta. B, placed at the end of the list of the chapter, also describes an article which apparently does not directly serve either as protection or clothing for the animal. C appears to be a gloss. Had there been a dispute between Eleazar and the sages it might have been preserved in the dispute form:

Eleazar: *hprh ywṣ'...*
Sages: *'yn hprh ywṣ'...*

Eleazar's rule has been preserved in the form of a third person report, not unusual for patriarchal material. We would expect it to be preserved in the *m'śh b* + narrative form as: *m'śh b: prtw šl...yṣh...* in the simple past tense. As it stands in M. it is unusual.

16. A. They [may] wash the child whether before or after the circumcision

B. and they [may] sprinkle it by hand but not with a vessel.

C. R. Eleazar b. Azariah says they [may] wash the child on the third day which falls on the Sabbath,

D. for it is written, "And it came to pass on the third day when they were sore (Gen. 34:25)."

M. Shab. 19:3 (b. Shab. 134b; B. R. 80:9, ed. Theodor-Albeck, p. 962, ls. 1-2, p. 963, ls. 1-2)

Comment: Where there is some danger to life or limb the prohibition against washing the entire body on the Sabbath may be abrogated. Thus the newly circumcised child may be washed after the circumcision as a therapeutic measure. Furthermore as 19:1-2 indicate, all preparations for the circumcision which cannot be performed before the Sabbath may be done on the Sabbath day. Thus the child may be washed before the circumcision.

B allows sprinkling to be performed by hand but not with a vessel. I do not know what the 'sprinkling' of our pericope was, nor what its purpose was. C presents Eleazar's ruling that the child may be washed on the Sabbath if it is the third day after the circumcision. As to the washing of the child on the day of the circumcision if it should fall on the Sabbath, Aqiva and Eliezer discuss the issue in 19:1-2. Although it is possible that Eleazar may hold that washing the baby on the day of the circumcision is permissible *a fortiori*, it is likely that he considered the third day as the most dangerous. (That is the implication of Gen. 34:25.) Hence no conclusion may be drawn from the ruling concerning the third day about the law of the day of the circumcision. b. correctly points out that the verse does not serve as a proof text for the law, but merely as an allusion to the fact that the third day is a critical time after the circumcision.

The law also appears anonymously in M. Shab. 9:3:

A. From whence do we know that we may wash the circumcised [child] on the third day which falls on the Sabbath?

B. For it is written...

There the pericope is fifth in the following series of seven questions:

1. R. Aqiva said: From whence do we learn of an idol that like a menstruant it conveys uncleanness by carrying? Because it is written, *Thou shalt cast them away like a menstruthing; thou shalt say unto it, Get thee hence*. Like a menstruant conveys uncleanness by carrying, so does an idol convey uncleanness by carrying.	1. R. Aqiva says: (an idol is) like a menstruant for it is written...as a menstruant conveys uncleanness by carrying, so does an idol convey uncleanness by carrying. M. A.Z. 3:6
2. From whence do we learn of a ship that it is not susceptible to uncleanness? Because it is written, *The way of a ship in the midst of the sea.*	2. Among earthenware utensils these are not susceptible to uncleanness...a ship. M. Kel. 2:3
3. From whence do we learn of a garden-bed, six handbreadths square, that five kinds of seed may be sown therein, four on the sides and one in the middle? Because it is written *For as the earth bringeth forth her bud and as the garden causeth the seeds sown in it to spring forth.* It is not written *its seeds* but the *seeds sown in it.*	3. " " " " M. Kil. 3:1
4. From whence do we learn of a woman who emits semen on the third day that she is unclean? (some MSS give "clean"). Because it is written, *And be ready against the third day.*	4. If a woman emits semen on the third day she is clean. So R. Eleazar b. Azariah. M. Miq. 8:3
5. (Eleazar/circumcised child on the third day.)	5. (Our pericope) M. Shab. 19:3
6. From whence do we learn that they tie a strip of crimson on the head of the scapegoat? Because it	6. He bound the thread of crimson on the head of the scapegoat... M. Yoma 4:2

is written, *Though your sins be as scarlet they shall be as white as snow.*	R. Ishmael said...A thread of crimson wool was tied to the door of the sanctuary and when the he goat reached the wilderness the thread turned white; for it is written... M. Yoma 6:8
7. From whence do we learn that on the Day of Atonement anointing is equal to drinking? Although there is no proof of the matter there is an indication in that it is written, *And it came into his inward parts like water and like oil into his bones.*	7. On the Day of Atonement eating, drinking, washing, anointing...are forbidden. M. Yoma 8:1

The second, sixth and seventh items have no direct parallel. Two and three can only be attested in the Ushan strata. The rest are attributed to Yavneans. The verse is added to all of them except to one and five. Four is interesting as its parallel gives the contradictory ruling in the name of Eleazar b. Azariah.

I can find no discernible pattern to the content or hermeneutic of the composite pericope. Though it may stem from an Aqivan redactional circle by the attribution at the outset, I see no internal reason to assume this. It is quite possible that the attribution was picked up through the parallel source of (1) and appended here.

Note that the concern of Eleazar's ruling in 19:3 stands independent of the issue disputed by Aqiva and Eliezer. This is further evidence that Eleazar stands outside of Aqivan redactional circles.

17. A. A bath house whose openings were stopped up on the eve of the Sabbath--one may wash in it immediately after the Sabbath.

B. [If its] openings were stopped up on the eve of the festival--one may enter on the festival day and sweat and go out and bathe in cold water.

C. Said R. Judah, "*m'šh b*: The bath house of *Benei Beraq*--they stopped up its openings on the eve of the festival and R. Aqiva and R. Eleazar b. Azariah would enter and sweat inside it and go out and bathe in cold water

D. "since (*'l' š*) its hot pools were covered with boards.

E. "When the transgressors multiplied they again forbade it."

Tos. Shab. 3:3, ed. Lieberman, p. 12, ls. 6-10 (b. Shab. 40a)

Comment: The pericope contains two separate issues. If on the Sabbath water had been heated up for bathing, one would have to wait for at least the amount of time that it would take to heat the water after the Sabbath before deriving any benefit from that water. A rules that if the openings of a bath house were stopped up before the Sabbath, there is no need to wait at all after the Sabbath before going in to bathe, since the water could not have been heated up on the Sabbath under those circumstances. Any heat that is present in the bath house had to have been generated before the Sabbath.

The standard near-eastern bath house in antiquity had rooms with hot pools, rooms with cold pools and steam rooms. B states that on the festival one may enter the steam room and sweat if its heat was not generated on the day of the festival (if its openings were stopped up). Furthermore, afterwards it was permissible to bathe in the cold baths. C tells us that Eleazar and Aqiva went into the bath house to sweat and then immersed themselves in the cold pool. There was no suspicion that they went into the hot pool since it had been covered with boards before the festival. E reports that because of the transgressors, they "forbade it." It is not clear whether the reference is to going in to sweat or to bathe in the cold pool.

There is a parallel version in b. Shab. 40a:

> A. *tnw rbnn*: A bath house the openings of which they plugged (*pqqw*) on the eve of the Sabbath--one may wash in it immediately after the Sabbath.
>
> B. [If its] openings were plugged on the eve of the festival--the next day he may go in and sweat and go out and immerse himself in the outer room.
>
> C. Said R. Judah, "*m'śh b*: The bath house of *Benei Beraq*--they plugged up its openings on the eve of the festival. The next day R. Eleazar b. Azariah and R. Aqiva went in and sweated, went out and immersed themselves in the outer room
>
> D. "since its hot pools were covered with boards."
>
> E. When the matter came before the sages they said even if its hot pools are not covered with boards [one may enter].
>
> F. And when the transgressors multiplied they began to prohibit.

The b. version is expanded and modified. Its conclusion is that what Eleazar and Aqiva did was proper and is permitted. The prohibition in F applies only to the case which the sages wanted to allow (E) and implies that since the hot pools were not covered, people began to immerse themselves in them.

Both the Tosefta and *beraita* assume that immersion in hot baths was forbidden even on the festival. The *beraita* implies that the transgressors would bathe in the hot baths if they were not covered with boards. Tosefta implies that in spite of all the precautions, the transgressors still took hot baths.

Here we find Eleazar and Aqiva together. The tradition has been preserved in the *m'śh b* + narrative form.

18. A. Once (*kbr*) R. Ishmael, R. Aqiva, and R. Eleazar b. Azariah were walking by the way and Levi the netmaker and Ishmael the son of R. Eleazar b. Azariah were following them.

B. The following question was put before them:

C. From whence do we know that mortal danger overrides the [prohibitions of the] Sabbath?

D. Answered R. Ishmael and said, "'If a thief is found breaking in, and is struck so that he dies, there shall be no bloodguilt for him (Ex. 22:2).' This is a case where there is doubt [whether the thief] came to steal or whether [the thief] came to kill

E. "and the spilling of blood defiles the land and causes the Divine Presence to depart from Israel,

F. "[yet] one may save himself by killing the thief (*nytn lhṣylw bnpšw*)

G. "we may infer *a fortiori* that [in a case of] mortal danger [one may] override the Sabbath [prohibitions to save a life]."

H. Answered R. Aqiva and said, "But if a man willfully attacks another to kill him treacherously, you shall take him from my altar that he may die (Ex. 21:14).' [Scripture says] 'From my altar' and not 'from upon my alter.'"

I. And said Rabbah bar bar Hannah said R. Yohanan, "This was the teaching only [regarding the removal of a priest] to be put to death. But [regarding the removal of a priest to give testimony] to save a life--he may even be taken 'from upon my altar.'

J. "And this is a case where it is doubtful whether there is substance to his words or not [if he is removed in order to testify]

K. "and the Temple service overrides the Sabbath [but we override the Temple service so that we may save a life].

L. "We may infer *a fortiori* that mortal danger overrides the Sabbath."

M. Answered R. Eleazar [b. Azariah] and said, "In the case of circumcision [which involves danger] to one of the two hundred and forty-eight limbs of the body--one may override the Sabbath.

N. "We may infer *a fortiori* that [where there is danger to] his entire body--one may override the Sabbath."

O. R. Yosé b. R. Judah says, "'*'k* you shall keep my Sabbaths (Ex. 31:13).' One might have thought thought that for all [Sabbaths there is no exception]. It says '*'k*' [which] distinguishes [between a normal Sabbath which must be kept, and one which must be violated because of mortal danger]."

P. R. Jonathan b. Joseph says, "'Because it is holy for you (Ex. 31:14).' It [the Sabbath] is given into your hands and you are not given into its hands."

Q. R. Simeon b. Menasiah says, "'The People of Israel shall keep the Sabbath observing the Sabbath throughout their generations (Ex. 31:16).' The Torah said that one may defile one Sabbath to save a life so that many other Sabbaths may be observed."

b. Yoma 85a-b (Mekh., *Shab.*, I, p. 340; b. Shab. 132a; Tanḥ. *VaYešeb*, 8, ed. Buber, p. 91a)

Comment: The pericope shows signs of sloppy redaction. Moreover, the attributions are questionable since T. Shab. 15:16 assigns the arguments of D-N to different masters. Let us turn first to the redactional structure of the pericope. A-C serves as the protasis. Of the five people mentioned in A, only Ishmael, Aqiva and Eleazar reappear later. The phrase "answered R. ... and said" is clearly a redactional convention which ties together three separate responses to the same issue. O-Q gives three more statements on the matter, tacked on because of their thematic content.

Before turning to an analysis of the content of the pericope, we look at the Toseftan version.

1. From whence do we know that mortal danger overrides the Sabbath?

2. For it is written, "You shall keep my Sabbaths (Ex. 31:13)." One might have thought that even circumcision, Temple service, and mortal danger [are not cause to violate the Sabbath]. It says, "*'k*": [implying that] there are times when you must "rest" and that there are times when you must not "rest."

3. R. Eliezer says, "Circumcision overrides the Sabbath--for what reason? Because one is liable to 'cutting off' [if it is performed] after its designated time.

4. "And can we not infer *a fortiori*: If one limb overrides the Sabbath, should not the whole body override the Sabbath?"

5. They said to him, "From the place you came [is the refutation to your argument]: Just as in your case [the Sabbath is set aside in a case of] certainty and not doubt, so here [one sets aside the Sabbath in a case of] certainty and not doubt.

6. "And (!) in what was the Torah more stringent? In the Temple service or in the Sabbath? It was more stringent in the Temple service than in the Sabbath. For the Temple service overrides the Sabbath and the Sabbath does not override the Temple service.

"Can we not infer *a fortiori*? Just as the service overrides the Sabbath, mortal doubt overrides it--the Sabbath--which the service overrides, is it not certain that the Sabbath which is overriden by the service should be overriden by mortal doubt. Thus we have learned that mortal doubt overrides the Sabbath."

7. R. Aḥa says in the name of R. Aqiva, "'If a thief is found breaking in' What is [the status of] the householder? Is he in certain or doubtful

[danger]? Thus we say if we allow the taking of a life where there is only doubtful mortal danger, do we not surely set aside the Sabbath for doubtful mortal danger?

8. "The commandments were given to live by them. As it says, 'all that a man may keep and live by them' and not die by them."

Ishmael's argument in the *beraita* (D-G) is given in Aqiva's name in T.(7). He argues that one may violate the prohibition against killing in order to save one's life. Killing is a greater transgression than violating the Sabbath. Therefore, one may certainly violate the Sabbath to save a life. Aqiva's argument (H-L and 6 in T.) is interrupted and interpreted by I. Service in the Cult overrides the Sabbath; mortal danger overrides the Cult (as I explains); therefore mortal danger certainly overrides the Sabbath.

Eleazar argues (M-N) that one may set aside the Sabbath to attend to the needs of circumcision which involves only part of the body and does not constitute mortal danger. Surely where the whole body is endangered the Sabbath may be overridden (3-4 of T. in Eliezer's name).

A-N of our pericope is an attempt to combine three responses to the same question in one artificial unit. We have seen three other instances in which Eleazar and Ishmael appear together, all more than likely late redactional creations (T. Ber. 1:4, M. Yad. 4:3 and M. Ker. 2:5). Even though T. does not attribute anything to Eleazar and seems in fact to assign his argument to Eliezer, the *beraita* evidence here and in b. Shab 132a makes it more likely that the attribution of M-N to Eleazar is accurate.

19. A. One who was taken out [beyond the Sabbath limit] by gentiles or an evil spirit, has but four cubits [to move within].

B. If they brought him back again it is as though he had never gone out.

C. If they brought him to another town or put him in a cattle-pen or a cattle-fold,

C1. [about this] Rabban Gamaliel and R. Eleazar b. Azariah say, "He may traverse their whole area."

D. R. Joshua and R. Aqiva say, "He has but four cubits [to move within]."

E. *m'śh š*: They came from Brundisium and their ship was at sea [on the Sabbath outside the Sabbath boundary].

F. Rabban Gamaliel and R. Eleazar b. Azariah traversed the whole area [of the ship].

G. R. Joshua and R. Aqiva did not move beyond four cubits

H. for they wished to adopt a stringent ruling for themselves.

M. Erub. 4:1

Comment: On the Sabbath one may not travel outside a radius of two thousand *'amot* of the place he was on sundown Friday. The Sabbath boundary is the diameter of the circle described by that radius. A presents a case of one who was taken out beyond the boundary. It rules that he may walk only within the confined space which he occupies (defined as four *'amot* in any direction) but no further. However if he was carried back to his point of origin he may again walk anywhere within his Sabbath boundary. C presents a middle case. If he was forcibly removed beyond the limit and placed in a confined area such as a cattle pen, Gamaliel and Eleazar rule that he may walk within the entire enclosed area. Joshua and Aqiva rule that he may walk only four *'amot* in any direction within the enclosed space.

E-H is a story in which the four disputants are on a ship which apparently travelled more than two thousand *'amot* on the Sabbath. The language of the rulings of C1-D is similar to that of F-G:

C1 -- *mhlk 't kwlh*	F -- *hlkw 't kwlh*
D -- *'yn lw 'l' 'rb' 'mwt*	G -- *l' zzw m'rb' 'mwt*

E-G probably generates C-D. H glosses the story. The conjunction of Eleazar and Gamaliel is significant as both were alleged to have been patriarchs. The story may have been preserved by patriarchal tradents who represent Joshua and Aqiva as adopting the stringent position. A statistically significant number of Gamaliel and Eleazar's tradition are preserved in the *m'śh b* + narrative form. The four Rabbis of this pericope appear together in M. M.S. 5:9. In M. Shab. 16:8 Gamaliel and "the elders" arrive on a ship. See also M. Erub. 4:1.

20. A. *dtny'*: "They shall eat flesh that night (Ex. 12:8)."

B. R. Eleazar b. Azariah says, "It says here 'that night' and it says further on, 'For I will pass through the land of Egypt *that night* (Ex. 12:12).'

C. "Just as in the latter [it refers to the time up] to midnight, so too here (*'p k'n*) [one may eat the Paschal lamb] until midnight."

D. Said to him R. Aqiva, "Does it not say, '(and you shall eat it in) haste (Ex. 12:11)'--implying [that it may be eaten] until the time of 'haste' [i.e., sunrise]?

E. "If so why does it say 'that night' (*mh tlmwd lwmr blylh*)?

F. "One might have thought that [the Paschal lamb] must be eaten as all sacrifices--during the day.

G. "It says [however] 'that night,' [implying] that it is eaten at night and not during the day."

b. Pes. 120b; b. Ber. 9a; b. Meg. 21a; b. Zeb. 57b (Mekh. de R. Simeon, *parshat Bo'*, ed. Epstein-Melamed, pp. 13, 15)

Comment: The pericope casts the conflicting opinions of Eleazar and Aqiva into a dispute. A-C give Eleazar's ruling that the Paschal sacrifice may only be eaten until midnight; D-F spell out Aqiva's view--they may be eaten all night. A simple statement of their opinions would have been:

> Until when may the Paschal lamb be eaten?
> R. Eleazar b. Azariah says, "Until midnight."
> R. Aqiva says, "Until sunrise."

Eleazar's ruling is not found cited in his name in M.-T. It is stated anonymously, however, in M. Zeb. 5:8b:

> The Paschal lamb is only eaten at night and is only eaten until midnight and is only eaten by those appointed for it and is only eaten roasted.

Eleazar's exegetical proof is based implicitly on Ex. 12:29, "And it came to pass at midnight and the Lord slew all the first born..." We find Eleazar connected with another ruling about the Paschal lamb in M. Zeb. 1:2--the sacrifice which was slaughtered not for its own sake.

21. A. *wm'śh b*: Rabban Gamaliel and R. Joshua and R. Eleazar b. Azariah and R. Aqiva were traveling on a boat.

B. Only R. Gamaliel had a *lulav* which he had bought for a thousand *zuz*.

C. R. Gamaliel took it and fulfilled his obligation and he gave it to R. Joshua as a gift.

R. Joshua took it and fulfilled his obligation and he gave it to R. Eleazar b. Azariah as a gift.

R. Eleazar b. Azariah took it and fulfilled his obligation and he gave it to R. Aqiva as a gift.

R. Aqiva took it and fulfilled his obligation and he gave it back to R. Gamaliel.

b. Suk. 41b; Sifra *'Emor, pereq* 16:2, ed. Weiss, p. 102b

Comment: The story is one of a genre which is characterized by the protasis that states "R. Gamaliel and the Elders were traveling on a boat." (See, for example, M. M.S. 5:9.) Here the Elders are listed in the protasis. The pericope is designed to illustrate two rulings: First, one may, if necessary, spend a great deal of money to procure a *lulav*; second, one may fulfill his obligation with the *lulav* of a second party but only if he receives it as a "gift."

This genre seems to stem from pro-Gamaliel sources as he is usually represented as the central figure of the group. Eleazar functions only as a name on a list here. Compare T. Suk. 2:11 which gives a parallel version of our pericope omitting all the names save Gamaliel's.

22. A. [There are] three things which R. Eleazar b. Azariah permits and the sages forbid:

B. His cow may go out on the Sabbath with the strap that is between its horns.

C. And they may curry [cattle] on the festival day.

D. And [they may] grind pepper in its mill.

E. R. Judah says, "One may not curry [cattle] on the festival day

F. "because it creates a wound [on the animal],

G. "but they may comb them."

H. And the sages say, "One may neither curry nor may one comb."

M. Beṣ. 2:8 (M. Ed. 3:12)

Comment: This pericope is part of a series of pericopae each of which lists three rulings. A introduces the pericope. B differs from C and D in tense as C and D are in the present participle form and B is in the third person singular possessive. It is likely that the redactor took B directly out of the source of M. Shab. 5:4. Here the redactor assumes that there was an explicit dispute on that matter. There the wording is simply that Eleazar allowed his cow to go out on the Sabbath "...against the wishes of the sages."

C and D relate to activity on the festival day. C permits the grooming of an animal with a curry comb. D rules that pepper may be ground on the festival day for use on that day. If it had been ground before the festival, it would have lost some of its pungency. All actions relating to the preparation of a meal for the festival may be performed on the day except those which may be effectively accomplished before the festival. Eleazar allows the grinding of pepper in its mill and the sages do not. Maimonides (*Yad*, *Hilkhot Yom Tob*, 3-12) assumes that they allow the grinding of pepper on the festival but prohibit the use of the mill. Eleazar follows the patriarchal tradition of Gamaliel's House. Tosefta Beṣ. 2:16 has: "[Those] of the House of Rabban Gamaliel used to grind pepper in its mill." The rationale behind the prohibition of the use of the mill is not clear.

C, E, and H present three differing opinions about currying cattle on the festival:

C -- (Eleazar) *mqrdyn 't hbhmh bywm ṭwb*
E -- (Judah) *'yn* " " " " "... *'bl mqrṣpyn*[5]
H -- (sages) " " *'p l'* "

G adds, "One may comb them." The reference is to use of a large comb which presumably would not scratch the animal. Tosefta (2:17) asks, "What is currying (*qyrwr*)? That is [combing with] small ones which create a scratch. What is combing? That is large ones which do not create a scratch."

The entire pericope has been extensively reworked by the redactor. It incorporates Eleazar's ruling about his cow with a dispute about currying and combing on the festival, and perhaps for the sake of completeness of a list of three items, adds Eleazar's ruling about grinding pepper. We thus have a pericope with three rulings which fits neatly into the list of M. Beṣ., Chapter Two.

The pericope actually contains two disputes. From A-C we can reconstruct:

Eleazar -- *mqrdyn*
sages -- *'yn mqrdyn*

E-H is simply a dispute about combing:

> Judah -- *mqrṣpyn*
> sages -- *ʾyn mqrṣpyn*

23. A. R. Eleazar b. Azariah says, "They may not newly dig a water channel during the festival or during the seventh year."

B. And the sages say, "They may newly dig a water channel during the seventh year

C. "and they may repair what has broken down during the festival;

D. "they may repair damaged waterways in the public domain and clean them out;

E. "and they may repair roads, open places, and pools of water, and perform all public needs, and mark the graves;

F. "and they may also go forth [to give warning] against the Diverse-Kinds."

M. M.Q. 1:2

Comment: A-B is in dispute form. It is unbalanced. A balanced dispute might have been:

A. A water channel
B. R. Eleazar b. Azariah says, "They may not dig."
C. The sages say, "They may dig."

The redactor, to make sense of the unspecific agricultural dispute, may then be responsible for assigning the ruling of the pericope to the seventh year and to the festival. Tosefta suggests that some agricultural laws were transmitted without specific referents, with the statement "Said Rabbi, I approve of the words of R. Judah concerning the festival and the words of the sages concerning the seventh year." Tosefta 1:1, 3, 4, 6 may also have been assigned by the redactor to the seventh year or to the festival.

C-E are festival laws which are independent of the preceding dispute. They are general rules for working the land on the festival and they permit repairs to be made (*mtqnyn*) but do not allow the initiation of new construction.

Alternatively, the redactor may have combined two separate disputes in our pericope (A-B):

A. A channel
B. Eleazar--may not dig in the seventh year
C. Sages--may dig in the seventh year

and:

A. A channel
B. Eleazar--may not dig on the festival
C. Sages--may dig on the festival.

The combined dispute was then placed in M. M.Q., Chapter One, where the redactor chose to attach the laws in C-E directly after our A-B. Those anonymous laws limit construction, but permit repairs on the festival. The sages' ruling concerning the festival had to be altered in order that it not contradict the laws of C-E. This disrupts the balance of the dispute and leaves Eleazar and the sages with identical rulings concerning the festival. They permit repairs only. The redactor was probably responsible for inserting the gloss "newly" (*btḥylh*) at this point in order to leave no contradiction between the rulings of A-B and of C-E.

We will now turn to the substance of the rulings. Eleazar's ruling as it appears in M. is consistent with his ruling in Tos. Moʿed 1:1 (see below). There also he prohibits initiatory activity on the festival, presumably because of the great exertion it would require. Repairs may be made so that a monetary loss may be averted. Eleazar's ruling is also consistent with his dictum of M. Sheb. 3:3. There he prohibits the storing of dung out on a field in the seventh year, lest it appear as if one is fertilizing the field. In our pericope he prohibits the digging of a new water channel on the seventh year lest it appear as if one is hoeing or plowing the field.

24. A. A newly flowing spring, "One may water a householder's (*byt hbʿl*) field from it," [those were] the words of R. Meir.

B. And the sages say, "One waters only an irrigated field (*byt hšlḥyn*) whose ditches had collapsed."

C. R. Eleazar b. Azariah says, "One does not water from it."

Tos. Mo'ed 1:1, ed. Lieberman, p. 365, ls. 1-3

Comment: The issue here is what may one do in order to irrigate his fields on the intermediate days of the festival. The Tosefta distinguishes between two types of fields: *byt hšlḥyn* and *byt hb'l*. Lieberman explains that the former is a field which must be artificially irrigated and the latter is naturally irrigated by rain water. Babli M.Q. 2a provides a similar interpretation.

A *beraita* (b. M.Q. 2a) has a slightly different version of the pericope:

> A. A newly flowing spring, "One may even (*'pylw*) water a householder's field from it," the words of R. Meir.
>
> B. And R. Judah says, "One only waters an irrigated field whose ditches had collapsed."
>
> C. R. Eleazar b. Azariah says, "Neither so nor so (*l' kk wl' kk*)."

Following the attributions, the earliest law allowed no watering. Then, watering of irrigated fields was permitted (B = sages = Judah). Finally even the householder's field could be watered. The *beraita* version of Eleazar's lemma indicates that it is dependent on A-B for its meaning, surely a later revision.

Maimonides explains the sages' (= Judah's = B) opinion (*Yad*, *Hilkhot Yom Tob*, 7-2): "If he does not water it (the irrigated land) as it is dry land, he will lose the trees that are in it. When he waters it he should not draw water and water it from a pool or from rain water, since that requires much effort. Rather he should water it from a spring--either an existent or newly formed one. He may divert it and water with that water."

The pericope gives the latest ruling first and places Eleazar's opinion last. For another example of this reverse chronological order, see M. Sheb. 3:3.

25. A. A twelve month old [infant who died] goes out [for burial] in a bier.

B. R. Aqiva says, "If he is one year old and his body like a two year old [infant],

C. "[or] if he is two and his body like a one year old, he goes out in a bier."

D. R. Simeon b. Eleazar says, "If one goes out in a bier, the public grieves over him. If one does not go out in a bier, the public does not grieve over him."

E. R. Eleazar b. Azariah says, "If he is recognized by the public (Rashi: he normally goes out of the house), the public busies itself with him [and is involved in his funeral]. If he is not recognized by the public, the public does not busy itself with him."

b. M.Q. 24b

Comment: Eleazar's ruling in E gives the criterion for determining whether the community participates in the funeral of an infant. Neither age nor manner of burial enters into his criterion. The determining factor is whether the infant has reached the stage of maturity at which time he appears in public. It is not clear whether this means he must be able to walk out on his own or whether it is the time when he is taken out.

D is an independent ruling specifying another criterion for the participation of the public in the funeral--that of whether the child is buried in a coffin. This is the issue of A and Aqiva's gloss B-C. The three rulings in the pericope are independent but related thematically.

A. If he is three years old, he is taken out in a bier.

B. R. Aqiva said, "If he is three, but his limbs are like a two-year-old, or if he is two, but his limbs are like a three-year-old he is carried out in a bier."

C. Simeon the brother of Azariah said, "For anyone who is taken out in a bier the people grieve."

D. R. Meir said in the name of R. Eleazar b. Azariah, "If he is recognized by the public, the public busies itself with him. If not, they do not busy themselves with him."

M. Sem. 3:3

E. R. Judah said in the name of R. Eleazar b. Azariah, "For the purpose of a eulogy, it is sufficient that his neighbors [know him].

F. "In the case of the poor, a eulogy is delivered for a child of three, and in the case of the rich, for a child of four."

G. R. Aqiva said, "In the case of the poor, for a child of six, and in the case of the rich, for a child of seven."

H. The children of the rich are like the children of scholars, and the children of scholars like the children of kings and they busy themselves with them.

M. Sem. 3:4, ed. Higger, pp. 110-111

Comment: Meir is Eleazar's tradent in D. In E Judah, as the tradent of Eleazar, cites a ruling on a related matter, the eulogy. The criterion is the same as that of D--if the child was accustomed to venture out of the house, he is eulogized.

F gives a contrary law basing the matter on age. In G Aqiva disputes F, but also uses age as the criterion for his ruling, as he does in B. The gloss H explains why there is a distinction between the rich and the poor.

iii. *Nasḥim*

26. A. The father is not liable for his daughter's maintenance.

B. This exposition was expounded by R. Eleazar b. Azariah before the rabbis at *Kerem beYavneh*:

C. "'The sons shall inherit and the daughters shall receive maintenance.'

D. "Just as the sons do not inherit until after the death of the father

E. "so too (*'p*) the daughters do not receive maintenance until after the death of their father."

M. Ket. 4:6

Comment: A is the statement of the law that a father is not responsible for the support of his daughter. The redactor elucidates the ruling with the tradition B-E. B tells us that Eleazar expounded the matter before the sages at the "vineyard at Yavneh." In C he expounds the words of the *ketubah* as if they were from a biblical verse. This implies that exegetical methods were not restricted to biblical material. M. Ket. 4:10 and 11 gives us the Aramaic form of some parts of the *ketubah*: *bnyn dkryn...yrtwn... bnn nqbyn...myznn mnksy*--male children...inherit...female children receive maintenance from the property. C has a Hebrew version. D-E explains the exposition.

The ruling could have had great social ramifications since it implies that a father need not support his daughters. If he so desires he may allow them to go begging from door to door for their maintenance. Such a ruling is quite harsh on the children and certainly warrants at least exegetical support. We have contrary rulings on the same issue in the name of Tannaim of the next generation. Yoḥanan b. Beroqa says that it is an obligation (*ḥwbh*) to maintain the daughters (Tos. Ket. 4:8). Judah maintains that it is a *miṣwah* to maintain the daughters because it would be a disgrace for them to go begging for food (b. Ket. 49a). If the attributions are reliable, these may represent a reaction against the earlier ruling and its social ramifications. On *Kerem beYavneh*, see Epstein, *Tan.*, pp. 425ff.

A. R. Leazar b. Azariah expounded upon the *ketubah* (*'bd ktwbh mdrš*):

B. R. Eleazar b. Azariah expounded: "The sons will inherit and the daughters will be maintained. Just as the sons do not inherit until the death of their father, so too (*'p*) the daughters are not maintained until after the death of their father."

y. Yeb. 15:3; y. Ket. 4:8

Comment: The pericope appears in the context of a series of illustrations of how various masters expounded the *ketubah*. B is a citation of M. Ket. 4:6 with one variation. The protasis of the exposition in M. is "This exposition was expounded by R. Eleazar b. Azariah before the Rabbis at the Yavneh." It is not likely that y. preserves another version of M. though, since the stylistic requirements of the sugya in which our pericope appears dictate that each example be introduced by the protasis "x *'bdyn ktwbh mdrš: drš* x."

On the issue of the tradition see comment to M.

27. A. Even though they said, "A virgin [who marries] collects two hundred [*zuz* if her husband divorces her or dies] and a widow [who marries collects] one hundred

B. "if he [the husband] wished to add on even ten thousand [*zuz*] he may add on [to his total liability to her]."

C. [If a woman] was widowed or divorced, whether she had [only] been betrothed or [even] married, she collects the entire amount [one hundred plus any additional amount].

D. R. Eleazar b. Azariah says, "A married woman [who was widowed or divorced] collects the entire amount [of two hundred].

E. "A betrothed woman [who was widowed or divorced] collects two hundred [if she had been a] virgin [when she was betrothed] and one hundred [if she had been a] widow.

F. "since he only wrote [the additional sum into her *ketubah*] on the condition that he bring her in [to his home (i.e., that he actually marry her)]."

M. Ket. 5:1

Comment: A-B rules that a husband may voluntarily add on as much as he wishes to the indebtedness he assumes in his wife's *ketubah*. The anonymous law of C states that under all circumstances a widow or divorcée collects one hundred plus any additional sum that had been stipulated ("the entire amount"). Eleazar distinguishes between the case of a betrothed woman and a married woman. The married woman whose husband divorces her or dies collects the standard amount plus any additional. However, a betrothed woman cannot collect the additional sum. The gloss F explains that the husband assumes liability for the additional sum on the implicit condition that they marry. If they never marry he need not pay the additional. Eleazar, therefore, disagrees with C. The pericope is in the form of an anonymous ruling followed by a citation of Eleazar's opinion, common in the preservation of Eleazar's tradition.

28. A. ...And all produce of the vine combines together

B. and one [a Nazirite] is not liable until he eats an olive's bulk of the grapes.

C. *mšnh r'šwnh*: "Until one drinks a quarter-*log* of wine."

D. R. Aqiva says, "Even if one dipped his bread into the wine and there was enough to combine for an olive's bulk--he is liable."

M. Naz. 6:1

E. And one [a Nazirite] is liable on the wine alone, on the grapes alone, on the insides (*ḥrṣnym*) alone or on the outsides (*zgym*) alone.

F. R. Eleazar b. Azariah says, "One is not liable until he eats two insides and their outsides (i.e., two whole grapes)."

M. Naz. 6:2

A. "All the days of his Naziriteship from all that is made from the grape vine, from the insides [of the grapes] to the outsides he shall not eat (Num. 6:4)."...Why does it say "From the inside to the outside he shall not eat"?

B. "It excludes [the case of where he ate only] two insides and one outside, [and is free of liability]"

C. the words of R. Eleazar b. Azariah.

Sifré Num., ed. Horowitz-Rabin, p. 29, ls. 11-12 (Num. R. 10:9)

Comment: M. combines two separate disputes concerning the minimum quantity of produce of the vine that a Nazirite must consume before becoming liable to stripes. The first dispute consists of A, B, and F. The dispute centers around the question of how much solid grape produce must be eaten for liability. B gives an anonymous law in the form *he is not liable until he eats + quantity*. B requires an olive's bulk as the minimum. In F, R. Eleazar b. Azariah's opinion is given in the same form: *not liable until + quantity*. He requires a minimum of two whole grapes. The two rulings are well balanced:

B. [The Nazirite] is not liable until he eats an olive's bulk of the grapes.

F. R. Eleazar b. Azariah says, "He is not liable until he eats two insides and their outsides."

In most elementary form the dispute becomes *kzyt/šnym* (an olive's bulk/two grapes).

A glosses the pericope. It introduces the concept of connection or combination. Neusner has suggested that this is an Ushan concept (see *HMLP*, Vol. 3, pp. 298ff.). It is likely that A is also an Ushan gloss.

C, D, and E form a second dispute. The issue is the amount of liquid that must be consumed for liability.

mšnh r'šwnh is C's authority. T. assigns this ruling to Eleazar (see below). In D, Aqiva's ruling presupposes an olive's bulk as the minimum liquid measure. D looks as if it has been heavily interpolated. In simplest form a dispute could have been formulated: *rby'yt/kzyt*:

C. *mšnh r'šwnh*: "Until he drinks a quarter of wine."
D. R. Aqiva says, "Even...an olive's bulk he is liable."

D explains how one may measure liquids in terms of the solid measure, an olive's bulk. The amount which an olive sized piece of bread absorbs is equivalent to an olive's bulk of liquids. E, a redactional convention, explains that the same law applies to both liquids and solids.

Before turning to the question of the redaction of this pericope, we will examine Tosefta's version.

A. ...And how much is their measure [of all of those things which a Nazirite is prohibited to eat]? An olive's bulk.

B. And all combine together to form an olive's bulk.

C. The wine and vinegar as well [are prohibited in an olive's bulk].

D. "What does one do [to measure an olive's bulk of liquid]? He brings a full cup of wine and he brings a standard [medium] sized olive and puts it in [the cup] and it overflows. If he drinks a like amount he is liable. And if not he is free [of liability]."

E. The words of R. Aqiva.

F. R. Eleazar b. Azariah exempts [the Nazirite] until he drinks a quarter-*log* of wine

G. Whether he mixed it and drank it or whether he drank it undiluted (*ḥṣ'yn*).

Tos. Nez. 4:1, ed. Lieberman, p. 136, ls. 3-6

Comment: Tosefta has both issues, liability for solids and for liquids. We will first examine the structure of the Toseftan version and then compare it to the version of Mishnah.

A rules that an olive's bulk is the minimum for solid liability. Eleazar's contrary ruling of M. (F) is absent from T. The gloss B introduces the question of combination for liability. C serves as the link between the issues of solids and liquids. D, E, and F give the dispute about liquids. Here Aqiva's ruling comes first. It accompanies an alternative explanation of how to go about converting solid measures for use with liquid. D suggests that the displacement of a solid the size of an olive is equivalent to an olive's bulk of liquids. F gives the minimum as a quarter *log*. Here the ruling is in Eleazar's name. G glosses F. It has no parallel in M. It asserts that the strength of the wine has no bearing on the minimum required for liability.

The following chart will facilitate the comparison of M. and T.:

M.	*T.*
1. (A) All the produce of the vine combines together	1. (A) And how much...? An olive's bulk.
2. (B) and he is not liable until he eats an olive's bulk of the grapes.	2. (B) And all combine together to form an olive's bulk.
3. - - - -	3. (C) The wine and the vinegar as well.
4. (C) *mšnh r'šwnh*: until he drinks a quarter-*log* of wine.	4. (D) What does one do?... (E) The words of R. Aqiva.
5. (D) R. Aqiva says, "Even if he dipped...for an olive's bulk--he is liable."	5. (F) R. Eleazar b. Azariah exempts until he drinks a quarter-*log* of wine.
6. - - - -	6. (G) Whether he mixed it and drank or whether he drank it undiluted.

7. (E) And he is liable on the wine...	7. - - - -
8. (F) R. Eleazar b. Azariah says... "two grapes and their skins."	8. - - - -

A and B Tosefta are nothing more than A-B of M. in reverse order. A of T. is formulated as a question whereas B of M. uses the formulary pattern of *not liable until*. C-D of M. parallels D-F of T. with several important variations. F of T. attributes its ruling to Eleazar. C of M. attributes the same ruling to *mšnh r'šwnh*. That phrase appears four times elsewhere in M. (Ket. 5:3; Giṭ. 5:6; San. 3:4; Ed. 7:2), none of which is associated with a ruling of Eleazar b. Azariah. M. places Aqiva's ruling second. M. also preserves E-F of which T. knows nothing.

M. has a smoother version of the pericope. It includes in F, Eleazar's ruling on the minimum for liability for consumption of solid grape produce. Its formulation of the statement differs from the parallel in Sifré. Whereas Sifré uses the phrases "it excludes" and "the words of," M. has "not liable until." As we have pointed out this formulation is also found in B of M. "he is not liable until he eats an olive's bulk of the grapes." The redactor of M. balanced B and F but did not interrupt the continuity of A-D by inserting F after B.

D of M. and D of T. give different versions of Aqiva's explanation of how to convert solid measures for use with liquids. The substitution of *mšnh r'šwnh* for Eleazar b. Azariah and the reversal of T.'s order of its D-F, leaves Aqiva's ruling second and implies that it is the "later" and hence more acceptable one, a result perhaps of the work of an Aqivan redactor. Although the structure of the pericope in M. looks unbalanced because of the separation of B and F, it is actually well redacted. Its form is in the pattern:

1. gloss--ruling about solids (A-B)
2. contradictory rulings about liquids (C-D)
3. connecting language--ruling about solids (E-F)

In sum, this pericope gives us two traditions of Eleazar on related subjects. M. assigns one tradition to *mšnh r'šwnh* implying its outdatedness. The other is given without comment as an alternative to the presupposed Aqivan view.

28a. A. *tmn tnynn*: There are three that must cut their hair and their cutting is a *miṣwah*. [They are:] the Nazirite, the leper and the levites; and if any of these cuts it off but not with a razor, or left two hairs remaining, they have done nothing [= M. Neg. 14:4].

B. Said R. Eleazar, "The mishnah speaks of an unclean Nazirite. But if a clean Nazirite cut the major part of his hair (*rwb r'šw*), even not with a razor, he fulfills his obligation."

C. In this [ruling of] R. Eleazar b. Azariah, R. Ami posed a question...

y. Naz. 6:3 (28b)

Comment: There is no other evidence to indicate that this teaching should be attributed to our Eleazar.

29. A. How much time is involved in intercourse, concerning which period of time witnesses must give testimony? Enough time for coition (*h'r'h*). And how much is [required for] coition?

B. R. Eliezer says, "As much as walking around a palm tree."

C. R. Joshua says, "Enough to mix a cup of wine."

D. Ben Azzai says, "Enough to drink it."

E. R. Aqiva says, "Enough time to roast an egg."

F. R. Judah b. Batyra says, "Enough time to swallow three eggs one after another."

G. R. Eleazar b. Azariah says [b.: Jeremiah; y.: Pinḥas], "Enough time for a weaver to tie a fringe."

H. Ḥanan b. Menaḥem says, "Enough time for her to put out her hand to take a loaf from the basket."

Tos. Soṭ. 1:2, ed. Zuckermandel, p. 293, ls. 6-9

Comment: The issue concerns the testimony given about a suspected woman which makes her liable to drink the bitter water and undergo its concommitant ordeal. The minimum time that the suspected woman must spend with the man to incur liability is defined seven different ways by seven different masters. The list is in no apparent order. Similar lists appear in Sifré Num., pis. 4; Sifré Zuṭa 5:13; y. Soṭ. 1:2; b. Soṭ. 4a; Num. Rab. 9:10; Tanḥuma, p. 16. All except Tosefta omit R. Eleazar b. Azariah.

30. A. He who divorces his wife and says to her, "Lo you are permitted to any man except for so-and-so."

B. R. Eliezer permits her to marry any man except for that man.

C. And R. Eliezer agrees that if she married another and was widowed or divorced, she [then] is permitted to marry that one to whom she had been prohibited [by the exclusionary clause].

D. And after the death of R. Eliezer, four elders came together to reply to his opinions, R. Ṭarfon, R. Yosé the Galilean, R. Eleazar b. Azariah, and R. Aqiva.

E. Said R. Ṭarfon, "If she went and married his brother [of the one forbidden to her], and he died without issue, how is she going to enter into the levirate marriage? Does it not result that he makes a condition against what is written in the Torah, and whoever makes a condition against what is written in the Torah--his condition is invalid. Thus we have learned that this is not divorce."

F. Said R. Yosé the Galilean, "Where have we found a forbidden connection (*'rwh*) in the Torah permitted to one [man] and prohibited to [another] one? But she who is permitted to one is permitted to every man, and who is prohibited to one is prohibited to every man. Thus we have learned that this is not divorce."

G. R. Eleazar b. Azariah says, "Divorce [lit.: cutting off]--a thing [document] which cuts [the tie] between her and between him."

H. Said R. Yosé the Galilean, "I prefer the words of R. Eleazar."

I. R. Simeon b. Eleazar says, "If she went and married another and he divorced her and said to her, 'Lo, you are permitted to every man'--how does this permit what the other has prohibited? Thus we have learned that this is not divorce."

J. Said R. Aqiva, "Lo, if the one to whom she was prohibited was a priest and the one who divorced her died--does it not come out that to him [that priest] she is a widow but to all his fellow priests, she is a divorcée?

K. "Another matter: And with whom did the Torah deal more stringently? Divorcées or widows? Divorcées are dealt with more stringently than widows. Now the divorcée, who is more stringently treated is not prohibited from the one who is prohibited, but a widow who is less stringently dealt with--is it not logical that she should be prohibited from him to whom she is permitted?

L. "Another matter: She went and married another and he had children from her and died, when she returns to this one to whom she is originally prohibited does it not come out that the children of the first are *mamzerim*? Thus you have learned that this is not divorce."

Tos. Giṭ. 9:1-5, ed. Zuckermandel, pp. 333-34, ls. 15-30, 1-3 (y. Giṭ. 9:1, b. Giṭ. 83a-b; Sifré Deut., 269, ed. Finkelstein, p. 289)

A. *tnw rbnn*: After the death of R. Eliezer, four elders came together to reply to his opinions. These are they: R. Yosé the Galilean, R. Ṭarfon, R. Eleazar b. Azariah and R. Aqiva.

B. R. Ṭarfon answered and said, "Lo, if she went and married the brother of the one who was forbidden to her, and he died without issue, does it not result that he uproots something from the Torah. Thus we have learned that it is not divorce."

C. R. Yosé the Galilean answered and said, "Where have we found [a case of a woman] forbidden to one and permitted to one? She who is forbidden, is forbidden to all and she who is permitted, is permitted to all. Thus we have learned that it is not divorce."

D. R. Eleazar b. Azariah answered and said, "Divorce--a thing which cuts [the tie] between her and him. Thus we have learned that it is not divorce."

E. R. Aqiva answered and said, "Lo, if this one went and married another from the market-place, and she had children and was widowed or divorced, and she [then] arose and married the one to whom she had been [previously] forbidden--does it not come out that the [original] writ of divorce is void and the children [from the second marriage] are *mamzerim*? Thus we have learned that it is not divorce.

F. "Another matter, Lo, if the one to whom she was forbidden, a priest, and the one who divorced her [subsequently] died, is she not found to be a widow with regard to him [the one to whom she was forbidden] and a divorcée with regard to all [other] men? Then there follows an argument *a fortiori*: Since she would be forbidden to the [forbidden] priest because she is a divorcée [*vis a vis* the other priests] even though it is only a minor [transgression], should she not certainly be forbidden to all men because [of the element of her status as] a married woman [*vis a vis* the one to whom she is prohibited] since that is a serious [transgression]? Thus we have learned that it is not divorce."

G. Said to them R. Joshua, "One does not answer the lion after his death."

H. Said Rava, "*All* [the above opinions] *are subject to objection except for R. Eleazar b. Azariah's which is not subject to objection.*

I. *tny' nmy hky*: Said R. Yosé, "I prefer the words of R. Eleazar b. Azariah over all the others."

b. Giṭ. 83a

Comment: A-C forms the first unit of the pericope. A serves as protasis for B's ruling. C glosses. D introduces E-J. H and I are interpolations. Simeon b. Eleazar in I is an Ushan and does not appear in D's list. Babli assigns H to Yosé b. Halafta and not to Yosé the Galilean who is a party to the preceding debate. At first glance I seems to respond to D-G and thus attests it at Usha. It is possible however that I responds only to A-C and attests it alone.

F and G present essentially the same argument. Eleazar bases his ruling on exegesis, and Yosé bases his on logic. Ṭarfon and Aqiva spell out specific objections to A-C. Ṭarfon points out that the case of A-C involves a writ which contains a clause potentially contrary to Torah law, for it may make the levirate marriage impossible. Aqiva points out the possible anomaly of the situation. If the woman is prohibited from marrying a priest and then the one who divorced her died, to that priest she is not regarded as a divorcée and to all others she is. She could therefore marry only one priest. The *qal veḥomer* in b. spells out the anomaly.

The formulation of G allows but does not necessitate its application to the problem of the pericope. G appears to be an exegetical remark. The opinions of Ṭarfon, Yosé, and Aqiva appear in the form "said x." G, however, is in the form "x says." The pericope is likely an artificial construction. G may come from an Eleazar-corpus of exegeses and is associated to the issue of our pericope by a redactor. T. preserves it in its pre-Ushan formulation in any event. T.'s editor here preserves the original tradition rather than reformulate it.

A, B, E, and F are likely the primary components of the pericope. J, L, and D were probably added last. C may respond to E or to J-L.

31. A. "[Then the former husband,] who sent her away, [may not take her again to be his wife, after she has been defiled (Deut. 24:4)]." I only know [from this verse that it is forbidden for the first husband to take back his wife after she] married [a second man]--for marriage [to himself], or after she was betrothed [to a second man]--for betrothal [to himself].

B. How do we know that [it is forbidden for him to take his wife back] after betrothal [to another] for marriage [to himself], and after marriage [to another] for betrothal [to himself]?

C. It comes to teach, "Then the former husband ..." the former husband may not take back [the woman] he sent away.

D. R. Yosé b. Kefar says in the name of R. Eleazar b. Azariah, "After betrothal she is permitted [to the former husband]. After marriage [to another] she is forbidden [to the former].

E. "For it is written, 'After she has been defiled.'"

F. And sages say, "Both after betrothal and after marriage [to another], she is forbidden [to the first]."

G. If so why does it say, "After she has been defiled"?

H. To include the *soṭah* who was secreted [with another man].

I. And so it says, "If a man divorces his wife and she goes from him [and becomes another man's wife, will he return to her?] (Jer. 3:1)."

Sifré Deut. 270, ed. Finkelstein, p. 291, ls. 4-10 (D-H = b. Yeb. 11b)

Comment: A-C provides the context for the dispute, D-F. G-H glosses F and provides an exegetical basis for it, and I is another gloss to F-H citing a verse from Jeremiah. E glosses D.

The issue is whether a man may remarry his former wife after her second husband has died. Eleazar says that only after marriage to a second man is she forbidden to the first husband (D). As the gloss explains (E), "defilement" is limited to marriage. If she was only betrothed to the second and he died, she may remarry the first. In F sages prohibit remarriage to the first even if she was only betrothed to the second before his death. The phrase "After she was defiled" is then "extra" and is used for a different teaching. If the woman was suspected of adultery (*soṭah*) and was found secreted with another man, she is forbidden to her husband (until the ritual of the bitter waters has been performed). The gloss I may be a support for D or for F depending on how it is interpreted.

Yosé b. Kefar appears as a tradent of Eleazar's tradition only in this pericope. (On him, see Neusner, *HJB*, I, Chapter Four, *passim*.)

32. A. ["Now these are the ordinances which you shall set before them (Ex. 21:1)."]...R. Eleazar b. Azariah says, "Behold the gentiles who judged according to the laws of Israel, should I understand that their judgments should be valid?

B. "It comes to teach, 'Now these are the ordinances.'

C. "You may judge their [judgments by their laws] but they may not judge your [judgments by your laws]."

D. From here they said, "A *geṭ* made by a Jew is valid; and by gentiles--it is invalid.

E. "But if gentiles force him and say to him, 'Do what the Jew says to you,'--it is valid (M. Giṭ. 9:8)."

Mekh. *Neziqin* 1, ed. Horowitz-Rabin, p. 246, ls. 7-10

Comment: A-B give a question and answer based on the verse. C presents a ruling. "R. Eleazar b. Azariah says + C" could stand alone but Mekh. links it to the verse. Eleazar reasons that Jews may judge cases by "these" ordinances. Gentiles may not. D-E cites the anonymous ruling of M. Giṭ. 9:8 as an illustration of Eleazar's ruling in C. D gives the case of a *geṭ*. If the writ is made by Jews, it is valid. If it is made by gentiles, it is not, for they may not adjudicate cases of Jewish law--they may not serve as judges for Jews in such cases.

According to Bert., TYT and TYY, M. speaks of cases in which the court is involved in forcing the husband to divorce his wife. Actual divorce proceedings do not go through the court but are a matter only between the husband and wife. D then rules that if Jewish judges force him to divorce her, the divorce is valid. If gentile judges pressure the husband, it is not valid. D still serves as an illustration of C. For if Jews implement the ruling, it is a valid divorce. If gentiles force him, it is not.

E is an intermediate case, not directly relevant to the law of C. The Jews decide the matter-the husband must divorce his wife. The gentiles execute the judgment through their authority. E rules that in such a case the divorce is valid. Technically, the Jews decided the matter and the gentiles serve merely as agents to see that it is carried out (cf. TYT, *ad. loc.*).

It is unlikely that the ruling of D-E may be attributed to Eleazar. The joining language "from here they said" indicates that the association of D-E to A-C is probably redactional. It illustrates the general rule by providing a citation of an anonymous dictum.

33. A. *tnw rbnn*: "[If your brother, a Hebrew man, or a Hebrew woman, is sold to you, he shall serve you six years, and in the seventh year you shall let him go free from you. And when you let him go free from you, you shall not let him go empty handed; you shall furnish him liberally out of your flock, out of your threshing floor, and out of your wine press;] as the Lord your God has blessed you, [you shall give to him (Deut. 15:12-14)]."

B. You might say, "If the household was blessed on his account, then you must furnish him liberally; if the household was not blessed on his account, you need not furnish him liberally."

C. It comes to teach, "You shall furnish him liberally," in any event.

D. If so why does it say, "As [the Lord your God] has blessed"?

E. All that you must give him depends on the [extent of the] blessing.

F. R. Eleazar b. Azariah says, "The matters [should be understood] literally.

G. "If the household was blessed on his account, you furnish him liberally. If the household was not blessed on his account, you do not furnish him liberally."

H. If so why does it say, "You shall furnish him liberally"?

I. The Torah used a colloquial idiom.

b. Qid. 17b (cf. b. B.M. 31b; M. Abadim 2:4; A-E = Sifré Deut., ed. Finkelstein, p. 178, ls. 15-17)

Comment: A gives the verse. B-E and F-I are independent exegeses of A. Each could stand alone. Indeed Sifré gives only A-E. B-E however may be dependent on F-I since B uses the exact wording of G and refutes it. It then presents a more liberal interpretation of A. Alternatively, F-I may have been expanded on the basis of B-E. Originally Eleazar's teaching could have consisted of only F, H, and I. G may have been added as a citation of B.

The issue is how much must be given to a Hebrew slave upon his release. B-E says that he must be furnished liberally but the exact amount depends on the extent of the slave's contribution to the prosperity of the household during his service. F-I proposes that only if the slave made some contribution to the household, must he then be given his just due upon his release. If his service contributed nothing he need be given nothing. Eleazar's exegesis and the principle cited in I are not related to any other tradition preserved in his name.

34. A. R. Eleazar b. Azariah says, "If he took sick while he was with his master, or his master took sick while with him, [his ear] is not pierced,

B. "since it says, 'Since he fares well with you (Deut. 15:16).'"

Mekh. de R. Simeon, ed. Epstein-Melamed, p. 163 (Sifré Deut. 121, ed. Finkelstein, p. 180)

Comment: If a Hebrew slave wishes to remain in the service of his master after six years of service, he must have his ear pierced at the door of the master's house. He then remains a slave to that master until the Jubilee year. Eleazar says that if either the slave or the master took sick during the period of the initial servitude, the slave may not elect to remain in the service of that master. Eleazar bases his ruling on a simple exegesis of the verse, "If he fares well with you." If either becomes sick, the slave goes free at the conclusion of the six years.

Sifré cites the tradition without any attribution.

35. A. R. Eliezer's students asked him, "May one drink from [a cup held in the hand of] a bride while her husband is sitting [with her]?"

B. He said to them, "Anyone who drinks from [the hand of a] bride, it is as if he drinks from a harlot's [hand]."

C. They said to him, "Do not the daughters of the sages have good manners (*drk 'rṣ*)?"

D. He said to them, "God forbid! Anyone who does not have the scent of Torah on his mouth, does not have good manners."

E. R. Eleazar b. Azariah decreed with four hundred *shofrot* that anyone who receives a cup from the hands of a bride will never be forgiven.

Kallah Rabbati 1:5, ed. Higger, p. 175

[A-D = A-D above]

E. R. Eleazar b. Azariah decreed with three hundred *shofrot*, Whether a bride be of the daughters of a scholar or of an *'am ha'areṣ*, he who drinks from her [hand] is as though he drinks from [the hand of] a harlot.

F. He further said, "Whoever takes a cup from [the hand of] a bride and drinks from it, has no share in the world to come."

M. Kallah, 1:3 (trans. Rabbinowitz, p. 402)

Comment: A-B provide a ruling on a law of modesty for the wife of a sage in the form of a question and answer. C-D, possibly an interpolation, are reminiscent of a tradition attributed elsewhere to Eleazar b. Azariah ("If there is no Torah, there is no seemly behavior (*drk ʼrṣ*)," M. Abot 3:17). The two versions of the pericope diverge at E. M. Kallah provides a direct statement in E and another in F. Kallah Rabbati puts the decree in indirect discourse.

The attribution of the tradition to Eliezer in A is questionable. As pointed out, D cites a teaching of Eleazar. Furthermore, E of M. Kallah attributes the law of B to Eleazar. It is possible that D generated E, but it remains likely that the entire tradition is Eleazar's. In either case, the ruling of the pericope is repeated. The second time it is stated with a warning attached. There is no hint of Eleazar's concern with matters of modesty in any earlier compilation.

iv. *Neziqin*

36. A. If a man kindled [a fire] within his own domain, how far may the fire spread [before he is no longer liable for the damage which it causes]?

B. R. Eleazar b. Azariah says, "They regard it as if it is in the middle of a *beit kor* [of land]."

C. R. Eliezer says, "Sixteen cubits [in every direction], like the public road."

D. R. Aqiva says, "Fifty cubits."

E. R. Simeon says, "*The one who makes the fire will certainly pay* (Ex. 22:5)--all goes according to the fire."

M. B.Q. 6:4 (y. B.Q. 6:6, b. B.Q. 61a-b; Mekh. *Nez*. 14, ed. Horowitz-Rabin, p. 297)

Comment: C and D respond directly to the question of the protasis, A. The most common dispute form has a protasis and two conflicting opinions. In our case A, C, D would have formed a perfect example of that form. B does not respond as directly to the question of A as C and D do. B formulates the ruling differently. Instead of giving a distance with an explanatory gloss as in C, Eleazar rules that liability extends to an area of 75,000 square cubits.

That is an area of a *beit kor* in which thirty *seah* are planted, which covers a cubic area of 274 by 274 cubits. Eleazar considers liability to extend approximately 137 cubits in each direction. (If a circular area is considered it would be approximately 155 cubits in each direction.) Thus B and C-D are related rulings probably emanating from different circles which have been nicely redacted into one pericope. The principle is that one is responsible for normal but not abnormal conditions.

E is a general rule which probably was not meant to respond to A's question. If we turn to T.'s version of the pericope we find that E serves as an independent ruling and precedes the pericope:

> 1. R. Simeon says...
>
> 2. He who kindles a fire in his own property, how far may the fire burn?
>
> 3. R. Eliezer says, "Sixteen cubits, like the public road; when there is wind, thirty cubits."
>
> 4. R. Judah says, "Thirty cubits; when there is wind, fifty."
>
> 5. R. Aqiva says, "Fifty cubits; when there is wind three hundred [y.: one hundred] cubits."
>
> Tos. B.Q. 2:22, ed. Zuckermandel, p. 356, ls. 18-21 (y. B.Q. 6:6)

T. bears out the contention that Simeon's ruling is not part of the dispute. What is more interesting is that T. omits Eleazar's opinion entirely. Judah's ruling (4) looks like an artificial construction taking Eliezer's highest number and Aqiva's lowest. Eliezer and Aqiva are demonstrably the primary disputants in our pericope.

There are several other instances in which the redactor placed Eleazar's name first in a triple dispute (see pp. 24 and 99). Eleazar's ruling that one is responsible for the damage which a fire causes within a *beit kor* may be related to the definition of the size of a garden or outer area given in M. Erub. 2:6. There Ilai quotes a ruling in the name of Eliezer that one may carry in a garden on the Sabbath if it is walled and is no larger than a *beit kor*. That was apparently the size of an average garden or field and thus may serve as the basis for Eleazar's standard for measuring the distance within which one is liable for the damages caused by one's fire.

37. A. "But the owner of the ox shall be clear (Ex. 21:28)."

B. Ben Azzai says, "Completely free of any benefit [from it], as one who says, 'So and so went out, clear of his possessions'--he has no benefit at all from them."

C. R. Eleazar b. Azariah says, "[It means] clear of culpability for the fetus."

D. Said to him Aqiva, "Why do I need [these words to teach me that]? Did it not already say, 'men' and not 'oxen'?..."

Mekh. De R. Simeon, ed. Epstein-Melamed, p. 179 (Mekh. *Mishpatim* 10, ed. Horowitz-Rabin, p. 283 attributes C to Aqiva)

Comment: The context of the pericope is a discussion of various legal exegeses of Ex. 21:28. Ben Azzai rules that the owner may derive no benefit from the carcass of a goring ox. In C, Eleazar says that if the ox caused a woman to have a miscarriage while it was goring another ox, no fine is to be assessed of the owner of the ox. C is independent of A-B. The allusion here is to a preceding verse, "When men strive together and hurt a woman with child, so that there is a miscarriage...the one who hurt her shall be fined (Ex. 21:22)."

In D Aqiva glosses and disagrees with Eleazar's exegeses. There is no necessity for deriving that ruling from Ex. 21:28, he says, since Ex. 21:22 specifically refers to a case of *men* striving together and not of *oxen* striving. Curiously, Eleazar's ruling in B here is attributed to Aqiva in Mekh. with no directly opposing view appended to it. The attribution to Eleazar here is thus uncertain.

38. A. If one owed another money and he signed over his field to him [as if it was an outright] sale,

B. as long as the seller eats the fruit [i.e., receives the profits from the produce of the land] it [the transaction] is permissible,

C. and if the buyer eats the fruit it is forbidden.

D. R. Judah says, "Both are permissible."

E. Said R. Judah, "So Boethus b. Zunin would do according to [the ruling of] R. Eleazar b. Azariah."

F. They said to him, "From there is proof? But [in that case] the seller eats the fruit."

Tos. B.M. 4:2, ed. Zuckermandel, p. 379, ls. 10-14

A. *dtny'*: Behold if one owed his fellow a hundred (*mnh*) and he [signed over] his field [as if it was] a sale for him [the creditor];

B. as long as the seller eats the fruits it is permissible;

C. [and if the] buyer eats the fruits it is forbidden.

D. R. Judah says, "Even when the buyer eats the fruit it is permissible."

E. Said R. Judah, "*m'śh b*: Boethus b. Zunin [signed over] his field [as if it were] a sale according to R. Eleazar b. Azariah and the buyer used to eat the fruit."

F. They said to him, "From there is proof? [In that case] the seller ate the fruit and not the buyer."

b. Meg. 27b; b. B.M. 63a; b. Arak. 31a

Comment: The issue of the pericope is how one may avoid usury in a case in which the borrower mortgages his land to the creditor. The mortgage is effected through the outright transference of the land to the creditor. Judah, in D, disputes the anonymous ruling of A-C, which prohibits a transaction in which the creditor acquires the rights to the profits ("fruit"). In such a case after repayment of the loan and subsequent return of the land to the borrower, the creditor will have in retrospect received profits on his loan. That is tantamount to usury.

Judah holds that it makes no difference whether the creditor or the borrower receives the profits. If the creditor gets them it is through entirely permissible means since the borrower signed the field over to him. E-F are autonomous of A-D. In T.'s version, E is not preserved in the *m'śh b* form. The *beraita* supplies that form and gives a fuller version of the precedent. Following b.'s version, it is apparent that E serves as proof for Judah's position. Judah asserts that Eleazar authorized loans through which the creditor receives the profits of the land, if the field is sold to the creditor. T.'s version of E seems to be truncated.

F of T. may be seen as a question and answer which interprets the significance of E. It then explains that E is no proof to Judah's position since the creditor did not receive the fruit in that case. Alternatively, F may be a statement of fact. Without Eleazar b. Azariah's ruling, the borrower has to retain the profits. Eleazar's ruling allows a case in which the creditor got the profits, thus modifying the law.

In any case, E seems to have been an independent statement which is used in our pericope as proof for Judah's ruling. In M., a similar version of the statement appears. M. B.M. 5:3 has:

> If a man lent to another on the security of his field and said to him, "If you do not pay me within three years it will be mine," then it becomes his.
> Thus Boethus b. Zunin does (!) with the consent of the sages.

The application of this apparent variant of our statement to a completely different case further suggests that it circulated separately.

Boethus b. Zunin appears elsewhere in M. A.Z. 5:2 and Tos. Pes. 1:31 as one who poses a question for the sages. Tos. Shab. 3:4 and Tos. Pes. 10:12 have stories about him. He appears in conjunction with Eleazar in our pericope and in b. B.B. 13b.

39. A. *tnw rbnn*: One may attach together [the scrolls of] the Torah, the Prophets and the Writings. The words of R. Meir.

B. R. Judah says, "The Torah by itself; the Prophets by themselves; and the Writings by themselves."

C. And sages say, "Each one by itself."

D. And said R. Judah, "*m'śh b*: Boethus b. Zunin had eight [scrolls of the] Prophets attached together according to the words of R. Eleazar b. Azariah."

E. And some say, "He had each one separate."

F. Said Rabbi, "*m'śh w*: They brought before us [the scrolls of the] Torah, Prophets and Writings attached together and we declared them fit."

b. B.B. 13b (M. Sof. 3:5)

Comment: The pericope is a composite combining together two sets of rulings. A plus F discuss the issue of whether one may combine together the three divisions of Scripture, but the issue of whether the separate books may be combined in each division is no problem. B-E addresses itself to that issue. B-C is a dispute. In D Judah brings evidence to support his opinion that the books may be combined into divisions. Presumably we are speaking here of scrolls, although codices are known to have existed in the second century.[6]

Boethus b. Zunin's practice is cited by Judah as evidence in T. B.M. 4:2 and its parallels. There too, he acts "according to the words of R. Eleazar b. Azariah."

40. A. A sanhedrin that executes one in seven years is called destructive (*ḥblnyt*).

B. R. Eleazar b. Azariah says, "Once in seventy years."

C. R. Ṭarfon and R. Aqiva say, "Had we been in the sanhedrin no one would ever have been executed."

D. R. Simeon b. Gamaliel says, "Even they increase the shedding of blood in Israel."

M. Mak. 1:10

Comment: Eleazar contrasts the anonymous opinion of A. C is related to A-B in content but not dependent on A as a protasis. D comments on C. The word *ḥblnyt* does not appear elsewhere in M. Eleazar apparently stands outside the circle of Aqiva and Ṭarfon. The two statements, B and C, have been preserved in different forms even though there is little substantive difference between them.

A-B reflect opposition to capital punishment. In C, Aqiva and Ṭarfon present an even more radical view. Simeon b. Gamaliel in D alludes to the deterrent capability of capital punishment.

41. A. Said R. Sheshet in the name of R. Eleazar b. Azariah, "From whence do we know that the strap [used to administer lashes] is [made] of calf [skin]?

B. "As it is written, 'Forty stripes may be given to him' (Deut. 25:3) *and next it says* (*wsmyk lyh*) 'You shall not muzzle an ox when it treads out the grain (Deut. 25:4).'"

b. Mak. 23a

Comment: The pericope is in the form: "From whence" + statement + "as it is written" + verse + "next it says" + verse. R. Sheshet cites four such traditions in the name of R. Eleazar b. Azariah. Each of the four deduces a law or teaching from two consecutive and unrelated verses. The form is a variation of that found in M. Shab. Ch. 9 where several rulings are given in the form "From whence"

+ law + "As it is written" + verse. Two rulings cited there anonymously appear elsewhere in Eleazar's name.

The law deduced in the pericope is found in M. Mak. 3:12: "How does one administer lashes [to one who has violated a negative prohibition]?...[With] the strap of a calf in his hand." The proximity of "stripes" and "ox" serves as basis for this ruling.

42. A. And said R. Sheshet, [b. Mak. omits: said R. Eleazar] in the name of R. Eleazar b. Azariah, "From whence do we know that in the case of a *yebamah* who fell to [a levir who was] afflicted with boils we do not 'muzzle' her [i.e., we do not force her to enter into the levirite marriage]?

B. "As it is written, 'You shall not muzzle an ox when it treads out the grain (Deut. 25:4)' *and next it says*, 'If brothers dwell together and one of them dies and has no son (Deut. 25:5).'"

b. Yeb. 4a; b. Mak. 23a

Comment: The form of the pericope is "From whence" + law + "As it is written" + verse + "And next it says" + verse. The law is derived from a play on the word "muzzle"--the woman should not be bound to the levir in a specific case. It is not clear how the inference is drawn that the reference is to a man who is afflicted with boils.

M. Ket. 7:10 rules on a case of a woman married to such a man. He is forced to divorce her. M. does not rule on a case of one so afflicted who is the levir of a woman.

43. A. All the [divine] names written in the Torah in connection with Abraham are sacred except for this one which is profane.

B. As it says, "[When he saw them, he ran from the tent to meet them, and bowed himself to the earth,] and said, 'My Lord, (*'dny*) if I have found favor in your sight, [do not pass your servant] (Gen. 18:3).'"

C. Haninah the son of R. Joshua's brother and R. Eleazar b. Azariah in the name of R. Eleazar the Modaite said, "Even this [one] is sacred."

b. Shabuot 35b

Comment: C appears as a gloss to A-B. Eleazar appears with Eleazar the Modaite only in the two pericopae in Pesikta DeRav Kahana, but not as a tradent aside from this instance (see p. 204). Haninah does not appear elsewhere as the tradent of Eleazar's traditions.

The vocalization of *'dny* in the verse cited is the same as the vocalization of the word when it appears as one of the divine names. This may account for the ruling in C that holds it to be sacred.

44. [One does not store up staples in the Land of Israel...]

A. They do not deal in grain but they do deal in wine and oil and beans.

B. They said concerning R. Eleazar b. Azariah that he used to deal in wine and oil all of his days.

Tos. A.Z. 4:1, ed. Zuckermandel, p. 465, ls. 29-30

A. One does not deal in the Land of Israel in staples such as wines, oils and flours.

B. They said concerning R. Eleazar b. Azariah that he used to deal in wine and oil.

b. B.B. 91a

Comment: B supports the anonymous ruling of A in Tos. In b., B contradicts A. The ruling addresses the question of whether or not one may become a dealer in oil and wine, buying from the producer and selling to the consumer. B is neither in direct discourse nor in the *m'śh b* form. It is in the third person report form which we find in several other instances related to Eleazar. It is striking that while in T., B serves as a precedent; in b. it does not.

v. *Qodoshim*

45. A. [If one said,] "I pledge a Burnt-offering,"

B. he should bring a lamb.

C. R. Eleazar b. Azariah says, "Either a turtle dove or a young pigeon."

D. [If one said,] "I specified [what I would bring] from the cattle, but I do not know what I specified,"

E. he should bring a bullock and a calf.

F. [If one said, "I specified what I would bring] from the animals, but I do not know what I specified,"

G. he should bring a bullock and a young bullock, a ram, a goat, a kid, and a lamb.

H. [If one said,] "I specified [what I would bring] but I do not know what I specified,"

I. [he should bring all the animals mentioned above and] add to them a turtle dove and a young pigeon.

M. Men. 13:6

Comment: A-C stands as a separate unit. A-B assumes that an undefined pledge of a Burnt-offering minimally requires the bringing of the smallest animal allowed--the lamb. Eleazar in C is more lenient. He allows the undefined pledge to be interpreted as a statement of intention of bringing the smallest possible sacrifice for a Burnt-offering--the turtle dove or pigeon.

D-I discusses an entirely different issue. It presents cases of one who pledged and forgot what he had pledged. Eleazar's ruling in C is dependent on the protasis, A. b. Men. 107b points out that the dispute between B and C is one of defining prevalent literary usage and not a legal dispute *per se*. It is striking that Eleazar, a rich man according to other traditions, here prescribes the smaller offering.

46. A. *tny'*: R. Aqiva says, "Why does it say 'with oil' (Lev. 7:12) twice [regarding the Thanksgiving-offering]?

B. "If it said, 'with oil' only once, I would have said, 'Behold, it is as all Meal-offerings [requiring with it] a *log* [of oil].' Now that it said 'with oil' twice, it is an added phrase (*rybwy*) after an added phrase; and [the rule is] an added phrase after an added phrase comes only to limit.

C. "Scripture limited [the requirement of oil for the Thanksgiving-offering] to a half *log*.

D. "[Is it] an added phrase after an added phrase? It is one added phrase!

E. "But if it had not said 'with oil' at all, I would have said, Behold, it is like all Meal-offerings [requiring with it] a *log*. Now that it says 'with oil' twice, it is an added phrase after an added phrase. [The rule is] an added phrase after an added phrase only limits. Scripture limits it to a half *log*.

F. "We might have thought that this half *log* was to be divided among the three types [of sacrifice mentioned in the verse]: unleavened cakes, unleavened wafers and cakes of fine flour.

G. "When it says 'with oil' [in reference to] cakes of fine flour, about which we need not be taught [that it must be brought with oil, since Lev. 6:21 says to do so, the added phrase teaches then that the amount of] oil for the cakes of fine flour should be increased.

H. "Thus how [does he proceed]? He brings a half *log* of oil and he divides it: half for the unleavened cakes and wafers and half for the cakes of fine flour."

I. Said to him R. Eleazar b. Azariah, "Aqiva, even if you claim the verse adds 'with oil' all day long, I will not listen to you.

J. "Because (*'l'*) [the law concerning the following quantities:] a half *log* of oil for the Thanksgiving-offering; a quarter *log* of oil for the Nazirite's offering; and eleven days between [the end of one period of] menstruation and [the beginning of the next period of] menstruation are traditions to Moses from Sinai."

b. Men. 89a; Sifra *Ṣav*, 11: 4-6, pp. 34, 35 (I-J: b. Nid. 72b)

Comment: The pericope consists of an extended legal exegesis in Aqiva's name (A-H) and brief response by Eleazar citing three rulings, among them Aqiva's conclusion in C, on the basis of ancient traditions.

Aqiva's exegesis is based on Lev. 7:12: "If he offers it [the peace-offering] as a Thanksgiving, then he shall offer with the Thank-offering unleavened cakes mixed *with oil*, unleavened wafers spread *with oil*, and cakes of fine flour well mixed *with oil*." A-C deduces that the Thanksgiving requires less than the usual amount of oil brought with a Meal-offering from the unnecessary repetition of the words "with oil." D-E is an interpolation (not found in the Sifra parallel) clarifying the exegetical process of A-C. F-H deduces from the third appearance of "with oil" that cakes of fine flour require more oil than the other elements of the offering. The third repetition increases the amount because it follows an exclusion or diminishing based on the first two occurrences of the phrase "with oil." The entire unit appears to be a *post facto* process of connecting a known ruling with a specific verse.

Eleazar objects to the exegetical process, claiming the superiority and independence of tradition (I-J). I is formulated to allow Eleazar's statement in J to be appended to the rest of the pericope. It is conceivable that I-J could have circulated independently with the simple protasis "R. Eleazar b. Azariah says." As it stands it is a direct critique of Aqiva's position. Let us turn now to the substance of the three rulings cited in J.

All three refer to numerical quantities (which is characteristic of traditions ascribed to Sinaitic authority). We have spelled out the context of the first ruling. It specifies a half *log* of oil for the Thanksgiving. A-C of the pericope spells out the same law using exegetical methods. The ruling derived in F-H is not reflected or presumed in J.

The second ruling, that a quarter *log* of oil is the proper quantity for the Nazirite's offering, probably refers to the oil mentioned in Num. 6:15. B. Niddah 72b prescribes "a quarter-*log* of *wine* for the Nazirite." If this is the correct reading, the law then may refer to the wine the Nazirite drinks after the sacrifices are offered. Num. 6:20 says, "after [the offering] he drinks wine." It is, however, possible that the ruling refers only to the libation which is offered with the sacrifice. Whether the reading is "oil" or "wine," in either case the quantity is not specified in M., nor is this ruling discussed in b.

The third ruling specifies that there are eleven days between menstrual periods. This law has two implications. First, if in that period a woman sees a flow of blood she does not acquire the status of a menstruant and she need not wait seven days, but may immerse herself on the next day. She is considered instead "a woman watching day by day" for a flow. On the other hand, if during these eleven days she experiences a flow for three consecutive days, she is considered a *zabah* and must wait a full seven clean days and then bring a sacrifice. After the eleven day period, any flow whether for one day or for seven days renders her a menstruant. She must then wait until the eighth day and immerse herself and need not bring a sacrifice.

Eleazar bases his ruling on Sinaitic tradition in two other instances: T. Peah 3:2--concerning forgotten sheaves in connection with a Houses dispute and T. Ḥal. 1:6.

47. A. "A man may dedicate part of his flock and part of his herd, some of his Canaanite man-servants and maid-servants. But if he declared all of them to be dedicated, they are not dedicated."

B. The words of R. Eleazar (N: R. Eliezer).

C. Said R. Eleazar b. Azariah, "If to God men may not dedicate all of their property, how much more so then must men no squander their goods (*ḥs ʿl nksyw*)."

M. Arak. 8:4 (b. Arak. 28a)

A. One is not permitted to consecrate all of his goods. And if he consecrated all of them they are consecrated.

B. One is not permitted to dedicate all of his goods. And if he dedicated all of them they are dedicated.

C. R. Eliezer says, "(Lev. 27:28: 'That a man devotes to the Lord of anything that he has, whether of man or of beast or of his inherited field.') 'Of man'--and not all the man; 'of beast'--and not all the beasts; 'an inherited field'--and not all the inherited fields.

D. "Therefore if he dedicated all of them, they are not dedicated."

E. Said R. Eleazar b. Azariah, "If to God one is not permitted to dedicate all of his property

F. "since the Omnipresent has mercy (*ḥs*) on him

G. "how much more so then must men not squander their goods."

T. Arak. 4:23, 24; ed. Zuckermandel, p. 548, ls. 27-32

Comment: M.'s version of the pericope consists of two sections; T.'s of three. A-B of M. are Eliezer's (or Eleazar's) ruling that one may not dedicate all of his goods in any one category to the Temple. T. provides an alternative to this ruling: Ideally one should not dedicate all his goods, but if he does, they are considered dedicated

(A-B in T.). Eliezer's statement is based on exegesis of Lev. 27:28.

Eleazar's teaching presupposes that of Eliezer. M.'s version of Eleazar's statement does not spell out the link between the law that one may not dedicate all of one's goods and the advice that one should not squander his possessions. T.'s gloss (F) attempts to find the logic of the pericope. God has mercy on the individual, he should then have mercy on his belongings.

48. A. R. Eleazar b. Azariah says: Lo, it says, "When the Lord your God enlarges your territory as he has promised you, [and you say, 'I will eat flesh,' because you crave flesh, you may eat as much flesh as you desire (Deut. 12:20)]."

B. It is possible that the meat is decaying in the pot and he does not hunger for it [should he then eat it?].

C. Hence it does not say that "you say, 'I will eat flesh'" [without any qualification. Rather one should only eat] according to one's appetite [--"as you desire"].

D. One might have thought that he could buy [meat] from the marketplace and eat,

E. it comes to teach (*tlmwd lwmr*) ["If the place which the Lord your God will choose to put his name there is too far from you,] then you may kill any of your herd or your flock, [which the Lord has given you as I commanded you; and you may eat within your towns as much as you desire (Deut. 12:21)]."

F. One might have thought that one should slaughter all of them and offer them up [as sacrifices],

G. it comes to teach--"of your herd" and not all of your herd; "of your flock" and not all of your flock.

Tos. Arak. 4:26, ed. Zuckermandel, p. 548, ls. 32-37

Comment: The pericope contains three exegetical remarks on Deut. 12:20-21. In A-B Eleazar directs that meat be eaten only when one craves it. Here it would seem that he suggests that rotten meat need not be eaten. D-E points out that one may not eat meat until he has a flock of his own--an astounding ruling. F-G links this pericope to the preceding one (4:25). One may sacrifice or slaughter part of his flock or herd, but not all of it, just as in the preceding pericope Eleazar rules that one may dedicate part of his possessions, but not all of them.

The pericope's rulings all address themselves to the question of how one must be temperate in his consumption of meat. D-E and F-G make use of the dialectical formulary *ykwl...tlmwd lwmr*.

ARN A, 20 attributes the pericope to Hananiah, prefect of the priests.

> A. (Deut. 12:20) R. Eleazar b. Azariah says, "The verse came only to teach you proper conduct--that one should only eat meat according to his appetite.
>
> B. "One might have thought that one might buy meat from the market and eat
>
> C. "it comes to teach 'then you may kill any of your herd and your flock.'
>
> D. "hence one does not eat meat until he has a herd and flock.
>
> E. "One might have thought that one may sacrifice all of his herd and all of his flock
>
> F. "it comes to teach--'from your herd' and not all of your herd; 'From your flock' and not all of your flock."

Sifré Deut. 75, ed. Finkelstein, p. 140, ls. 1-5 (b. Ḥul. 84a)

Comment: Sifré reformulates the first exegetical comment of the pericope. Meat should only be eaten when one craves it--but the implication here is that one should develop an appetite for it. It should not be too commonplace. B-F repeats D-G of T.

49. A. And so R. Eleazar b. Azariah would say, "Whoever has ten *maneh*s may arrange to have vegetables in the pot every day.

B. "Twenty *maneh*s--may arrange to have vegetables in the pot and stew (*'lps*).

C. "Fifty *maneh*s--a pound of meat from Sabbath eve to Sabbath eve.

D. "One hundred *maneh*s--a pound of meat every day.

E. "Even though there is no proof for this, there is a suggestion of it, for it is written, 'In that day a man will keep alive a young cow and two sheep and because of the abundance of milk which they give, he will eat curds (Isa. 7:21-22).'

F. "From one hundred *log*s of milk comes out one *log* of curds."

Tos. Arak. 4:27; ed. Zuckermandel, pp. 548-49, ls. 27, 1-40 (A-D: Tanh. *Aḥaré* 17, ed. Buber, p. 70)

Comment: The pericope concludes the collection of rulings given in the name of Eleazar b. Azariah concerning temperateness and "proper conduct" in the consumption of food. The list prescribes different diets depending on one's income. The proof of E-F is based on the fact that the ratio of milk required to produce curds is one hundred to one. Thus if one has one hundred *maneh*s he may buy a pound of meat every day. The argument may also relate back to T. Arak. 4:26.

A. From here (!) said R. Eleazar b. Azariah, "Whoever has a *maneh* should buy a pound of vegetables for his stew.

B. "Ten *maneh*s--he should buy a pound of fish for his stew.

C. "Fifty *maneh*s--he should buy a pound of meat for his stew.

D. "One hundred *maneh*s--he should pour out for himself a pot every day.

E. "*And the others, when* [should they buy the food mentioned]?

F. "Each Sabbath eve (*m'rb šbt l'rb šbt*)."

b. Ḥul. 84a

Comment: b. omits T.'s proof text. It also presents a different list:

b.	*T.*
(1) one *maneh*/pound of vegetables for his stew	(1) ten/vegetables in the pot every day
(2) ten/pound of fish for stew	(2) twenty/vegetables in the pot and stew
(3) fifty/pound of meat for stew	(3) fifty/pound of meat from Sabbath to Sabbath
(4) hundred/pour out a pot every day	(4) hundred/pound of meat every day

50. A. What [manner of] bondwoman [is referred to in M. Ker. 2:2-4]?

B. "Whoever is half bondwoman and half freedwoman,

C. as it is written, 'And she hath not yet been altogether redeemed (Lev. 19:20).'"

D. The words of R. Aqiva.

E. R. Ishmael says, "She [the bondwoman mentioned in Lev.] is a complete bondwoman."

F. R. Eleazar b. Azariah says, "All the [other] forbidden connections are expressly set forth [in Lev.]

G. "and what was left?

H. "only the [case of a connection with] a half bondwoman and half freedwoman."

M. Ker. 2:5

Comment: The pericope gives three definitions of the bondwoman mentioned in Leviticus 19 and in M. Ker. Ch. 2. Both Aqiva's and Ishmael's opinions can stand independently in their present formulation. Ishmael's responds more directly to the protasis A. Eleazar's lemma takes the form of a gloss to Ishmael's view. Thus in essence E and F-H present contrasting opinions, with Aqiva's ruling in B-D offering the same definition as Eleazar's.

The contradictory views grow out of the ambiguity in Lev. 19:20-21: "If a man lies carnally with a woman who is a slave, betrothed to another man and not yet redeemed (*whpdh l' npdth*: lit.: redeemed and not redeemed) or given her freedom, an inquiry shall be held. They shall not be put to death because she was not free but he shall bring a Guilt-offering for himself..." Ishmael interprets the verse as referring to a betrothed bondwoman who is therefore to be considered a forbidden connection. Eleazar disagrees and explains that all forbidden connections are listed elsewhere. Hence this cannot be a new definition of prohibited relations. Thus he constructs the case of a half freedwoman and half bondwoman which is the referent of our verse in Leviticus.

Aqiva presents an identical definition. By placing Aqiva's lemma first, the redactor constructed an artificial dispute between Aqiva and Ishmael. It is likely that Aqiva's view precedes the other two in the pericope because of the citation of the biblical verse which focuses on its ambiguous language.

Eleazar also appears with Ishmael in Tos. Ber. 1:4 and M. Yad. 4:3.

> A. *tnw rbnn*: "Redeemed" (*whpdh*)--one might have thought [from that word that Lev. 19:20 was referring to a bondwoman who was] fully [redeemed]. It comes to teach (*tlmwd lwmr*) "not yet altogether redeemed" (*l' npdth*) [that the verse is not referring to such a bondwoman.]

B. One might have thought [it referred to a bondwoman who] was not at all redeemed (*ykwl l' npdth*). It comes to teach [that she was somehow] "redeemed."

C. How could she be redeemed and not redeemed [at the same time]?

D. "[In a case where she was a] half bondwoman and half freedwoman and betrothed to an Israelite slave."

E. The words of R. Aqiva.

F. R. Ishmael says, "Scripture here speaks of a Canaanite bondwoman who was betrothed to an Israelite slave."

G. If so why does it say (*mh tlmwd lwmr*) "and she has not yet been altogether redeemed"?

H. Scripture here makes use of a colloquial expression (*dbrh twrh klšwn bny 'dm*).

I. R. Eleazar b. Azariah says, "All the [other] forbidden connections are expressly set forth for us.

J. "And what was left for us?

K. "[The case of a connection with] a half bondwoman and a half freedwoman

L. "who is betrothed to an Israelite slave."

M. And others say, "'They shall not be put to death because she was not free'--Scripture speaks of a Canaanite bondwoman who was betrothed to a Canaanite slave."

b. Ker. 11a (Sifra, *Parshat Qedoshim*, *pereq* 5)

Comment: The *beraita* spells out the mechanics of the dispute. Ishmael explains that nothing may be learned from the grammatical usage of the verse--it is a common colloquialism (H). The exegetical process behind Aqiva's ruling is spelled out (A-E). Eleazar's lemma is glossed with the qualification "who is betrothed to an Israelite slave" (L) the only possible legitimate husband for a half bondwoman and half freedwoman. b. also adds M to balance

Eleazar's view with a contrary opinion, thus creating two parallel disputes: Aqiva/Ishmael and Eleazar/Others.

51. A. *tnw rbnn*: "[But the person who does anything with a high hand, whether he is a native or a sojourner,] reviles the Lord, [and that person shall be cut off from among his people] (Num. 15:30)." Isi b. Judah says, "It is like one who says to his fellow, '*you scraped out the bowl and you have diminished it*.'"

B. *He thinks* that "reviling" is cursing God.

C. R. Eleazar b. Azariah says, "It is like one who says to his fellow, '*you scraped out the bowl and have not diminished it*.'"

D. *He thinks that* "reviling" is worshipping idols.

E. *tny' 'ydk*: "Reviles the Lord": R. Eleazar b. Azariah says, "Scripture speaks of an idolater."

F. And sages say, "Scripture comes only to prescribe cutting off for one who curses God."

b. Ker. 7b

Comment: The pericope contains two separate, related traditions. A-D gives two metaphors to interpret Num. 15:30. Isi makes a comparison between one who "reviles" God and one who scrapes out the contents of a bowl and in so doing also scrapes out part of the wood (Rashi). In C Eleazar compares the reviler with one who does not scrape the body of the bowl but just removes its contents. The glosses B and D interpret the analogies of the two masters in light of the second tradition in E-F. F makes the issue of the pericope apparent--for whom is Scripture prescribing the punishment of "cutting off"?

The attribution of C to Eleazar b. Azariah is open to question on two accounts. First, Isi was a contemporary of Judah the Patriarch.[7] Second, y. San. 25b cites a similar parable in the name of Simeon b. Eleazar, also a contemporary of Judah. It is however possible that the tradition cited in E-F was picked up and incorporated with Isi's tradition and is in fact attributed accurately.

Below I cite the parallel to A-D in Sifré Num. and the near parallel in y. San.:

> A. "Reviles the Lord": R. Eleazar b. Azariah says, "It is like one who says to his fellow, '*You have scraped out the bowl and diminished it.*'"
>
> B. Isi b. Akabiah says, "It is like one who says to his fellow, '*You have scraped out the bowl entirely and left nothing in it.*'"
>
> (Sifré Num. 15, ed. Horowitz, p. 120, ls. 15-17)

> A. From whence do we know "cutting off" [is he punishment for worshipping idols]?
>
> B. "He reviles the Lord"--it is not written [just] "reviles the Lord."
>
> C. [It is] like one who says to his fellow, "*You have scraped out the whole bowl and not left anything in it.*"
>
> D. A parable: R. Simeon b. Eleazar says to two who were sitting and a bowl of pounded grains was between them. One stretched out his hand and scraped out the entire bowl and left nothing.
>
> E. So too one who curses the Lord and worships idols does not leave [for himself] afterwards any commandments [to observe].
>
> (y. San. (25b), 7:11)

vi. *Ṭohorot*

52. A. A barrel that was punctured and mended with more pitch than necessary:

B. whatever touches the [necessary] pitch is unclean;

C. [whatever touches] the unnecessary [pitch] is clean.

D. [If] pitch dripped onto a jar whatever touches it [the pitch] is clean.

E. A wooden or earthenware funnel that one stopped up with pitch:

F. R. Eleazar b. Azariah declares it unclean.

G. R. Aqiva declares unclean that which is of wood and declares clean that which is of earthenware.

H. R. Yosé declares both clean.

M. Kel. 3:8

Comment: The pericope E-H combines two independent rulings and a gloss. In its simplest form, Eleazar's ruling can stand alone as:

mšpk šppqw bzpt - R. Eleazar b. Azariah mṭm'.

Likewise Aqiva's may have stood independently with a similar protasis and *R. Aqiva mṭm' bšl 'ṣ wmṭhr bšl ḥrs*. Yosé clearly glosses Aqiva's ruling. As is common the redactor introduced Aqiva's distinction into the protasis of the entire pericope (E).

As MA points out, the issue of the pericope depends on which of the two types of funnels mentioned in M. Kel. 2:8 is under consideration here. If our pericope refers to the householder's funnel, which is not usually classified as a container, the issue is whether the stopper transforms it into one. Yosé denies that the funnel can ever attain the status of a container. It always remains no more than a 'sherd' (*šbr kly*). Eleazar, on the other hand, holds that if it is stopped up with pitch, it becomes a container and thus susceptible to uncleanness (so MA).

Aqiva distinguishes between wood and earthenware since only in the former is the pitch seal permanent. The earthenware funnel can never be removed from its status as a funnel and transformed into a 'vessel,' since it has been glazed in an oven and will not be permanently sealed by the pitch.

The alternative is that the pericope deals with a tradesman's funnel which from the outset is susceptible to uncleanness since it serves as a container as well. The issue then is whether uncleanness which touches the stopper is conveyed to the funnel. Yosé holds there is no connection. Eleazar holds there is. Aqiva adds the consideration that pitch and wood may be considered connected since there is adhesion--the wood is porous. Earthenware will not connect to pitch in the case of a funnel because it is glazed at the spout. The issue is then related to A-D. There, however, there is connection in both wood and earthenware since the pitch is used in a crack where it is certainly absorbed in any case.

In either alternative the issue is a Yavnean one--whether there is connection or whether an object may attain the status of a new vessel. (See Neusner, *HMLP*, Vol. III, pp. 298ff.) It seems likely that Eleazar's concern is the latter issue--whether the vessel may be considered a receptacle. The redactor has complicated the issue by combining several rulings.

53. A. ...Said R. Yosah, "*m'śh b*: Four elders were sitting in the store of (*ḥrs*--see Neusner, *HMLP*, Vol. II, p. 209) R. Eleazar b. Azariah in Sepphoris--R. Ḥuspit and R. Yeshebav and R. Ḥalafta and R. Yoḥanan b. Nuri

B. "and someone brought before them the head of a post which was removed with a chisel (*rhytny*).

C. "He said to them, 'On this I was sitting,'

D. "and they declared it clean for him."

T. Kel. B.B. 2:2

Comment: The pericope is preceded in T. Kel. by a story in which Aqiva declares unclean a stump which Simeon brought before him. The four elders mentioned do not appear in any pericope with Eleazar, nor does he play an active role in this tradition. He is represented merely as the owner of the store in which this incident takes place.

The story follows two others which are thematically related. They discuss objects which were used for sitting and were brought before the sages for a ruling on their susceptibility to uncleanness.

On the ruling of D, compare M. Kel. 22:9.

54. A. (1) The ball; (2) and the shoe last; (3) and the amulet; (4) and phylacteries; (5) and the round pillow, which were torn, if they hold what is in them, are unclean.

B. R. Joshua b. Qorḥa says in the name of R. Eleazar b. Azariah, "One immerses them just as they are (*kl šhn*)."

T. Kel. B.B. 2:6

Comment: T. explains M. Kel. 23:1:

> The ball, the shoe last, the amulet, and the phylacteries which were torn--He that touches them is unclean and what is in them is clean.

T. qualifies the list by adding "if they hold what is in them" which explains that the containers remain unclean even though torn since they are able to retain their contents.

Eleazar's opinion, cited by Joshua b. Qorḥa as a gloss to the list and its ruling, is that both the objects and their contents may be purified by immersing them together. The implication is that the stuffing does not interpose during the immersion since the container and its contents are considered to be connected. According to Eleazar then, if one touches the contents of the objects, he becomes unclean--contrary to M. Kel. 23:1. (So MS and Bert.) MA explains, however, that Eleazar's ruling may have no bearing on his opinion as to whether the stuffing is connected to the container or not. He cites M. Miq. 10:2 which rules that in the case of containers which are generally meant to remain sealed "one may immerse them sealed." Connection then is no issue since the inside of the container need never touch the water during immersion.

The fact that they are torn is mentioned in A only to allow the possibility of touching the stuffing so that the ruling that the stuffing is not connected may be spelled out. Eleazar therefore need not be expressing a contradictory ruling. (See MA to M. Kel. 23:1.)

b. San. 68a assigns the ruling of B to Eliezer b. Hyrcanus and assumed that Eleazar learned it from him (see ARN A, 19). Joshua b. Qorḥa appears with Eleazar in M. Ned. 3:11, but not as a tradent, and in T. Neg. 7:3.

55. A. Said R. Eleazar b. Azariah, "Five things we learned from R. Eliezer [on his deathbed].

B. "And we rejoiced in them more than we rejoiced in them in his lifetime.

C. "These are they:

D. "The round pillow, and the ball, and the shoe last, and the amulet, and the phylactery which were torn,

E. "of which you told us, what are they [clean or unclean]?

F. "He said to them, 'They are unclean and be careful with them and immerse them as they are,

G. "'For these are established laws which were spoken to Moses at Sinai.'"

ARN A 19, ed. Schechter, p. 70 (Kallah Rabbati 6:1; Derekh Ereṣ Rabbah 3:5)

A. When R. Eliezer took sick [and was on his deathbed, of that instance] they said, That day was the eve of the Sabbath and R. Aqiva and his colleagues arrived to visit him...

B. When the sages saw that his mind was clear, they entered and sat down before him, at a distance of four cubits.

C. They said to him, "Rabbi, a round cushion, a ball, a shoe last, an amulet, phylacteries which were torn--do they become unclean?"

D. He said to them, "They become unclean and immerse them as they are, and be careful with them,

E. "for these are great laws which were spoken to Moses at Sinai."

F. And they asked him about [the laws of] cleanness, uncleanness and immersion pools...

G. Said to him R. Eleazar b. Azariah, "Rabbi, what of the shoe attached to the shoe last?"

H. He said to him, "Clean."

I. And he answered on the clean, "clean" and on the unclean, "unclean" until his soul went forth in purity.

J. Immediately R. Eleazar b. Azariah tore his clothes and wept and went out and said to the sages, "My rabbis, come and see that R. Eliezer is in a state of purity for the world to come, for his soul has gone forth in purity (lit.: clean--*ṭhwr*)..."

ARN A 25, ed. Schechter, pp. 80-81 (b. San. 68a)

Comment: T.'s law is attributed by Eleazar to Eliezer in ARN A 19. D provides the list, and F gives the ruling. ARN A 25 (C-E) and b. San. 68a omit reference to Eleazar b. Azariah and attribute the ruling directly to Eliezer.

G-I of ARN A 25 is a secondary question related to the law of T. Eliezer tells Eleazar that the shoe last is clean, presumably because it is easily removable and therefore not deemed to be attached to the shoe. Thus it does not carry the uncleanness of the shoe. G-I may have been generated by ARN A 19 which links T.'s ruling to Eliezer through Eleazar. In b. however Aqiva is substituted, Eleazar omitted. Clearly this makes more sense, since Eleazar does not appear elsewhere represented as a student or even in any close relationship with Eliezer. Eleazar's name is likely brought in only because of its association with T.'s ruling. It is not clear why T.'s ruling is associated with Eliezer's death.

56. A. Their appearance [color] changed,

B. whether to produce a lenient or to produce a stringent decision--

C. How to produce a lenient decision?

It was as white as snow and became as white as the lime of the Temple, as white as white wool and as white as the skin of an egg and became [as white as] the second shade of a swelling or the second shade of bright white (Lev. 13:6-8).

D. How to produce a stringent decision?

It was as white as the skin of an egg and became as white as wool, as white as the lime of the Temple and as white as snow--

E. R. Eleazar b. Azariah declares clean [= M. 4:7].

F. R. Eleazar Ḥisma says, "To produce a lenient decision it is clean and to produce a strict decision --let it be examined as in the beginning."

G. R. Aqiva says, "Whether to produce a lenient decision or to produce a strict decision--let it be examined as in the beginning [as a new spot]."

M. Neg. 7:2; Sifra, *Neg. pereq* 1:1

Comment: As Neusner points out (*HMLP*, Vol. VI, pp. 124f.) the pericope "shows clearly how a glossator does his work." A and E-G are primary. B is introduced to accord with the distinction made in F-G between a lenient and a strict decision. E does not depend on B. Eleazar's opinion can stand by itself, as a simple version of the law would be "If their appearance changed," they would be nonetheless "clean" or "unclean." Both F and G differ from E. C and D represent a tertiary level of interpolation and were likely introduced on the basis of the distinction of B.

The commentators following Sifra (Bert., MA, etc.) explain that the law of A applies to the list of M. 7:1: "These bright spots are clean: any that were on a man before the law was given [at Sinai]; or that were on a gentile when he converted; or that were on a child when it was born; or that were on a crease and were [later] laid bare..." In all of those cases concerning the bright spot the person is insusceptible at the time of its appearance. The issue then is what is its status if it later changes color. Eleazar states flatly that it retains its status as a clean bright spot no matter what occurs.

This ruling agrees in principle with the anonymous law of M. Neg. 4:7: "...If [the bright spot] had been bright white but was now dull white, or dull white but was now bright white, it is regarded as though it had remained as it was; provided that it does not become less white than the four colors [of M. Neg. 1:1]." In fact our pericope may be applied to the more general case of bright spot as that of Chapter Four, rather than to the cases of 7:1. The redactor however saw its place in Chapter Seven.

Both Eleazar Ḥisma and Aqiva presuppose that the bright spot can become unclean and subject to decision. In essence, they rule that it is a new bright spot. That is also the supposition of B-D. We take account of the history of the spot. Eleazar says that we do not--therefore the spot is clean. If it is subject to decision then we may have either a lenient or a stringent ruling as B-D spells out to elucidate F-G.

Eleazar Ḥisma rules that only where the color whitens, do we have the possibility of uncleanness. Where it grew dull it must be viewed as a continuation of the old "clean" spot. Aqiva holds that any color change denotes a new spot. Aqiva and Eleazar b. Azariah are the two extreme rulings: "clean" or "let it be examined as in the beginning." Eleazar Ḥisma's view is a compromise, agreeing with both and using the apodoses of both.

Eleazar takes the strong and lenient position that since the spot was insusceptible before the period of susceptibility commenced, the bright spot can never be declared unclean since the color change does not indicate a new bright spot.

57. A. He who comes [before the priest] when he is entirely white,

B. and on him is quick flesh the size of a lentil [so he is unclean]--

C. it broke forth over all of him [so he is clean]--

D. and afterwards the tips of the limbs reappear--

E. R. Ishmael says, "It is like the restoration of the tips of the limbs in the case of a large bright spot [such that covered the whole body, so he is unclean]."

F. R. Eleazar b. Azariah says, "It is like the restoration of the tips of the limbs in the case of a small bright spot [on part of the skin, and he is clean]."

M. Neg. 8:9

Comment: The exegesis of this pericope depends on the understanding of the chain of events which is spelled out in A-D. Maimonides understands the case as follows: First there is a decision for uncleanness because of the token of uncleanness, the quickflesh. Then there was spreading over the entire body. He should therefore be clean, since the rule is that if there is spreading from a status of uncleanness, it is clean. Next the fingertips receded. Here we have the dispute. Ishmael rules that even though the initial covering of the entire body came as a result of spreading from unclean signs, we still consider the case as one who came all white to the priest (i.e., the large bright spot). 8:1 tells us that he is unclean. Eleazar disagrees. The case here, he says, is one of a small bright spot. The spreading renders him clean. Recession of the signs from the fingertips is of no consequence *vis a vis* the small bright spot since that is a place where it does not apply (see 6:7).

TYY explains that there is no disagreement between the two as to whether the afflicted person is clean or unclean. Either the case is one in which the fingertips recede and both declare it unclean or it is a case of where the quickflesh spread in which case both say clean, since the quickflesh may not spread into itself. They disagree rather over what the status of the signs are if there is another change afterwards.

TYB sees the dispute in a case where there had not been a decision. The man has signs of uncleanness but according to Ishmael he is judged simply as one who came all white. He is unclean then because of the recession. Eleazar also judges him unclean but because it is spreading from a small spot. The recession in this case is of no consequence.

MA understands the dispute as follows. The man comes before any decision was made. The question is whether there is spreading before the recession from the fingertips or not. Ishmael considers the man clean because he sees the spread of the quickflesh as of no consequence. The man was totally white to begin with. Therefore the recession does not render him unclean. Eleazar sees the spreading as pertinent even though it is only from one sign of uncleanness into another. Therefore the recession of the signs from the fingertips renders him unclean. Ishmael bases his ruling on M. 8:3.

The interpretive question boils down to deciding at what stage the man comes to the priest and when the spreading took place. Then it must be clarified as to whether we may consider there to be spreading or not. Maimonides and TYY adhere to the language of the pericope and explain how the views consider the case either one of a "large" or "small" bright spot. MA is more problematical in this respect.

58. A. "A house which shades (*msk*) a house which bears the plague [and is certified unclean],

B. "and so a tree which shades a house which bears the plague--

C. "he that enters the outer [house] is clean,"

D. thè words of R. Eleazar b. Azariah.

E. Said R. Eleazar, "If a single stone from it renders unclean by entering in, will the house itself not render unclean by entering in?"

M. Neg. 13:6

Comment: A and C are primary to R. Eleazar b. Azariah's opinion. B is clearly interpolated, since C ignores B and refers only to A. E is phrased as a gloss to A plus C-D and also ignores B, which must then have been inserted at a later stage.

The issue is the status of one who enters a house which shades another house afflicted with plague. Eleazar b. Azariah rules that the person that enters is clean. Likewise if someone stood under a tree which shaded the afflicted house he is clean. R. Eleazar in E replies that if a single stone from the afflicted house was brought into the outer house, which then forms a Tent over the stone, it would be unclean. Surely then where the outer shades the entire inner house, all that comes into the outer will be unclean.

MA observes that Eleazar's argument is compelling whether the inner house was already subject to decision or had only been shut up. In the former case each and every stone from the inner house is unclean. In the latter we may assume that Eleazar refers to the afflicted stone of the inner house. Eleazar b. Azariah declares clean since he rules that entry into the outer house in this case does not convey uncleanness. MA relates this ruling to M. Neg. 13:11.

Sens compares A-C to the house and the upper room of M. 13:3. Neusner points out that the issue is whether the outer house forms a Tent over the inner (*HMLP*, Vol. VI, p. 254). Eleazar b. Azariah bases his view on the supposition of overshadowing. The Tent spreads uncleanness, thus anything in the afflicted house is unclean. It also interposes against uncleanness and does not allow the contamination to spread to the outer house. Eleazar argues that a stone which serves as part of the structure of a Tent cannot be considered to be contained within it. Thus the inner Tent does not interpose. Maimonides ties the ruling to M. 13:4 (see MS). T. Neg. 7:4B gives the dispute but lacks any attribution to Eleazar b. Azariah.

59. A. He who puts his hand into a house afflicted with plague and touched it on the inside--

B. Rabbi declares unclean.

C. And R. Leazar b. R. Simeon declares clean

D. until he puts in his head and the greater part of his body.

E. And so did R. Joshua b. Qorḥa declare clean in the name of R. Leazar b. Azariah.

T. Neg. 7:3, ed. Zuckermandel, p. 626, ls. 23-25

Comment: A serves as the protasis for the dispute B-C. The issue is whether uncleanness is conveyed to one who inserts his hand into a house afflicted with the plague. Lev. 14:46 tells us that entry conveys uncleanness. What is the status of a person who puts only part of his body (e.g., his hand) into the house? Can the hand contain the uncleanness of the house and transmit it to the individual? The dispute is then how much of the body must enter the house: the hand or the head and greater part of the body? Both of these positions extend the simple definition of "entry" in Lev. Presumably entry should involve the whole body.

The referent of Eleazar's ruling is not clear. From the formulation of the citation he seems to agree with C-D. However, it is possible that he declares clean even in a case of entry of the greater part of the body and requires full entry for the conveyance of uncleanness.

M. Neg. 13:6 above also shows Eleazar's concern for the transmission of the uncleanness of the plague of houses through entry. There, however, his ruling concerns "a house which shades a house which bears the plague." The Tent does not convey the uncleanness there. Here too the hand and perhaps the majority of the body does not convey it. Hence Eleazar displays in these two rulings a consistent demand for the more literal understanding of Scripture which leads to leniency in his rulings in both cases.

60. A. One who leaves his clothes in the wall-niche of the bath attendant (*hlwn šl' wly' ryn*): [K: *'wlyydyn*; P: *'wryyryn*; N,L,G: *'wry'ryn*].

B. R. Eleazar b. Azariah declares [them] clean.

C. And the sages say, "[The clothes are considered unclean] until he gives him the key, or the seal or until he made a sign [on the niche so that he would know if it had been opened]..."

M. Ṭoh. 7:7

Comment: A serves as the protasis for B and C. B + C, however, seem to be independent. Had the opinions been balanced they would have had apodoses "clean"/"unclean." As C stands in its present form it lacks the word "unclean" which is implicit.

The issue is whether we consider the niches of the bath attendant to be accessible to all who enter into the bathhouse. If, as MA points out, it is normal for all those who enter to bathe to open all of the niches to see if they are empty so that they may put their clothes there, then we have here a case of doubt as to whether or not an unclean person touched the clothes. In such a case we rule that they are unclean. Eleazar holds that it is doubtful whether the niches were opened and therefore the clothes are clean. MA compares this case to the one in M. Ṭoh. 6:3: "If one put his hand into a recess which contained uncleanness--if it is doubtful whether he touched it or not--that doubt [we decide is] unclean." However, if there is doubt as to whether he put his hand in--he is clean. Eleazar considers our case to be one of doubtful entry--thus clean. The sages consider it to be one of doubtful contact--thus unclean--unless he had a way of determining that no one opened the niche.

TYY explains that the sages' ruling in effect is that if the attendant gives the bather the key, or if the user makes a sign on the niche, it is considered to be his domain. This is enough of a guarantee that the niche will not be opened.

A. One who leaves an *ʿam haʾareṣ* in his house to guard it and he [the watchman] is unable to move (*mwwl*: lit.: footless) or tied up

B. as long as he is able to see those who enter and leave [the house]

C. it [the contents of the house] is unclean up to the place which they can [reach] to cause uncleanness.

D. Said R. Judah, "R. Eleazar b. Azariah admits to the sages [that in the case of] the wall-niches of the bath attendants

E. "which were opened one to the other

F. "if all take out from them

G. "that they are unclean."

H. And the sages say, "In either case (*bn kk wbn kk*) they are unclean."

T. Ṭoh. 8:7

Comment: D-H is related to M. Ṭoh. 7:7. Judah explains that Eleazar's ruling there (that the clothes in the niche are clean) applies only to a case of separate niches. If however they are all connected and each person who takes his clothes out has access to the other niches, Eleazar would admit that they are unclean. There is no doubt in such a case that others may have opened the niche. Therefore the clothes are unclean.

Both the rulings of M. and of T. are based on the presupposition that unguarded clothing is unclean since an unclean person is presumed to have touched them. A-C of

T., for example, is another of the series of rulings based on this supposition and common to M.-T. Ṭoh.

Eleazar's ruling is well attested.

61. A. [R. Joshua used to say that any pool (*mqwh*) containing less than forty *seah*s into which fell three *log*s [of drawn water] and even a *qartob* (1/64 *log*) was removed, is valid--since it [what remains] lacks the full three *log*s [of drawn water]. And the sages say, It remains invalid until all its contents and a bit more go out of it.]

How so? The cistern in the courtyard: into it fell three *log*s

B. it remains invalid

C. until its contents and a bit more go out of it

D. or until he will set up [a pool of] forty *seah*s in the courtyard [below it] and purify the upper one with the lower one.

E. R. Eleazar b. Azariah declares it invalid unless he stopped it up (*pqq*: K,N,G,L; *psq*: P, PB) [i.e., the upper, invalid pool from the lower, valid pool].

M. Miq. 3:2

Comment: The pericope addresses the question of how one may purify water in a cistern into which fell drawn water so that it may be used for ritual immersion. A gives the case: three *log*s of drawn water fell into a cistern (*bwr*). B-D has an anonymous ruling in the formulary pattern "it is invalid until...or until..." Eleazar's ruling in E follows a similar pattern: "invalid unless..." The pericope, however, is not balanced. B-D gives two options for purifying the water in the cistern. E has one. Moreover, the language differs: B has "it remains invalid" (*l'wlm hw' bpswlw*); E has "declares invalid" (*pwsl*). In addition C and D have "until" (*'d š*) and E has "unless" (*'l' 'm kn*). Likewise the former has the verb in the imperfect tense and the latter in the perfect. Thus E is independent of A-D.

A balanced version of the pericope might have been:

The cistern...is invalid (or sages declare invalid)
  until its contents go out...
or until he sets up...
R. Eleazar b. Azariah says:
  until he stops it up.

A-C of the pericope is better balanced formally by A-C of M. 3:3:

A. The cistern which is filled with drawn water and a channel led into it and out of it
B. it remains invalid
C. until it is estimated that there do not remain three *log*s of the original [drawn water].

It is therefore possible that A-C of M. 3:3 and of 3:2 formed a balanced, separate pericope, summarizing how one may purify a cistern either of part or all drawn water. D and E of M. 3:2 are simply glosses introduced into this unit. The "How so?" of A then serves to alert the reader to the fact that a general statement of law follows the specific case of M. 3:1. (So TYY.) MA correctly notes that *kyṣd* usually precedes an explanatory pericope--one which further elucidates a specific case. This is not the case in our pericope as we have seen. M. Ohalot 16:2 has a similar use of *kyṣd*. It serves there to introduce a distinct ruling of general nature. In either case the joining language is a tenuous link between 3:1 and 3:2.

Let us turn to the issue of the pericope. GRA stands alone in his explanation since he bases it on a proposed emendation of the text. He places E before D, thus assigning both rulings to Eleazar. According to the sages then, once water equivalent to the volume of the cistern has flowed out allowing undrawn water to displace it, we may assume that the invalid water has left the cistern and that now it is valid. Eleazar, on the other hand, makes no such assumption. He has instead two alternatives. One may either stop up the invalid pool and allow it to drain without being replenished or one may purify the pool intact by allowing another, valid one to come into contact with it, allowing the water to intermingle.

If we do not resort to GRA's emendation, the issue is a bit more complex. Eleazar surely makes no assumption that if the volume of the pool turns over, the invalid water has flowed out. Nor does he accept the suggestion that one may purify one pool through contact with another. This he rejects because he does not hold the concept of *gwd 'syq*. The upper pool may not be purified by the lower. Maimonides' [MSS. K,G,L] reading of D ("the upper purifies the lower") necessitates the assumption that he also does not hold *gwd 'ḥyt*.

As MA points out, C is out of place in this chapter and belongs in Chapter 6. GRA may have emended the pericope in order to avoid having Eleazar reject the ruling of C.

Eleazar's lemma is dependent on A-C for its context. The literary considerations suggest that this was not its original setting. For another ruling of Eleazar's on pools, see T. Shab. 3:3.

62. A. "If one discharged thick drops from his member he is unclean." The words of R. Eleazar Ḥisma.

B. If one suffered impure thoughts at night and got up and found his flesh heated, he is unclean.

C. "[If a woman] discharged semen on the third day [after intercourse] [she] is clean."

D. The words of R. Eleazar b. Azariah.

E. R. Ishmael says, "Sometimes they are four periods, sometimes they are five and sometimes they are six."

F. R. Aqiva says, "Always five."

M. Miq. 8:3 (Mekh. *Baḥodeš*, 3, ed. Horowitz-Rabin, p. 214; Mekh. De R. Simeon, p. 142)

Comment: C-D gives the ruling of Eleazar b. Azariah. If a woman discharges semen on the third day she is clean.

The implication is that if she does so on the first or second, she is unclean. M. Shab. 9:3 explains the source of Eleazar's ruling:

> "From whence do we know that one who discharges semen on the third day is clean (so K, other MSS. give 'unclean')? For it is written, 'Be ready by the third day; do not go near a woman (Ex. 19:15).'"

Potent semen is classified as one of the fathers of uncleanness (M. Kel. 1:1). After the second day the presumption is that it is no longer considered potent semen. Hence if it is discharged she (and it) is clean.

E is phrased as a gloss to C-D and F disputes E. It is likely that E-F referred originally to another protasis since the word "they" in the present context has no antecedent. A possible protasis might be: "A woman who discharges semen in the first three days after intercourse is unclean." Then Ishmael could introduce the question of how many "periods" are encompassed in the "three days."

Each day consists of two "periods"--the daytime and the night. Ishmael points out that three days can be either four, five, or six periods, depending on whether intercourse last occurred at night, during the day, or at the end of the day. If it was, for example, late Wednesday afternoon we can count two periods on Thursday and two on Friday so that on Saturday, the third day, if she discharged semen she would be clean. It is possible to add on two more periods on Wednesday giving either five or six altogether until Saturday. Aqiva, on the other hand, simply holds that no matter when you start, if you count five periods you have spanned three days.

A. "[If a woman] discharges semen on the third day [after intercourse, she] is clean."

B. The words of R. Eleazar b. Azariah.

C. R. Ishmael says, "Sometimes they [i.e., the three days] are four periods, sometimes they are five, sometimes they are six."

D. R. Aqiva says, "Always five,

E. "and if part of the first period elapsed we complete it with part of the sixth."

T. Miq. 6:6

Comment: A-D simply repeats M. Miq. 8:3. E is then T.'s comment on M. It modifies Aqiva's ruling. In each case the time span is a full sixty hours (five periods). If intercourse occurred late on Wednesday, for example, any semen discharged until late on Saturday is unclean. Without T.'s comment we would have considered any discharge from the morning on (the beginning of the fifth period) as clean.

63. A. *tny*: R. Eleazar b. Azariah says, "A day and a night constitute a period.

B. "And part of a period is [treated] like an entire one."

C. *wtny*: Concerning the teaching of R. Eleazar b. Azariah, "Sometimes there is one day and a bit and she is clean; [sometimes there are] two days minus a bit and she is unclean."

y. Shab. 9:3

Comment: The pericope refers to M. Miq. 8:3: "[If a woman] discharged semen on the third day [after intercourse she] is clean; the words of R. Eleazar b. Azariah." A-B is in direct discourse. C is a comment on the ruling of A-B.

The issue is how we add up the time between intercourse and the time the woman becomes clean. According to A-B any fraction of a period, that is the day or the night, counts for the reckoning as a full period. Therefore as C points out, one day plus a small amount of time the night before and the night after is enough of a lapse of time for the woman to be considered clean. There are then three days in all. On the other hand if two full days are elapsed from just after sunrise on one day to just before sunset on the second, she is still unclean, for only two days can be counted.

It is strange, however, that Eleazar speaks of "periods" since in M. only Ishmael and Aqiva reckon on that basis. Eleazar's counting there is confined to days (cf. comment to M. Miq. 8:3).

64. A. These [liquids] render unclean and render susceptible to uncleanness: The flux of a *zab*, and his spit, and his semen, and his urine, and a quarter-*log* [of blood] from a corpse, and the blood of a menstruant.

B. R. Eliezer says, "Semen does not render susceptible."

C. R. Eleazar b. Azariah says, "The blood of a menstruant [P adds: does not render susceptible]."

D. R. Simeon says, "The blood of a corpse does not render susceptible."

M. Maksh. 6:6

Comment: The pericope consists of a protasis followed by a list of six items. B-D gives three independent rulings. According to the list of A, the items mentioned are unclean and considered 'liquids.' They can therefore render an object susceptible to uncleanness and transmit uncleanness to it at one time. M. Kel. 1:3 lists the flux of a *zab*, his spit, his semen, his urine and the blood of a menstruant as items which render objects unclean through both contact and carrying. [M. Ohal. 2:2 states that a quarter-*log* of blood renders unclean in a Tent, and the implication is that it certainly renders unclean through contact.] There is then no question that these items render unclean.

The central question of our pericope is whether they render susceptible to uncleanness. A presumes they do. M. 6:4 lists the seven primary liquids which render an object susceptible to uncleanness: dew, water, wine, oil, blood, milk, and bee's honey. Secretions of the body are included as derivatives of the category of "water" according to M. 6:5. [The author of the list of A apparently presumes that the first four items of his list fall into this category.] Blood of a corpse and the blood of a menstruant are included in the primary category of blood.

However, flux and semen are not listed as derivatives of any primary category. Therefore, what we may have are two contradictory lists of liquids which render susceptible. (MA harmonizes the two lists; see him on 6:6.) Eliezer's rule need not be taken as a gloss to A referring only to *zab*, but may be a general statement about the status of semen. Likewise, Simeon's rule in D.

Eleazar too, in C, seems to state a general rule. He distinguishes between menstrual blood and other blood. We find a similar distinction in M. Niddah 7:1: "The blood of a menstruant and flesh from a corpse render unclean [when they are] moist and [when they are] dry." Clearly a distinction is drawn between types of blood. Menstrual blood is conceived of as a separate entity, a separate "life," which renders objects unclean but is not to be considered in the same category as ordinary blood but as an equal to the flesh of a corpse. Therefore it certainly is not subsumed under the category of blood which defines those liquids that render an object susceptible to uncleanness.

The redactor placed these three rulings (B-D) between two lists. The first is our list in A. The second follows immediately and lists the items which neither render unclean nor render susceptible. B-D is actually a "list" of items which render unclean but do not render susceptible. 6:4, of course, lists those liquids which render susceptible but do not render unclean.

65. A. ...All the holy Scriptures render the hands unclean.

B. The Song of Songs and Qoheleth render the hands unclean.

C. R. Judah says, "The Song of Songs renders the hands unclean, but [concerning] Qoheleth there is a dispute."

D. R. Yosé says, "Qoheleth does not render the hands unclean, but [concerning] the Song of Songs there is a dispute."

E. R. Simeon says, "[The status of] Qoheleth is among the lenient [rulings] of the House of Shammai and the stringent [rulings] of the House of Hillel (M. Ed. 5:3)."

F. Said R. Simeon b. Azzai, "I have a tradition from seventy-two elders that on the day that they placed R. Eleazar b. Azariah in the academy [K omits: *byšybh*]

G. "that the Song of Songs and Qoheleth render the hands unclean."

H. Said R. Aqiva, "God forbid! No man in Israel ever disputed that the Song of Songs should render the hands unclean;

I. "for all the ages are not worth the day on which the Song of Songs was given to Israel;

J. "for all the Writings are holy but the Song of Songs is holy of holies.

K. "But if they disputed, they only disputed [the status of] Qoheleth."

L. Said R. Yoḥanan b. Joshua [K: Shamuʿa], the son of R. Aqiva's father-in-law, "According to the words of b. Azzai, so did they dispute and so did they decide."

M. Yad. 3:5

Comment: F attributes to b. Azzai the tradition that the ruling on the status of Song of Songs and Qoheleth is connected to "the day that they placed R. Eleazar b. Azariah in the Academy." F appears in the same form in M. Zeb. 1:3 and in M. Yad. 4:2. There it is connected to a ruling concerning sacrifices which were slaughtered not for their own sake.

The redactor here placed the tradition concerning a dispute about the status of the Song of Songs side by side with a tradition in Aqiva's name that there was never a dispute about its status (H-K). L decides the matter.

66. A. On that day they said,

B. "All the sacrifices which were slaughtered not for their own sake are fit

C. "but they do not count for the owners for [fulfillment of their] obligations

D. "except for the Passover and Sin-[offerings]

E. "the Passover in its [specified] time

F. "and the Sin-[offering] at any time."

G. R. Eliezer says, "Even [*'p*] the Guilt-offering."

H. The Passover in its [specified] time

I. and the Sin and Guilt-[offerings] at any time.

J. Said R. Simeon b. Azzai, "I have a tradition from seventy-two elders that on the day that they placed R. Eleazar b. Azariah in the academy

K. "that all the sacrifices that are eaten, which were slaughtered not for their own sake are fit

L. "but they do not count for the owners for [fulfillment of their] obligations

M. "except for the Passover and Sin-[offerings]."

N. And b. Azzai added only the Burnt-[offering]

O. and the sages did not agree with him.

M. Yad. 4:2

A. The Passover [sacrifice] that one slaughtered on the morning of the fourteenth [of Nisan]

B. not for its own sake

C. R. Joshua declares it fit

D. as if it were slaughtered on the thirteenth

E. Ben Batyra declares it unfit

F. as if it were slaughtered at twilight.

G. Said Simeon b. Azzai, "I have a tradition from seventy-two elders [*zqn*] that on the day that they placed [*hwšybw*] R. Eleazar b. Azariah in the academy [*yšybh*]

H. "that all the sacrifices that are eaten, which were slaughtered not for their own sake are fit

I. "but they do not count for the owners for [fulfillment of their] obligations

J. "except for the Passover and Sin-[offerings]."

K. And b. Azzai added only the Burnt-offering

L. and the sages did not agree with him.

M. Zeb. 1:3

Comment: The pericope contains two versions of the same ruling. A introduces our pericope as well as several others in the chapter. B-D and K-M are identical except for the words "that are eaten" in K. E-F glosses D. G-I gives Eliezer's ruling and N-O gives b. Azzai's.

The two versions also appear in M. Zeb. 1:1-3. M. Zeb. 1:1 is an exact parallel of A-I and M. Zeb. 1:3 repeats J-O. The following synopsis illustrates the parallels:

M.Yad. 4:2A-1	M.Zeb. 1:1	M.Zeb. 1:3 = M.Yad. 4:2J-O
A. On that day they said,	- - - -	- - - -
- - - -		J. Said Simeon b. Azzai, I have a tradition from 72 elders that on the day that they placed R. Eleazar b. Azariah in the academy
B. all the sacrifices which were slaughtered not for their own sake are fit	" " " "	K. that all sacrifices *that are eaten*...
C. But do not count for the owners for [fulfillment of their] obligations	" " " "	L. " " " "
D. except for the Passover and Sin-[offerings]	" " " "	M. " " " "

M.Yad. 4:2A-1	M.Zeb. 1:1	M.Zeb. 1:3 = M.Yad. 4:2J-O
E. the Passover in its time	" " " "	- - - -
F. and the Sin-[offering] at any time.	" " " "	- - - -
G. R. Eliezer says, Even the Guilt-offering.	" " " "	- - - -
H. The Passover in its time	" " " "	- - - -
I. and the Sin- and Guilt-offerings at any time.	" " " "	- - - -
- - - -	- - - -	N. and b. Azzai added only the Burnt-[offering].
- - - -	- - - -	O. and the sages did not agree with him.

The issue of the pericope is as follows: If a sacrifice is offered with improper intention it may still be eaten as if it were a Peace-offering. The owner, however, must bring another sacrifice since his original obligation is still outstanding. The Passover and Sin-offerings are exceptions to this rule. They must be slaughtered at the outset with proper intention or they will be completely invalid. The Passover is subject to this rule only if it is offered in "its time" (i.e., on the fourteenth of Nisan, at twilight).

In J-O, b. Azzai quotes this ruling, adding the words "that are eaten" in K. The implication of this formulation of the ruling is that a sacrifice which is wholly consumed on the altar, such as the Burnt-offering, is invalid if offered with improper intention. This is spelled out in N. O simply notes that the sages demur, probably on the basis of the alternative version of the ruling cited in A-I. Since b. Azzai's opinion derives from the additional word in his variant of the ruling and was not preserved in lemma form, it was not redacted into the dispute form as was Eliezer's in G-H.

The protasis, J, appears in M. Yad. 3:5 as well. In both instances the protasis is not germane to the ruling.

To b. Azzai is attributed the tradition that this ruling connected to "the day that they placed R. Eleazar b. Azariah in the academy." On this, see pp. 146-59.

67. A. On that day they said:

B. "What of Ammon and Moab in the Sabbatical year?"

C. Decreed R. Ṭarfon: "Poorman's tithe [must be given from the crop]."

D. And decreed R. Eleazar b. Azariah: "Second tithe [must be given]."

E. Said R. Ishmael, "Eleazar b. Azariah, you must bring forth proof, for you give a stringent ruling;

F. "for every one that gives a stringent ruling must bring forth proof."

G. (1) Said to him R. Eleazar b. Azariah, "Ishmael, my brother, I have not changed the order of the years.

(2) "Ṭarfon, my brother, changed it, and he must bring forth proof."

H. Answered R. Ṭarfon, "Egypt is outside the Land [of Israel] and Ammon and Moab are outside the Land; just as in Egypt Poorman's tithe [must be given] in the Sabbatical year, so in Ammon and Moab Poorman's tithe [must be given] in the Sabbatical year."

I. Answered R. Eleazar b. Azariah, "Babylonia is outside of the Land and Ammon and Moab are outside of the Land; just as in Babylonia Second tithe [must be given] in the Sabbatical year, so in Ammon and Moab Second tithe [must be given] in the Sabbatical year."

J. Said R. Ṭarfon, "Egypt which is near [the Land of Israel] they have made [liable for] Poorman's tithe so that the poor of Israel may rely on it [for sustenance] in the Sabbatical year; so too, Ammon and Moab, which are near [the Land of Israel] have been made [liable for] Poorman's tithe, so that the poor of Israel may rely upon it in the Sabbatical year."

K. Said to him R. Eleazar b. Azariah, "Lo, you are like one that would bestow [on them] worldly gain, and you are like one that would suffer lives to perish. You prevent (*qwb'*) the heavens from sending down dew and rain, as it is written, 'Will a man rob God? Yet you rob me. But you say, Wherein have we robbed thee? In tithes and Heave-offerings (Malachi 3:8).'"

L. Responded R. Ṭarfon (so K,L,P,PB,N,M):

M. Said R. Joshua, "Lo, I am as one who will answer on behalf of Ṭarfon my brother, but not according to the subject of his words.

N. "[The rule concerning] Egypt is a new decision, and [the rule concerning] Babylonia is an old decision and the argument before us is a new decision. Let a new decision be derived from a new decision, but do not let a new decision be derived from an old decision.

O. "[The rule concering] Egypt is a decision of the Elders; and [concerning] Babylonia is a decision of the Prophets, and the issue before us is a decision of the Elders. Let a decision of the Elders be derived from a decision of the Elders, but do not let a decision of the Elders be derived from a decision of the Prophets."

P. They were polled and decided: "Ammon and Moab [are liable to] tithe Poorman's tithe in the Sabbatical year."

Q. And when R. Yosé b. Durmasket came to R. Eliezer in Lydda, he said to him, "What new thing did you have today in the *Bet HaMidrash*?"

R. He said to him, "They were polled and decided: 'Ammon and Moab tithe Poorman's tithe in the Sabbatical year.'"

S. Wept R. Eliezer and said, "'The secret of the Lord is with them that fear him, and he will show them his covenant (Ps. 25:14).' Go and tell them, 'Be not anxious because of your voting; I have a tradition from Yoḥanan b. Zakkai, who heard it from his teacher, and his teacher from his teacher, [back to] a *halakhah* given to Moses at Sinai, That Ammon and Moab tithe Poorman's tithe in the Sabbatical year.'"

M. Yad. 4:3

A. Ammon and Moab tithe Poorman's tithe in the Seventh year and the rest of the lands and Babylonia [tithe Second] tithe.

B. Ammon and Moab in the rest of the years of the seven year cycle [follow Israel]: if [in Israel they tithe] Poorman's tithe [then in Ammon and Moab they tithe] Poorman's tithe; if Second-tithe--Second-tithe.

T. Yad. 2:15; ed. Zuckermandel, p. 683, ls. 16-18

C. Said R. Yosé b. Durmasket, "I was with the first Elders when they came from Yavneh to Lod. And I came and found R. Eliezer, who was sitting in the stall of the bakers of Lod.

D. "He said, 'What new thing did you have in the House of Study today?'

"I said to him, 'We are your students and drink from your waters.'

"He said to me, 'Even so, what new thing?'

"I told him the laws and the responses in the voting, and when I came to this one his eyes welled with tears.

E. "He said, '"The secret of the Lord is to those who fear him and he will show them his covenant (Ps. 25:14)," and it says, "For the Lord God will not do anything without revealing his secret to his servant and the prophets (Amos 3:2)."

"'Tell them, Be not anxious because of your voting. I have a tradition from Yoḥanan b. Zakkai, who received it as a tradition from the pairs, and the pairs from the Prophets, and the Prophets from Moses, as a law to Moses at Sinai, that Ammon and Moab tithe Poorman's tithe in the seventh year.'"

T. Yad. 2:16, ls. 18-26 (b. Ḥag. 3b)

Comment: The pericope seems to be a combination of a dispute, three debates and a story. A and P are redactional conventions of M. Yad. B-D presents a well balanced dispute using the attributive formula "decreed" (*gzr*) instead of "said." This formula does not appear elsewhere in M.

E-G is a debate between Eleazar and Ishmael. Ishmael's appearance here is problematical. Normally the parties to the dispute proceed to debate the issue. Ṭarfon rather than Ishmael should challenge Eleazar. B, D, E, F, and G(1) could form an independent pericope involving Eleazar and Ishmael. [It would not be well balanced since there is no ruling in Ishmael's name to balance Eleazar's lemma.]

If H-J followed B-D we would have an example of a common debate form: Statement of the issue, two opinions, first party argues, second party responds, first party argues again and remains unchallenged--hence the apparent victor in the debate.

K is odd. It does not directly answer Ṭarfon's argument. Rather it shifts to an attack on Ṭarfon. By not offering the correct tithe, Eleazar says, you offer no sustenance to the poor of Israel. Instead you cause lives to perish because the rains will be withheld. Formally K is not part of the debate of H-J. It is not phrased "answered R. Eleazar b. Azariah." Moreover, its presence destroys the structure of the common debate form. It does, however, refute the thrust of Ṭarfon's analogy and thus in context is appropriately placed.

L indicates that we have before us a defective text. The presence of a response by Ṭarfon might have restored at least the balance of the debate form (H-L). Joshua jumps into the discussion in M-O. Although he is not party to the debate until here, it is not out of character for him to "poke his head in" at this point in support of Ṭarfon. Actually Joshua presents two parallel arguments, N and O. Both insist that the analogy to Egypt is valid and the comparison to Babylonia is not. Joshua's intrusion completes the debate of H-K. P, redactional language, affirms that the law does indeed follow Ṭarfon. Q-S is, however, the climax of the pericope. The story may actually be a polemic claiming that Eliezer has the tradition which is superior to any decision based on reason. T. knows nothing of Eleazar, Ṭarfon or Joshua and the debate. It simply states the law and cites the story.[8]

Let us turn now to the issue of the pericope and the arguments of the debate. During the Sabbatical year the Land of Israel may not be cultivated. It is technically "ownerless" property and thus not subject to tithes. Neighboring lands may be cultivated and thus are subject to tithes. The presumption here is that these lands were regulated by the agricultural laws of the Land of Israel, hence considered part of Israel. Since these lands were not under Jewish control at the time these rules were redacted, such laws are particularly striking.[9]

The debate centers around the question of which tithe must be given in Ammon and Moab in the seventh year. In Israel, Poorman's-tithe is given in the third and sixth year of the seven year cycle in lieu of Second-tithe. H and I suggest comparison with other areas outside the Land (Egypt or Babylonia) will indicate whether Second-tithe or Poorman's-tithe must be separated. That is inconclusive, however. J suggests that sustenance of the poor is the key principle. K, as we have said, is best seen as an argument from Scripture tacked on to the pericope. On its own it indicates in favor of neither Second- nor Poorman's-tithe. M-O's operative argument is that new decisions, those of the Elders must be derived from like decisions. Therefore Ammon and Moab must be compared with Egypt and not Babylonia. H, I, J, and M-O all refer to the rules regulating Egypt and Babylonia which, however, appear nowhere in M.-T. Even though the arguments heavily favor Ṭarfon, the redactor attributes the final authority to Sinai. Revelation, however, leads the God-fearing Rabbis to the proper decision even though they are ignorant of the tradition.

68. A. ...The fruit stalk of a date palm that one stripped [of dates] is clean.

B. If he left one date [on the stalk] it is unclean.

C. And so with legumes.[10]

D. The fruit stalk that one stripped is clean.

E. If he left one pod on it, it is unlcean.

F. R. Eleazar b. Azariah declares clean [fruit stalks] of beans,[11]

G. and declares unclean [fruit stalks of other] legumes,

H. because he desires it for its use [in handling the pods].

M. Uqṣ. 1:5 (b. Ḥul. 119b)

Comment: F-H gives Eleazar's ruling on the status of stalks of legumes. M. Uqṣ. 1:1 begins, "Any [stalk] that serves as a handle...may become unclean and conveys uncleanness..." G tells us that the stalks of legumes in general receive and convey uncleanness because, as the gloss H says, they are useful in the handling of the vegetables. In F, Eleazar rules that *pul* is an exception. Its stalk is not considered a handle even if it is laden with fruit (MA). The ruling follows other specific laws concerning handles, such as those of A-E. F-G is a gloss on A-E.

NOTES

CHAPTER II

[1]On *ḥbr hyhwdym* and *ḥbr h'yr*, see E. Schurer, *The History of the Jewish People in the Age of Jesus Christ*, Vol. I, revised and edited by Geza Vermes and Fergus Millar, Edinburgh, 1973, p. 211, n. 25.

[2]Finkelstein suggests (Sifré, p. 53, s.v. *mykn 'mrw*) that both Yosé and Eleazar reflect an "early" ruling which was modified during Hadrian's persecution of the Jews. He cites Tos. Ber. 2:13 as an illustration of the change: (R. Meir says,)

> Once we were sitting before R. Aqiva and we were reciting the *shema'* and we did not hear our own words because a *questor* was standing in the doorway.

This practice was accepted as law by R. Meir and others, he says.

[3]Other evidence that some tithes were given to the priesthood can be found in Judith 11-13; Jubilees 13-25; Josephus, *Antiquities* 20:181, 20:206, *Vita* 63; Philo, *On the Virtues*, 95. Though the practice may have been common there is no other evidence that it was ever a formal obligation to give tithes exclusively to the priesthood.

[4]See Charles Primus, *Aqiva's Contribution to the Law. 1: Zera'im*, Ph.D. dissertation, Brown University, 1975, pp. 129ff. (his comment on this pericope).

[5]The gloss F explains Judah's opinion. B. (Beṣ. 23a) connects Judah's ruling to his general opinion regarding the unintentional performance of a prohibited act on the Sabbath or festival. In b. Shab. 41b Abaye states that Judah holds that unintentional acts are also prohibited. No source is given for Judah's general ruling about intention. It is likely that our pericope provided the original source for the Amoraic view that Judah discounted intention and held one culpable regardless, since he rules here that even though one may have intention only to curry the animal, he may not since he will probably scratch it in the process.

[6]See C. C. McCown, "The Earliest Christian Books," in *The Biblical Archaeologist Reader*, ed. G. E. Wright and D. N. Freedman, N.Y., 1951, p. 254.

[7]See Neusner, *HJB*, I, p. 147 and Appendix VII.

[8]Neusner (*Development*, pp. 58-60, 202; *Eliezer*, p. 334) says that "the content and the forms of the sayings are suspicious and are probably fraudulent."

[9]Neusner (*Eliezer*, p. 335) points out that all of these authorities [Ṭarfon, Eleazar, Joshua, and Yoḥanan] are represented as crypto-revolutionaries since they all lived in a period when these lands were not under Jewish control.

[10]*vicia faba* (Y. Feliks, *Agriculture in Palestine in the Period of the Mishnah and the Talmud*, (Hebrew), p. 156).

[11]*hülsen fruchte* (I. Löwe, *Die Flora der Juden*, Vol. IV, p. 73).

CHAPTER III

THE NON-LEGAL TRADITIONS

i. *Mishnah-Tosefta*

69. A. ...For sins between Man and the Omnipresent, the Day of Atonement atones. [But for] sins between Man and his fellow, the Day of Atonement does not atone, until one has appeased his fellow [and asked for his pardon].

B. This is what R. Eleazar b. Azariah expounded: "From all your sins shall you be clean before the Lord (Lev. 16:30)": "[For] those sins which are between Man and the Omnipresent, the Day of Atonement atones. [But for] sins between Man and his fellow, the Day of Atonement does not atone, until one has appeased his fellow."

M. Yoma 8:9

Comment: The end of tractate Yoma contains several pericopae on the nature of atonement on the Day of Atonement. In our pericope B repeats A and adds only the verse from Scripture. Thus we have two versions of one tradition. Eleazar's exegesis is simple. He reads "clean before the Lord"--but not clean before his fellow man. For that atonement he must beg forgiveness from his fellow. Eleazar thus qualifies the "all" of the verse "from all your sins." He reads the clause *lpny yhwh* as an adjectival clause referring to the clause which precedes it rather than reading it as an adverbial clause related to the phrase which follows it. He reads, "*mkl hṭ'tykm lpny yhwh--tṭhrw*" and not "*mkl hṭ'tykm--lpny yhwh tṭhrw*."[1]

A. For sins between Man and the Omnipresent, the Day of Atonement atones. But for sins between Man and his fellow, the Day of Atonement does not atone until one has appeased his fellow.

B. This is what R. Eleazar b. Azariah expounded: "From all your sins you shall be clean before the Lord (Lev. 16:30)."

C. "For matters between you and the Omnipresent [the Day of Atonement] grants pardon (*mwḥlyn*) for you.

D. "For matters between you and your fellow, it does not grant pardon until you appease your fellow."

Sifra, *Aḥaré*, *pereq* 8:1-2

Comment: Sifra gives a slightly different version of Eleazar's comment. The language of Eleazar's lemma has not been revised precisely to follow M.'s anonymous ruling.

69a. A. Asked R. Mattiah b. Ḥeresh of R. Eleazar b. Azariah in Rome,

B. "You have heard of the four types of atonement that R. Ishmael used to expound?"

C. Said [R. Eleazar b. Azariah], "They are three and repentance must go with each one..."

b. Yoma 86a; ARN 29; y. Yoma 8:7; y. San. 10:1; y. Shabuot 1:6

Comment: Eleazar is cast in the role of a commentator on Ishmael's teaching (cf. T. Yom. 5:6-8, ed. Zuckermandel, p. 190, ls. 15-23). Eleazar's comment is unclear. ARN attributes the tradition to R. Eleazar Hakefar at Laodicea. That attribution of the teaching is probably more accurate since it is unlikely that Eleazar b. Azariah would comment on a teaching of Ishmael. Moreover, Mattiah b. Ḥeresh does not appear elsewhere with Eleazar b. Azariah.

70. A. R. Eleazar b. Azariah says, "Repulsive is the uncircumcision, for through it the wicked have been disgraced.

B. "As it is written, 'For all these nations are uncircumcised (Jer. 9:26).'"

M. Ned. 3:11 (Mekh. *'Amaleq*, 1, ed. Horowitz-Rabin, p. 191, ls. 15-16)

Comment: Eleazar's exegesis of the verse in Jeremiah equates "the nations" with "the wicked." His remark is followed in M. Ned. by six statements, each prefaced by the phrase "great is circumcision." Eleazar's comment is the only one in M. which attaches the connotation of "repulsive" to the nations because of their uncircumcised status.[2]

71. When R. Eleazar b. Azariah died, riches departed from amongst the sages.

M. Soṭ. 9:15

A. When Eleazar b. Azariah died the crown of glory of the sages was abolished

B. for the crown of the sages is their wealth.

T. Soṭ. 15:3, ed. Zuckermandel, p. 321, ls. 20-21; ed. Lieberman, p. 240

Comment: In both M. and T. the tradition is set in the context of several other statements all formulated "When X died...". The tradition attributing wealth to Eleazar is further developed in b. Ber. 27b and b. Ber. 57b. T. either glosses M. or presents a separate version.

72. A. There are three sages [whose appearance in a dream is meaningful].

B. If one sees Rabbi in a dream, he should expect wisdom.

C. [If one sees] R. Eleazar b. Azariah [in a dream], he should expect wealth.

D. [If one sees] R. Ishmael b. Elisha [in a dream], he should fear punishment [will come upon him].

b. Ber. 57b

Comment: The pericope appears in a long section of b. Ber. which deals explicitly with the interpretation of dreams. Eleazar appears in a list of three sages. To each is assigned a conventional meaning as a symbol in a dream. The association of Eleazar with wealth is found in M. Soṭ. 9:15 and T. Soṭ. 15:3. The tradition here seems to be a natural development of the tradition in Soṭ.

A. There are four sages:

B. One who sees R. Yoḥanan b. Nuri in a dream should expect [to acquire] fear of sin.

C. [One who sees] R. Eleazar b. Azariah should expect greatness and wealth.

D. [One who sees] R. Ishmael should expect wisdom.

E. [One who sees] Elisha b. Abuyah should fear punishment.

ARN A, 40, ed. Schechter, p. 128

Comment: Here Eleazar appears in a list of four sages, instead of three.

73. A. Eleazar b. Azariah's cow... [referring to M. Shab. 5:4]

B. *Did he have* [only] *one cow*?

C. "Lo," said Rav, and some say, said R. Judah, said Rav,

D. "R. Eleazar b. Azariah *used to tithe twelve thousand calves from his flock each year*."

E. [It was] *taught*, "*They were not his, but his neighbors; And because he did not mind, they were called* [*tithe*] *in his name*."

b. Shab. 54b; b. Beṣ. 23a

Comment: C-D builds on the tradition that attributes great wealth to Eleazar (T. Soṭ. 15:3 and M. Soṭ. 9:15). It of course presumes that the tithe-system continued after the destruction of the Temple. E is a comment on C-D.

It rejects the interpretation and insists that the statement of M. be taken literally. Eleazar had only one cow, but the tithes of others were given in his name.

74. A. *m'śh b*: R. Yoḥanan b. Beroqah and R. Eleazar Ḥisma came from Yavneh to Lod--

B. And they paid respect to R. Joshua in Peki'in.

C. He said to them, "What new teaching was there in the house of study today?"

D. They said to him, "We are your disciples and drink of your water."

E. He said to them, "It is not possible for the house of study [to convene] without [hearing] a new teaching.

F. "Whose week was it?"

G. "It was [the week of] R. Eleazar b. Azariah."

H. He said to them, "And concerning what did he expound?"

I. "'Assemble the people, men, women, and little ones (Deut. 31:12).' If the men come to learn and the women come to hear, why do the little ones come? To acquire reward for those who bring them."

J. And [R. Eleazar b. Azariah] further expounded: "You have declared this day concerning the Lord [that he is your God]...And the Lord has declared this day concerning you [that you are his people] (Deut. 26:16-17)." (MSS. Vienna and printed ed. Venice have: Said the Holy One to Israel, As you have made me the only object of your love in the world, so I shall make you the only object of my love in the world to come.)

K. And [R. Eleazar b. Azariah] further expounded: "The sayings of the wise are like goads (Qoh. 12:11)."

L. Just as a goad directs the cow to bring life to the world, so the words of Torah [direct man and] bring life to the world.

M. But if [you object and say] that a goad is moveable [and may be withdrawn, so too its analogue] the words of Torah [may be] "moveable,"

N. It comes to teach, "and like nails firmly fixed [are the collected sayings which are given by one shepherd] (*ibid*)."

O. [If you say that a nail is unchanging] not diminished or increased, it comes to teach, "firmly fixed" (lit.: planted).

P. (MSS. Vienna and printed ed. Venice have: Just as a plant is fruitful and multiplies, so too the words of Torah are fruitful and multiply.)

Q. "The collected sayings" (lit.: Members of the gatherings)--these are the disciples of the sages who sit in councils (lit.: gathered together)

R. and pronounce the unclean, unclean and the clean, clean.

S. One should not say to himself, "Since some forbid and others permit, why do I study [at all]?"

T. It comes to teach, "given by one shepherd." One shepherd received them, one God created them--so you should make your heart as the inner chamber and receive into the words of those who declare unclean and the words of those who declare clean.

U. He [R. Joshua] said to them, "The generation in whose midst is R. Eleazar b. Azariah is not an orphan."

T. Soṭ. 7:9-10, ed. Zuckermandel, p. 307, ls. 7-20; ed. Lieberman, pp. 193-95

Comment: The pericope is a composite, consisting of a story and exegeses on three separate verses. The story casts Eleazar in a favorable light. A-B sets the scene. C-E is a literary convention, perhaps denoting that the *Sitz im Leben* of the tradition which follows is the academy setting (cf. T. Yad. 2:16). F-G, the question of whose week it was, is alluded to in the deposition story in b. Ber. 28a-b and its parallels. In U, Eleazar is extolled for his teaching. In all, this section of the pericope is a highly artificial construction utilizing stereotyped phrases.

Let us turn to the exegeses. I comments on Deut. 31, the account of the assembly of the people of Israel every seven years to hear the law. Eleazar explains the gathering in contemporary terms. It is to be viewed not as a cultic event but rather as an occasion for Torah study. The presence of "little ones" in that context is puzzling. Eleazar explains that they are not direct participants. Rather, those who bring them receive reward. The underlying point is that youngsters who cannot understand, cannot participate in Torah study. J comments on the exclusive promise of salvation for the faithful in Israel. J is out of phase with the rest of the pericope, for its theme is salvation in the world to come, not Torah study.

K-T comments on the verses at the end of Qoheleth. L interprets the "sayings of the wise" as Torah. To it is attributed the role of maintaining life in the world. M-N speaks of the permanent fixture of Torah in the world. O-P points out the creative nature of Torah study. Unlike the nail, it grows like a living plant.

Q-R changes the focus of the subject matter of the pericope from Torah itself to the schoolhouse setting. R gives a picture of the activity of the Rabbis. They declare the law in matters of purity. That apparently typifies their work. S then turns to a large question. The nature of rabbinic traditions, especially the dispute form which leaves matters unresolved, seems to force the study of the "oral Torah" to become a mere academic exercise. The ultimate meaning of Torah study is called into question.

T answers the objection raised in S with a powerful polemic for the study of the "oral Torah." Along with the written, it was given to Moses by God. T does not suggest that the purpose of its study is the exercise of a pious action commanded by God. It simply takes it as a given that the creation of God should be taken into one's heart. Both the written Torah and the disputes of the Rabbis constitute parts of God's creation. Study therefore is transformed from an academic pursuit to a religious endeavor.

K-T then attaches a strongly pro-rabbinic teaching to the epilogue of Qoheleth. There was a controversy over the propriety of including Qoheleth in the canon (cf. M. Ed. 5:3). Establishing that it concludes with positive remarks about the centrality of Torah and the teachings of the Rabbis would have been important for the Rabbis who sought to preserve its inclusion.

U ends the pericope with a standard statement in praise of Eleazar. It could have just as well come after I or J.

A. *tnw rbnn*: *m'śh b*: R. Yoḥanan b. Beroqah and R. Eleazar Ḥisma went to pay respect to R. Joshua in Peki'in.

B. He said to them, "What new teaching was there in the house of study today?"

C. They said to him, "We are your disciples and drink of your water."

D. He said to them, "Even so it is not possible for the house of study [to convene] without [hearing] a new teaching.

E. "Whose week was it?"

F. "It was the week of R. Eleazar b. Azariah."

G. "And what was the teaching (*hgdh*) today?"

H. They said to him, "[It was] on the section concerning the assembly (*pršt hqhl*)."

I. "And what did he expound?"

J. "'Assemble the people, men, women and little ones (Deut. 31:12).' If the men come to learn and the women come to hear, why do the little ones come? To give reward to those who bring them."

K. He (Joshua) said to them, "You had a precious pearl in your possession and you wanted to deprive me of it (*l'bdh mmny*)."

L. And he (Eleazar) further expounded: "You have declared this day concerning the Lord [that he is your God]...And the Lord has declared this day concerning you [that you are his people] (Deut. 26: 16-17)." Said to them the Holy One to Israel, "You have made me the only object of your love in the world and I shall make you the only object of my love in the world."

M. "You have made me the only object of your love in the world," *as it is written*, "Hear, O Israel, the Lord our God, the Lord is one (Deut. 6:4)." "And I shall make you the only object of my love in the world," as it says, "What other nation on earth is like thy people Israel (I Chron. 17:21)."?

N. And even he (Eleazar) began and expounded, "The sayings of the wise are like goads and like nails firmly fixed are the collected sayings which are given by one shepherd (Qoh. 12:11)."

O. Why were the words of Torah compared to goads?

P. To tell you, "Just as the goad directs the cow to its furrow in order to bring life to the world, so the words of Torah direct its disciples from the ways of death to the ways of life."

Q. If [you object and say that] just as this goad is moveable [and may be withdrawn, so too its analogue] the words of Torah [may be] "moveable."

R. It comes to teach, "And like nails [firmly fixed]."

S. If [you object and say] just as this nail may be diminished but not increased, so too the words of Torah [by analogy] may be diminished but not increased.

T. It comes to teach, "Firmly fixed" (lit.: planted). Just as this plant is fruitful and multiplies, so too the words of Torah are fruitful and multiply.

U. "The collected sayings": These are the disciples of the sages who sit in councils (lit.: gathered together) involved in [the study of] Torah.

V. These declare unclean and these declare clean; these forbid and these permit; these declare unfit and these declare fit.

W. Lest one say, "How can I study Torah on this account?"

X. It comes to teach, "given by one shepherd." One leader (Moses) uttered them. [He received them] from the mouth of the Master of all actions, blessed be He. *As it is written*, "And God spoke all these words (Ex. 20:1)." So (*'p*) you should make your ear like a hopper and acquire for yourself an understanding heart to hear the words of those who declare unclean and the words of those who declare clean; the words of those who forbid and the words of those who permit; the words of those who declare unfit and those who declare fit.

Y. In these words (*blšwn hzh*) he (Joshua) said to them, "The generation in whose midst is R. Eleazar b. Azariah is not an orphan."

b. Hag. 3a-b [A-W = ARN A 18 (with slight variations at T, W, and X), ed. Schechter, pp. 67-68]

Comment: b. gives virtually the same version as T. Some embellishments by the *beraita* editor are apparent. K is a standard interpolation of praise. J seems hardly as profound as K makes it seem. M subtly shifts T.'s theme of the second exegesis from a promise of otherworldly salvation to a statement of this-worldly chosenness. M also adds appropriate verses.

P expands on T.'s version adding that Torah directs man away from the "way of death." T-X also expands on T.'s formulation of the pericope. U adds that those who "sit in councils" study Torah. V does not limit the Rabbis to ruling on matters of purity. They also forbid and permit, declare unfit and fit--all standard apodoses for disputes in M.-T. X adds an apt verse and removes the mystical connotations found in T. One should "acquire an understanding" rather than as T. puts it "make your heart an inner chamber to receive..."

A. Once (*kbr*) the students rested (*šbtw*) [for the Sabbath] in Yavneh.

B. And R. Joshua did not rest there.

C. And when the students came to him, he said to them, "What matters were discussed in Yavneh?"

D. They said to him, "After you Rabbi."

E. He said to them, "And who rested there?"

F. They said to him, "R. Eleazar b. Azariah."

G. He said to them, "Is it possible that R. Eleazar b. Azariah rested there and did not teach you anything new?"

H. They said to him, "Rabbi, he expounded this idea (*kll*):

I. "'You stand this day all of you [before the Lord your God]...your little ones, your wives... (Deut. 29:10).' Does a little one know the difference between good and evil?

J. "Rather [they stand there] to give those who bring them reward, to increase the reward of those who do his will.

K. "To fulfill what was said, 'The Lord was pleased for his righteousness' sake... (Isa. 42:21).'"

L. He said to them, "Is this not a new teaching? Moreover, behold I am as a seventy year old and I have not merited [hearing] this matter before today. Happy are you Abraham our father since Eleazar b. Azariah is your descendant. The generation in whose midst is R. Eleazar b. Azariah is not an orphan."

M. They said to him, "Rabbi, he also expounded this idea:

N. "'Therefore, behold, the days are coming, says the Lord, when it shall no longer be said, 'As the Lord lives who brought up the people of Israel out of the land of Egypt,' but 'As the Lord lives who brought up the people out of the north country and out of all the countries where he had driven them (Jer. 16:14-15).'

O. "To what may the matter be compared? To one who longed for sons and a daughter was born to him. He swore by the life of his daughter. Then a son was born to him and he set down [swearing by the life of] the daughter and swore by the life of the son."

P. R. Simeon b. Yohai says, "To what may the matter be compared? To one who was walking by the way and he encountered a wolf. He was saved from it and would tell (*mtnh*) the miracles that were done for him with regard to the wolf. He encountered a lion and was saved from him. He set aside the account of the wolf and would tell of the miracles that were done for him with regard to the lion."

Q. Similarly (*kywṣ' bw*) he expounded, "And he called the name of the place Bethel (Gen. 28:19)." The first name was removed and the second one was established.

R. Similarly he expounded, "No longer shall your name be Abram (Gen. 17:5)." The first name was removed and the second was established.

S. Similarly he expounded, "As for Sarai your wife, you shall not call her name Sarai, but Sarah shall be her name (Gen. 17:15)." The first name was removed and the second was established.

T. Similarly he expounded, "Then he said, 'Your name shall no more be called Jacob, but Israel (Gen. 32:28).'" The first name was established and the second was added to him.

U. [As to] Isaac, his name was not changed for it was called out from the mouth of the Holy One.

Mekh. *Pis*. 16, ed. Horowitz-Rabin, pp. 58-59, ls. 19-20, 1-17; cf. y. Ḥag. 1:1

Comment: A-K is another version of the tradition in T. Soṭ. 7:9-10 (A-I). Aside from several minor differences, there are three major changes. First, *šbt* is used here as a verb, thus removing any connotation of "week" which might be attached to it in the noun form in which it is found in the other versions. Second, the exposition in I-K is attached to different verses. Third, Joshua's praise of Eleazar in L is expanded to include references to the tradition associated with Eleazar in T. Ber. 1:12 ("Behold, I am as a seventy year old"; and the reference to Abraham). N-U is a thoroughly edited version of T. Ber. 1:13ff. which is clearly attributed there to b. Zoma and not to Eleazar. The pericope is thus a conflation of two sources attributing material to Eleazar which was probably not his.

A. On the day that they seated R. Eleazar b. Azariah in the academy he began and said,

B. "'You stand this day all of you [before the Lord your God]...your little ones, your wives (Deut. 29:10).' The men come to listen, the women come to receive reward for their journey, why do the little ones come? In order to give reward to those who bring them."

C. Based on this the young daughters of Israel learned the practice of coming to the synagogues, in order to give reward to those who bring them, and they come to receive reward.

M. Sof. 18:8 (42b), ed. Higger, p. 320

Comment: A uses the language attributed to b. Azzai in M. Yad. as a protasis for the tradition. The gloss C reports that the exegesis was used as the basis for a ruling.

75. [And what does "Until they came to the border of the land of Canaan (Ex. 16:35) teach"?--it teaches that if the manna had not stopped [coming down for them] they would not have wished to eat the produce of the land of Canaan.]

A. R. Eleazar b. Azariah says, "They drew a parable. To what is the matter similar? To a human king who said to his servant, 'Mix wine for me with warm water.'

"He said to him, 'I have no warm water.'

"He said to him, 'If not mix [wine] for me with cool water.'

B. "So too these [the Israelites. If] the manna had not stopped coming down, they would not have wished to eat from the produce of the Land of Israel.

Tos. Soṭ. 11:2-3, ed. Zuckermandel, p. 135, ls. 1-3; ed. Lieberman, p. 218

Comment: The tradition makes use of a parable for exegetical purposes. The verse does not directly precede the citation. B repeats the statement which immediately precedes the pericope and thus may be integral to it. The pericope may then have circulated independently.

76. A. R. Eleazar b. Azariah says,

1. "If there is no Torah, there is no seemly behaviour;
   "If there is no seemly behaviour, there is no Torah.
2. "If there is no wisdom, there is no fear;
   "If there is no fear, there is no wisdom.
3. "If there is no understanding, there is no knowledge;
   "If there is no knowledge, there is no understanding.
4. "If there is no flour, there is no Torah;
   "If there is no Torah, there is no flour."

B. He used to say, "All [those] whose wisdom is greater than his deeds--to what is he to be compared? To a tree whose branches are many and whose roots are few; when the wind comes it uproots it and tosses it over.

"As it is written, 'He is like a shrub in the desert and shall not see any good come. He shall dwell in the parched places of the wilderness in an uninhabited salt land (Jer. 17:6).'

"But anyone whose deeds are greater than his wisdom--to what is he to be compared? To a tree whose branches are few and whose roots are many. For even if all the winds in the world come and blow on it, they cannot move it from its place.

"As it is written, 'He is like a tree planted by water that sends out its roots by the stream, and does not fear when heat comes for its leaves remain green and is not anxious in the year of drought, for it does not cease to bear fruit (Jer. 17:8).'"

M. Abot 3:17; cf. ARN A 22, ARN B 34, ed. Schechter, pp. 75-76

Comment: The pericope consists of two separate traditions joined at B by "he used to say." A consists of four sets of pairs all arranged in a tight construction; *'m 'yn ...'yn*. The first two are related thematically. A1 apposes Torah and seemly behavior; A2 relates wisdom to fear. Both seem to be ethical commonplaces. Torah/wisdom lead to seemly behavior/fear and *vice versa*. ARN A gives only these two. A3 juxtaposes two intellectual virtues: understanding/knowledge. A4 makes material well being contingent with Torah: flour/Torah. Each of the virtues listed is bisyllabic except seemly behaviour which is quadri-syllabic (*drk 'rṣ*). ARN B breaks the four parts by inserting "he used to say" before A3, thus leaving us with two sets of two. Discussion of general and universal virtues was a usual characteristic of rhetorical training in the Hellenistic world.

B's exegesis of two verses in Jeremiah extolls deeds over wisdom. ARN A substitutes "learned Torah" for "wisdom." Here we have another commonplace polemic placing practice or ritual above wisdom (or Torah). Eleazar, the priest, as to be expected, comes down definitively on the side of cult as opposed to learning. B's form is highly stylized. Cf. also Matthew 7:24ff., Luke 6:47ff.

ii. *Babli and Yerushalmi*

77. A. *wm'śh b*: A student came and asked R. Joshua,

B. "What is [the law with regard to] the evening prayer?"

C. He said to him, "[It is] optional."

D. He [the student] came and asked R. Gamaliel,

E. "What is [the law with regard to] the evening prayer?"

F. He said to him, "[It is] compulsory."

G. He [the student] said to him, "But R. Joshua said to me, '[It is] optional.'"

H. He [R. Gamaliel] said to him, "Tomorrow when I enter the meeting house (*byt hww'd*) stand and ask about the law (*hlkh*)."

I. The next day the student stood and asked R. Gamaliel,

J. "What is [the law with regard to] the evening prayer?"

K. He said to him, "Compulsory."

L. He [the student] said to him, "But R. Joshua said to me, 'optional.'"

M. Said R. Gamaliel to R. Joshua, "Is it you who says, 'optional'?"

N. He [Joshua] said to him, "No."

O. He [Gamaliel] said to him, "Stand on your feet and they will testify against you."

P. And R. Gamaliel sat and expounded. And R. Joshua was standing on his feet until the entire assembly (*'m*) shouted.

Q. And they said to Ḥuspit the Meturgeman, "Dismiss the assembly."

R. They said to R. Zenon the Hazzan, "Say [the service]."

S. He began to say.

T. The whole assembly began and stood on their feet and said to him [Gamaliel], "For upon whom has not come your unceasing evil (Nahum 3:19)."

U. They went and appointed (*mynw*) R. Eleazar b. Azariah to the academy (*yšybh*).[3]

V. He was sixteen years old and all his hair turned grey (*ntml' kl r'šw sybyt*).

W. And R. Aqiva was sitting. And he was troubled and said, "It is not that he is [lit.: more of a son of Torah] more learned than I; rather he is more of a son of a great one [of more illustrious parentage] than I.

X. "Happy is the man whose fathers have gained him merit. Happy is the man who has a peg on whom to hang."

Y. And who was R. Eleazar b. Azariah's peg?

Z. [It was] that he was the tenth generation [in descent] from Ezra.

AA. And how many benches were there [in the academy]?[4]

BB. R. Jacob bar Sisi said, "There were eighty benches for the disciples of the sages [students] besides those standing behind the fence."

CC. R. Yosé b. R. Abun said, "There were three hundred besides those standing behind the fence."

DD. *This* [refers to] *what we learned elsewhere* (*kyy dtnynn tmn*): "On the day that they seated R. Eleazar b. Azariah in the academy."

EE. *We learned elsewhere* (*tmn tnynn*): "This teaching R. Eleazar b. Azariah expounded before the sages in the vineyard at Yavneh."

FF. And was there a vineyard there? Rather [it refers to] those disciples of the sages who were arranged in rows as in a vineyard.

GG. Immediately, R. Gamaliel went to each [rabbi] to appease him in his house.

HH. *He went to R. Joshua. He found him sitting making needles.*

II. *He said to him, "Is this how you make a living (hyy)?"*

JJ. *He said to him* [Gamaliel], "*Are you* [only] *now finding out* [how difficult it is to live]?

KK. "Woe to the generation of which you are the steward."

LL. He [Gamaliel] sent to him, "I submit to you (*n'nyty lk*)."

MM. *They sent a fuller* (*qṣr*) to R. Eleazar b. Azariah.

NN. *And some say it was R. Aqiva.*

OO. He said to him [Eleazar], "He who is a sprinkler the son of a sprinkler, let him sprinkle. He who is neither a sprinkler nor the son of a sprinkler [should he] say to the sprinkler, son of a sprinkler, 'Your water is water of a cave and your ashes are wood ashes [i.e., unfit]?'"

PP. He [Eleazar] said to them, "If you are satisfied (*ntrṣytm 'ny*) [you have appeased me]. Let you and I go up to the door of R. Gamaliel."

QQ. Even so they did not depose him from his high position (*mgdlwtw*). Rather they appointed him *av bet din.*

y. Ber. 4:1

Comment: We need not go through a detailed analysis of this entire pericope and its parallels since that ground has recently been covered.[5] We present a brief literary analysis of the pericope since several traditions relating to Eleazar are imbedded in it. As Goldenberg has demonstrated, y. gives us the primary version of the pericope.

b., which follows below, has a nicely edited and embellished version.

A-T is a story of a dispute between Joshua and Gamaliel over the status of the evening prayer. It represents the first major source of the pericope. The dispute results in the assembly's rising up against Gamaliel, leading nicely into the second major source of the unit--the narrative of Eleazar's rise to power. U begins this section. It serves as a fitting continuation to A-T and an apt introduction to the material which follows. V-FF is a series of loosely related independent traditions, all of which are secondary to the main account.

V glosses U and is likely (as b. points out, see below) a development of the puzzling statement at M. Ber. 1:5 where Eleazar says, "Lo, I am like a seventy year old..." From this, the tradition develops that he rose to a high position at an early age while at the same time giving the impression that he was much older because of his grey hair.

W introduces Aqiva, who has not been mentioned before. In W, Aqiva is represented as Eleazar's opponent. It is independent of the main narrative, but perhaps responds to U. It represents Aqiva as the common rabbi who is subservient to the priest-aristocrat. A similar role is assigned Aqiva at the gloss NN. There he is identified as the messenger sent by Gamaliel to appease Eleazar.

X-Z may be independent of W, thus another interpolation. If it is an independent tradition, it is cited here to illustrate Aqiva's remark attributing lofty parentage to Eleazar. The tradition that Eleazar is descended from Ezra appears independent of this context at b. Men. 53a, y. Yeb. 1:6, and y. Taan. 4:1.

AA-CC gives yet another interpolation, the dispute over how many benches were in the academy. DD, an Aramaic gloss, relates the dispute to the day of Eleazar's ascension, perhaps through an association with the word "seated" in the passage cited in it (cf. M. Zeb. 1:3, M. Yad. 3:5

and 4:2). It seems that the text is defective and that a statement such as the one b. supplies should have preceded AA ("On that day a number of benches were added."). EE and its gloss, FF, end this loosely connected section. EE cites part of M. Ket. 4:6, assuming that in the present context it is clear why Eleazar expounds before the sages. FF glosses and further clarifies the vineyard imagery.

At GG, we return to the story which was left off at T. Gamaliel is now cast in a subservient role. He goes to appease Joshua. This provides for a good opportunity for inserting a further polemic against the patriarch in HH to JJ. The Aramaic interpolation represents Gamaliel as oblivious to the living conditions of the average working rabbi, Joshua. KK could have followed GG with only the superscription, "Said R. Joshua," preceding it. As it stands, though, it fittingly caps off Joshua's condemnation in JJ.

LL is a fine conclusion to the story begun at A. Gamaliel submits to Joshua. The next unit, beginning at MM develops the final chapter to our story. Joshua has been appeased, but Eleazar remains to be dealt with. To this point, however, we have heard nothing of a rift between Gamaliel and Eleazar. All we have is the story of his ascension appended to the narrative of Gamaliel's misfortune. Indeed, MM-OO does not mention Gamaliel. He reappears only at PP.

MM-OO is a story of someone (Aqiva, according to the gloss, NN), who comes to Eleazar with an argument against his assuming authority. The argument is one which Eleazar, a Priest, could easily comprehend. A non-priest, the messenger argues, cannot take on the role of directing a priestly rite--the rite of the red cow. He has no authority to declare the ashes and water used in the ritual to be unfit. Only a member of the hereditary priesthood can so rule. The mention of Aqiva raises the question of whether MM-OO could actually be part of the interpolation inserted at W, where Aqiva is seen as Eleazar's opponent.

If so, we have two separate traditions combined in the pericope. One describes a dispute between Joshua and Gamaliel (A-T and GG-LL); the other a dispute between Eleazar and Aqiva (U-W and MM-OO). This, however, is conjecture.

PP relates the Eleazar story with Gamaliel. Eleazar, now appeased by the fuller (Aqiva?), goes with him humbly before Gamaliel. The gloss, QQ, reports that in the end, Eleazar maintains a high office.

This lengthy pericope purports to give us several important facts relevant to Eleazar. First, there are some singular traditions about the man which appear only here. He was appointed to the academy, presumably as Patriarch (U). Second, he was demoted to a lesser position, the *av bet din* (QQ). Third, he is represented as being at odds with Aqiva (W-X, perhaps NN-OO). Fourth, he is cast as subservient to Gamaliel (PP). Moreover, we note the exposition of two puzzling mishnaic statements about Eleazar. That he was "as a seventy year old" is the implicit referent of the tradition about his grey hair (V). The statement that he "expounded before the sages in the vineyard at Yavneh" is also taken up (EE-FF). Last, the tradition that he was a descendent of Ezra in its current context invests him with needed authority. We now turn to b.

A. *tnw rbnn*: *m'śh b*: A student came before R. Joshua.

B. He said to him, "Is the evening prayer optional or compulsory?"

C. He [Joshua] said to him, "Optional."

D. He came before R. Gamaliel.

E. He said to him, "Is the evening prayer optional or compulsory?"

F. He said to him, "Compulsory."

G. He said to him, "Did not R. Joshua say to me, 'Optional'?"

H. He [Gamaliel] said to him, "Wait until the shield bearers enter the study house."

I. When the shield bearers entered, the inquirer stood up and asked, "Is the evening prayer optional or compulsory?"

J. Said to him R. Gamaliel, "Compulsory."

K. Said R. Gamaliel to the sages, "Is there no one who disagrees in this matter?"

L. Said to him R. Joshua, "No."

M. He [Gamaliel] said to him, "Did they not say in your name, 'Optional'?"

N. He [Gamaliel] said to him, "Joshua, stand on your feet and they will bear witness against you."

O. R. Joshua stood on his feet and said, "If I were alive and he [the witness] dead--the living can contradict the dead. But now that I am alive and he is alive, how can the living contradict the living?"

P. R. Gamaliel sat and expounded and R. Joshua stood on his feet until the entire assembly shouted.

Q. And said to Ḥuspit the Turgeman, "Stop!"

R. And he stopped.

S. *They said,* "*How long will he go on troubling him*?

T. "*On the last New Year he troubled him*; [with regard to] *the firstling* [concerning] *the incident of R. Ṣadoq he troubled him*; *here too he has troubled him. Let us remove him.*

U. "*Whom shall we appoint* [in his stead]? *Shall we appoint R. Joshua*? [No since] *he is party to the dispute. Shall we appoint R. Aqiva*? [No] *he might be punished since he has no* ancestral merit.

V. "*Rather we shall appoint R. Eleazar b. Azariah.*

W. "For he is a sage and he is tenth [in descent] from Ezra.

X. "He is a sage--*for if one questions him, he can answer.*

Y. "He is rich--*if he must go pay honor to the caesar, he too can go.*

Z. "And he is tenth [in descent] from Ezra--*for he has* ancestral merit *and will not be punished.*"

AA. *They came and said to him, "Would it please the master to head the academy?*[6]"

BB. *He said to them,* "*I will go and consult the members of my household.*"

CC. *He went and consulted his wife.*

DD. *She said to him,* "*They may remove you.*"

EE. *He said to her,* "*Let a man use a valuable cup one day and let it be broken the next.*"

FF. *She said to him,* "*You have no white hair.*"

GG. *On that day he was eighteen years old. A miracle befell him and eighteen rows of his hair turned white.*

HH. *This is as R. Eleazar b. Azariah said,* "Behold I am as a seventy year old."

II. *tn'*: On that day they removed the door keeper, and permission was given for the students to enter.

JJ. For R. Gamaliel used to announce, "Any student whose inside is not like his outside--should not enter the house of study."

KK. *On that day a number of benches were added.*

LL. *Said R. Yoḥanan,* "*The matter is disputed by Abba b. Dostai and the Rabbis.*

MM. "*One said, 'Four hundred benches were ad-added.'*

NN. "*And one said, 'Seven hundred* [*were added*].'"

OO. *R. Gamaliel was disturbed* (*q' hlš' d'tyh*). *He said,* "*Perhaps, God forbid, I have withheld Torah from Israel.*"

PP. *He saw in a dream white casks filled with ashes* (a good sign).

QQ. *But that was not the case. He was shown that only to calm his mind.*

RR. *tn'*: Eduyyot was under review that day. And *whenever it* says "on that day" *the reference is to that day.*

SS. And there was no law pending in the house of study which was not explained (*prš*) [on the day].

TT. And even R. Gamaliel did not absent himself from the house of study for one hour [on the day].

UU. *dtnn*: On that day Judah, an Ammonite proselyte came before them in the house of study.

He said to them, "Am I permitted to enter the congregation?"

Said to him R. Gamaliel, "Is it not said, 'An Ammonite shall not enter the congregation of the Lord (Deut. 23:4)'?"

Said to him R. Joshua, "Do Ammon and Moab yet dwell in their places? Sennacherib the king of Assyria has already arisen and mixed all the nations together. As it says, 'And I have removed the boundaries of peoples and have plundered their treasures; like a bull I have brought down those who sat on thrones (Isa. 10:13).'

"*And anything which comes out* [of a mixture is judged as if] *it comes out of the major part.* [A standard legal principle.]"

Said to him R. Gamaliel, "Has it not already been said, 'And afterward I shall bring back the captivity of the children of Ammon says the Lord (Jer. 49:6)'? They have already returned [to their original places]."

Said to him R. Joshua, "Has it not already been said, 'And I shall return the captivity of my people Israel (Amos 9:4),' and they have not yet returned."

They immediately permitted him to enter the congreation.

VV. Said R. Gamaliel, "*Since this is the case* [they deposed me] *I shall go and appease R. Joshua.*"

WW. *When he came to his house he saw the walls of his house were black.*

XX. He said to him [Joshua], "From the walls of your house one can tell you are a smith [or charcoal maker]."

YY. He [Joshua] said to him, "Woe to the generation of which you are the steward (*prns*). You do not know the troubles of the disciples of the sages--with what they support themselves and with what they feed themselves."

ZZ. He [Gamaliel] said to him, "I submit (*n'nyty*) to you. Forgive me."

AAA. [Joshua] *paid him no heed.*

BBB. [Said Gamaliel,] "Do it for the honor of my father."

CCC. [Joshua] *was appeased.*

DDD. *They said, "Who will go and tell the Rabbis?"*

EEE. *A washerman (kwbs) said, "I shall go."*

FFF. *R. Joshua sent him to the house of study* [with a message]: "*He who wears the garment* (*md'*) *should wear the garment.* [Should] *he who does not wear the garment say to him who wears the garment, 'Send me your garment and I shall wear it'?*"

GGG. *Said R. Aqiva, "Shut the doors so as not to allow the servant of R. Gamaliel to trouble the Rabbis."*

HHH. *Said R. Joshua, "It is better that I go to him* [Gamaliel] *myself.*"

III. *He came and knocked on the door.*

JJJ. *He said to him,* [Gamaliel], "The sprinkler, son of a sprinkler should sprinkle. And he who is neither a sprinkler nor the son of a sprinkler, shall he say to the sprinkler, son of a sprinkler, 'Your water is cave water and your ashes are wood ashes?'"

KKK. Said to him R. Aqiva, "R. Joshua, have you been appeased? We have only acted for your honor. Tomorrow you and I shall wait at [Gamaliel's] door."

LLL. *They said, "What shall we do? Shall we remove him* [Eleazar]?"

MMM. "*We have a tradition*: One may increase the sanctity of an object, but not decrease it.

NNN. "*If each master will expound one week, that will lead to jealousy.*

OOO. "[Then] *let R. Gamaliel expound three weeks* [MSS. M: two] *and R. Eleazar b. Azariah, one week.*"

PPP. *This is what is meant by* (*hyynw d'mr mr*): "Whose week was it? R. Eleazar b. Azariah's."

QQQ. And the student [who came to Joshua with the question in A] was R. Simeon b. Yohai.

b. Ber. 27b-28a

Comment: Goldenberg has shown, as mentioned above, that b. is an expanded version of y. A-T gives its slightly altered account of the Joshua-Gamaliel incident. It has little bearing on the traditions relating to Eleazar. In the rest of the pericope, the *beraita* editor accomplishes two major goals. He clears up some of the ambiguities of y. and places the Rabbis in the position of final authority.

In T, an obvious Aramaic insertion, the redactor makes the fact of the deposition more explicit. S-U gives the Rabbis the authority to depose and appoint the patriarch. U answers the most obvious questions: If the story of the deposition grows out of a dispute with Joshua, who wins out, why does he not succeed Gamaliel? Moreover, why not appoint the Rabbi *par excellence*, Aqiva, to the patriarchate? In V the rabbis appoint Eleazar. W then lists the two virtues which qualify Eleazar for the position, both present in y. (For the relationship between y. and b., see the chart below and see especially Goldenberg's analysis.) Y-Z however lists the three virtues of Eleazar along with their respective Aramaic glosses. On X, compare a similar statement in ARN 18; on Y, compare M. Soṭ. 9:15 and T. Soṭ. 15:3. Z, the tradition concerning descent from Ezra, is also in y.

AA-HH is an Aramaic addition to the story. The offer of authority is humbly offered and carefully considered. FF-HH spells out the tradition of Eleazar's grey hair. II-JJ is a new addition to the pericope. Gamaliel's strictures are relaxed. In the benches dispute, b. gives different names and numbers (KK-NN) and a motivation for the dispute's inclusion in the narrative (KK).

Another Aramaic interpolation is introduced at OO-QQ. Perhaps this was part of the door-keeper story given above (II-JJ). The theme of associating the cryptic references in M. to "that day" with the day of Gamaliel's deposition is then developed (RR-UU).

The narrative of the dispute between Gamaliel and Joshua is resumed at VV. Gamaliel submits to Joshua (ZZ), represented here as a smith. AAA-CCC carefully shifts the implication of Gamaliel's motive for submission. Ostensibly, in y., he gave in because of political pressure. Here in b., however, concession is represented as a humble one, accepted by Joshua only for the purpose of granting honor to Gamaliel's father (BBB).

Joshua and Gamaliel now confront the problem of how to inform the Rabbis of their reconciliation (DDD). In FFF, in Aramaic, the messenger brings a variation of the "sprinkler" argument to the rabbis, not to Eleazar. The one who wears the priest's cloak or garment, does so by a hereditary office too, should be respected, and cannot be transferred.

In GGG, Aqiva speaks as a member of the opposition to Gamaliel's authority. HHH-III puts Joshua himself in the role of the one who ultimately goes to the Rabbis with the case for restoring Gamaliel to his rightful place. Aqiva is the spokesman again at KKK. Honor is reiterated as the motivation for the deposition, not politics. It is Aqiva who finally goes with Joshua to Gamaliel in this version, not Eleazar.

The Rabbis effect the final reconciliation. Their solution--sharing the patriarchate--serves to explain one more abstruse phrase associated with Eleazar, "Whose week was it"? (PPP) (cf. T. Soṭ. 7:9 and its parallels).

Before summarizing the main points in b. relevant to Eleazar, let us turn to the following chart for a comparison with y.

y. Ber. 4:1	b. Ber. 27b-28a
U. They went and appointed Eleazar to the academy	S-V. *They said, How long...whom shall we appoint?...Rather we shall appoint Eleazar.*
V. He was sixteen...	(see below FF-GG)
W. And R. Aqiva was sitting.	- - - -
X. Happy is the man...	- - - -
Y-Z. What was Eleazar's peg? ...tenth generation.	W. He is a sage and tenth from Ezra.
- - - -	X. He is a sage...
- - - -	Y. He is rich...
- - - -	Z. He is tenth...
- - - -	AA. *They came and said to him Would it please the master...*
- - - -	BB-EE. *...consult my household...*
(see V above)	FF-GG. *...white hair...miracle*
- - - -	HH. "Lo, I am as a 70 year old."
- - - -	II-JJ. Removed the door keeper.
AA-CC. How many benches?	KK. *On that day benches were added*
DD. Refers to, "on that day they seated Eleazar."	- - - -
EE-FF. Vineyard/sages seated in rows	- - - -
- - - -	OO-QQ.
- - - -	RR-UU. Eduyyot under review
GG. appease each	VV. appease Joshua
HH-KK. *Joshua the needlemaker*	WW-YY. *Joshua the smith*
LL. Gamaliel submits	ZZ. *Gamaliel submits*
- - - -	AAA-CCC. *Joshua argues*
- - - -	DDD. *Who will tell rabbis?*
MM. *They sent a fuller*	EEE. *A washerman said, I shall go*

y. Ber. 4:1	b. Ber. 27b-28a
- - - -	FFF. *Joshua sent him to house of study...He who wears...*
- - - -	GGG. *Said Aqiva, Shut the doors*
- - - -	HHH. *Said Joshua, I will go*
- - - -	III. *He came and knocked...*
OO. Sprinkler argument	JJJ. Sprinkler argument
PP. Eleazar says to them, Let you and I...	KKK. Said Aqiva to Joshua...You and I shall wait
- - - -	LLL. *They said, What shall we do?*
- - - -	MMM. May increase sanctity...
- - - -	NNN-OOO. *3 weeks/one week*
- - - -	PPP. *Meaning of* "Whose week..."
QQ. Appointed him *av bet din*	- - - -
- - - -	QQQ. The student was Simeon b. Yoḥai

Specifically in reference to the traditions concerning Eleazar, we see several important shifts in b.'s version. The role of Aqiva, *vis a vis* Eleazar, undergoes a major change. The hint at conflict between the masters (W-X in y.) is deleted in b. Furthermore, from FFF on in b., Aqiva assumes Eleazar's role. He is appeased, not Eleazar. In b., Joshua appeases him, not a messenger. The two then go to Gamaliel (in y., Eleazar and the messenger go to him).

There are also two additions in b. First, an Aramaic story is developed concerning Eleazar and his wife (AA-HH in b.). NNN-OOO add the exposition of the phrase "Whose week was it"? The explanation of the shared patriarchate necessitates the omission of y.'s claim that Eleazar was appointed *av bet din*. Finally, the trifold virtue of Eleazar is neatly formulated at X-Z from three separate traditions.

78. A. Three relinquished their crown in this world and inherited life in the world to come.

And these are they: Jonathan b. Saul and Eleazar b. Azariah and the elders of Bathyra.

B. [Concerning] Jonathan b. Saul--Said Rabbi, "*No, even the women* [winetreaders] *behind the pressers knew that David was to be king.*

C. "[Concerning] Eleazar b. Azariah--*it was a conditional* [deposition which he consented to].

D. "*There is no* [other instance therefore] *comparable to the* [one which took place concerning] *the sons of Bathyra who freed themselves from the Patriarchate and appointed* [Hillel] *the Patriarch.*"

y. Pes. 6:1

Comment: The tradition in A asserts that three personalities gave up their rights to rule and for that act inherited life in the world to come. The order of the list is not chronological and may have been rearranged to suit Rabbi's comments in B-D. A refers to the narrative at the beginning of II Sam., the deposition story in y. Ber. 4:1 (and b. Ber. 27a-b), and the account in T. Pisḥa 4:13 (and its parallels).

In C, Rabbi alludes to the compromise described at the end of the deposition-narrative in b. which says that Eleazar and Gamaliel shared the patriarchate. y. only mentions that Eleazar became *av bet din* but makes no mention of a shared office. The attribution of this tradition (B-D) is to Rabbi. If it is reliable we then have quite an early attestation of one element of the deposition story. It is not surprising that Rabbi, the Patriarch, knows of the deposition incident. It was probably an important story in the history of the patriarchate. The pericope yields a simple polemic favoring Eleazar for allowing the patriarchal succession to continue unbroken. The mythic event *par excellence* in the history of the patriarchate is of course the ascension of Hillel (D).

79. [R. Jacob bar Idi in the name of R. Joshua b. Levi: *m'śh b*: The elders came to R. Dosa b. Hyrcanus

to ask about the co-wife of the daughter... He said to them, "On this seat sat Haggai the prophet and testified three things..."]

A. He said, "Let my eyes be brightened so that I might see the sages of Israel."

B. He saw R. Joshua and recited of him, "'Whom will he teach knowledge (Isa. 28:9).' I recall that his mother used to bring his cradle to the synagogue so that his ears should be attuned to the words of Torah."

C. [He saw] R. Aqiva and recited of him, "'The young lions suffer want and hunger (Ps. 34:10).' I recognize that he is a mighty man of Torah."

D. He saw R. Eleazar b. Azariah and recited of him, "'I have been young now I am old (Ps. 37:25).' I recognize that he is the tenth generation to Ezra and his eyes resemble his."

E. Said R. Haninah of Sepphoris, "Even R. Tarfon was among them and he recited of him as that which he recited of R. Eleazar b. Azariah."

y. Yeb. 1:6

Comment: The pericope presents a tradition which ascribes remarks about three sages to Dosa b. Hyrcanus. Joshua, Aqiva, and Eleazar commonly appear together as a group. As Haninah indirectly points out in E, Tarfon is sometimes the fourth member of this group.

The description of Eleazar in D is probably related to two traditions about him in y. Ber. 4:1 and b. Ber. 27a-b. There he is described as having turned prematurely grey. This may explain the verse quoted about him here. He is also said there to have been tenth in descent from Ezra. We cannot say which of the two sources is primary since we cannot firmly establish a date for the deposition story. However, if the deposition story does generate our pericope, we have a firm attestation of it here. On the other hand, if the deposition story grows out of this pericope, it must be shown that the two elements of tradition here are central to it.

A. [*gwp'*] In the days of R. Dosa b. Hyrcanus, the co-wife of the daughter was permitted [by him] to the brothers.

B. And the matter was troublesome (*qšh*) for the sages, because he was a great sage, and his eyes were dim so that he was unable to come into the house of study.

C. They said, "Who will go to inform him [of their distress]?"

D. Said to them R. Joshua, "I will go."

E. "And who will go after him?" R. Eleazar b. Azariah.

F. "And who will go after him?" R. Aqiva.

G. They went and stood by his door. His handmaid entered and said to him, "Rabbi, the sages of Israel have come to you."

H. He said to her, "Let them enter."

I. They entered. He took hold of R. Joshua and seated him on a golden couch. He [Joshua] said to him, "Speak to your other student so that he may be seated."

J. He said to him, "Who is he?"

K. [He answered,] "R. Eleazar b. Azariah."

L. He said, "Does Azariah our comrade have a son?" He recited about him this verse, "I have been young, and now am old; yet I have not seen the righteous forsaken or his children begging bread (Ps. 37:25)."

M. He took hold of him and seated him on a golden couch. He said to him, "Rabbi speak to your other student so that he may be seated."

N. "And who is he?" "Aqiva b. Joseph." He said to him, "Are you the Aqiva b. Joseph whose name travels from one end of the world to the other? Sit my son, sit. May the like of you be multiplied in Israel."

O. They began addressing him legal questions (*hyw mšbbym 'wtw bhlkwt*) until they reached [the question of] the co-wife of the daughter...

b. Yeb. 16a

Comment: The pericope is a second version of the tradition in y. Yeb. 1:6. A links Dosa's remarks about the sages to his ruling on the co-wife of the daughter. In y. Dosa says, "Let my eyes be brightened..." b. expands this into an explanation of why the sages go to visit Dosa. C-F lists the three rabbis. G-I is a standard formula. In I, L and N the three masters enter. The following chart shows the difference between the versions in y. and b.:

y. Yeb. 1:6	b. Yeb. 16a
A. Let my eyes be brightened...	B. eyes were dim...
- - - -	C-H. Who will go? Stood by door...
B. Joshua + Isa. 28:9	I. Joshua + golden couch
C. Aqiva + Ps. 34:10 + mighty man of Torah	- - - - (see N)
D. Eleazar + Ps. 37:25 + tenth generation to Ezra	J-M. Golden couch + Ps. 37:25
- - - - (see C)	N. Name travels + may you be multiplied.
E. Haninah of Sepphoris-Tarfon	- - - -
- - - -	O. Addressed legal questions

The praises are different in the two versions and a framework has been added to the b. account. Aqiva appears last there as is common. The reference to Eleazar's ancestry is dropped. On the relation between this and other traditions about Eleazar, see previous comment.

Said the sages to R. Peraida, "R. Ezra the son of R. Avtolus, who was the tenth [generation in descent] from R. Eleazar b. Azariah, who was the tenth from Ezra stands behind the tradition."

b. Men. 53a (Song of Songs R., ed. Grünhut, p. 36)

Comment: Cf. comments to y. Ber. 4:1 and y. Yeb. 1:6.

80. A. Said R. Shizbi in the name of R. Eleazar b. Azariah, "*Why is it written*, 'A slothful man will not catch his prey [but the diligent man will get his precious wealth (Prov. 12:27)]'?

B. "[It means] *the deceiver shall not live or prolong his days* (a reference to the student whose object is to dazzle people with his erudition)."

C. R. Sheshet said, "The shrewd hunter will roast his game (i.e., become a scholar)."

(D. When R. Dimi came [from Palestine] he said, "A parable--to a man who snares birds. If he breaks the wings of the first [each as they are caught] then he may keep all of them. If not, then he may not [be able to] keep them.")

b. Erub. 54b (b. A.Z. 19a)

Comment: A-B gives an exegesis of Prov. 12:27 in the form of a question and answer. Shizbi, Rav's grandson (c. 300), cites the tradition. The exegesis is based on the word *yḥrwk* in the verse. It is viewed as a contraction of *yḥyh* and *y'ryk*. The phrase in Prov. is taken as a declarative sentence. C provides an alternative reading of the verse as a rhetorical question. B.R. 67:2 (ed. Albeck, p. 753) cites the tradition in the name of R. Eleazar b. R. Simeon.

81. A. Said R. Sheshet in the name of R. Eleazar b. Azariah,

B. "I can free the entire world from judgment from the day the Temple was destroyed until today.

C. "As it is written, 'Therefore hear this, you who are afflicted, who are drunk but not with wine (Isa. 51:21).'"

b. Erub. 64b-65a

Comment: The remark takes the form of *statement + verse* as proof text. The basic assumption of the exegesis is that one who is drunk is not responsible for his actions. Israel, in the verse, is referred to as if it were a drunken nation. Sheshet cites traditions in Eleazar's name in b. Pes. 118a and b. Mak. 32a as well.

82. A. This Hallel--who said it [first]?

B. R. Eleazar says, "Moses and Israel said it at the time they stood at the sea. They said, 'Not to us O Lord, not to us [but to thy name give glory] (Ps. 115).' And He said to them, 'For my own sake, for my own sake I do it [for how should my name be profaned? My glory I will not give to another (Isa. 48:11)].'"

C. R. Judah says, "Joshua and Israel said it at the time that the Kings of Canaan opposed them. They said, 'Not to us O Lord...' And He answered, 'For my own sake...'"

D. R. Eleazar HaModai says, "Debora and Baraq said it at the time that Sisra opposed them. They said, 'Not to us, O Lord...' And He answered, 'For my own sake...'"

E. R. Eleazar b. Azariah says, "Hezekiah and his company said it at the time that Sennacherib opposed them. They said, 'Not to us O Lord...' And He answered, 'For my own sake...'"

F. R. Aqiva says, "Hananiah, Mishael and Azariah said it at the time that Nebuchadnezzar the evil one opposed them. They said, 'Not to us O Lord...' And He answered, 'For my own sake...'"

G. R. Yosé the Galilean says, "Mordechai and Esther said it at the time that Haman the evil one opposed them. They said, 'Not to us O Lord...' And He answered, 'For my own sake...'"

H. And sages say, "The Prophets among them established for Israel that they say it at each trial and at every distress [which confronts them] that it may not come upon Israel. And when they are redeemed they [should] say it on [the occasion of] their redemption."

b. Pes. 117a

Comment: The pericope consists of the statement of the issue, A, followed by six separate statements, identical in form except for the name of the speaker, the suggested author of the Hallel and the instance at which time it was supposed to have been initially said. The six statements are arranged chronologically, by the order of the suggested authors of the Hallel. The six opinions are attributed to both Yavneans and Ushans. The entire unit A-G either may have been generated out of H or H is a summary of A-G. We have no other traditions assigned to Eleazar dealing with matters of a historical nature, but he is concerned with parts of the liturgy (cf. M. Ber. 1:5, 4:7, T. Ber. 1:2, 1:4, 1:12).

83. A. Said R. Shizbi in the name of R. Eleazar b. Azariah, "[Gaining] the sustenance of man is as difficult as the splitting of the Red Sea, *as it is written*, 'He who gives food to all flesh (Ps. 136:25),' *and nearby it says*, 'to him who divided the Red Sea asunder (Ps. 136:13).'"

B. Said R. Eleazar b. Azariah, "[Insuring the functioning of] the orifices of man is as difficult as the day of death and the splitting of the Red Sea, as it says, 'He who is bowed down shall speedily be released (Ps. 51:14),' *and after it is written*, 'who stirs up the sea so that the waves roar (Ps. 51:15).'"

C. And said R. Sheshet in the name of R. Eleazar b. Azariah, "[Concerning] all those who mock the festivals--it is as if they worship idols. As it says, 'You shall make for yourselves no molten gods (Ex. 34:17),' *and after it it is written*, 'The feast of unleavened bread you shall keep (Ex. 34:18).'"

D. And said R. Sheshet in the name of R. Eleazar b. Azariah, "All those who speak maliciously and all those who accept malicious talk, and all those who swear falsely concerning their fellow, they are worthy of being cast to the dogs, as it says, 'You shall cast it to the dogs (Ex. 22:31),' *and after it it is written*, 'You shall not utter a false report (Ex. 23:1).'

E. "*And read it* [rather], 'You shall not whisper (*tsy'*).'"

b. Pes. 118a

Comment: The pericope contains four traditions attributed to Eleazar containing exegetical remarks based on the proximity of two verses. A is cited by R. Shizbi (cf. comment on b. Erub. 54b). It is the only one of the four traditions in the pericope which utilizes nonconsecutive verses. Eleazar remarks that God's maintenance of man's existence is as miraculous as the splitting of the Red Sea.

Sheshet is the tradent in C and D (cf. comment on b. Mak. 23a and b. Erub. 65a). C compares those who mock the festivals (Rashi, *ad. loc.*: those who do work on the intermediate days of the festivals) to idolaters. D deprecates those who utter evil reports or swear falsely. E is an amoraic gloss. On C, cf. Galatians 4:9-11.

84. A. *dtny*: *m'śh b*: R. Eleazar b. Azariah and R. Aqiva were on a ship.

B. And R. Aqiva built a sukkah on the bow and the wind came and carried it off.

C. Said to him R. Eleazar b. Azariah, "Aqiva, where is your sukkah?"

y. Suk. 2:4; y. Erub. 1:7

Comment: Our pericope is in the *m'śh b* form. At first glance the text seems to be defective, breaking off abruptly at C. However, I can conceive of no adequate response for Aqiva. Therefore, the pericope is probably complete as it stands. As such it is a humorous albeit biting polemic against Aqiva. There are several other indications of Eleazar's antagonism towards Aqiva in the material which has been preserved (see comment to y. Soṭ. 5:6).

M. Suk. 2:3 rules, "One who builds a sukkah...on the bow of a ship--it is valid." It may be that the issue of its validity was the subject of our pericope. b. Suk. 23a substitutes Gamaliel for Eleazar.

85. A. *tnw rbnn*: When the sons of R. Ishmael died [these] four elders went in to console him: R. Tarfon, and R. Yosé the Galilean, and R. Eleazar b. Azariah and R. Aqiva.

B1. Said to them R. Tarfon, "Know that he is a great sage and is well versed in *aggadot*.

B2. "Let no one of you enter the words of his fellow."

C. Said R. Aqiva, "And may I be the last."

D. R. Ishmael opened the discourse and said, "His sins are many. His sorrows follow closely upon one another. He has bothered his masters [to console him] one time and then another."

E. Answered R. Tarfon and said, "'But your brethren the whole house of Israel may bewail the burning [which the Lord has kindled] (Lev. 10:6).'

F. "Is not the matter a *qal veḥomer*?

G. "Nadab and Abihu fulfilled only one commandment, as it is written, 'And the sons of Aaron presented the blood to him (Lev. 9:9).' So the sons of R. Ishmael how much more so [are they worthy of being mourned because of all the commandments they fulfilled]."

H. Answered R. Yosé the Galilean and said, "'And all Israel shall mourn for him and bury him (II Kings 14:13).'

I. "Is not the matter a *qal veḥomer*?

J. "Abiyah the son of Jeroboam performed only one good act as it is written, 'Because in him there is something pleasing [to the Lord, God of Israel in the house of Jeroboam] (*ibid.*).' So the sons of R. Ishmael, how much more so [should they be mourned]." ...[an Amoraic interpolation follows.]

K. Answered R. Eleazar b. Azariah and said "'You shall die in peace. And as spices were burned for your fathers, the former kings who were before you, so men shall burn spices for you [and lament for you, saying, Alas, Lord!] (Jer. 34:5).'

L. "Is not the matter a *qal veḥomer*?

M. "Zedekiah the king of Judah fulfilled only one commandment. He raised Jermiah up from the mortar. So the sons of R. Ishmael, how much more so [should they be mourned]."

N. Answered R. Aqiva and said, "'On that day the mourning in Jerusalem will be as great as the mourning for Hadadrimmon in the plain of Meggido (Zech. 12:11).' ...[An Amoraic interpolation follows.]

O. "Is not the matter a *qal veḥomer*?

P. "Ahab the king of Israel who did only one good deed as it is written, 'And the king was propped up in his chariot facing the Syrians (I Kings 22:35).' So the sons of R. Ishmael how much more so [should they be mourned]."

b. M.Q. 28b

Comment: The pericope uses formalized language and structure to give four arguments justifying mourning over Ishmael's sons and consoling him. A is a standard introductory sentence which tells us the setting and the names of the Rabbis involved in the incident. It is commonly associated with the *mʿśh b* form. That phrase is absent here. B is a warning by Tarfon that the sages should interrupt one another's expositions. C explains why Aqiva speaks last.

The form of each master's remarks is identical. E, H, K, and N all cite verses. F, I, L, and O are identical. In G, J, M, and P the biblical personality used is shown to have performed only one commandment, good deed or good act by the citation of another verse. The conclusion is then drawn in each case that the sons of R. Ishmael must be mourned since they presumably fulfilled many commandments and did many good deeds in their lifetimes.

Eleazar's role in the tradition is not a personal one. He serves merely as a name in a list of four sages, as is common.

86. A. *tʾ šmʿ*: "One [throne] for justice; one [throne] for charity [a reference to Dan. 7:9]."

B. The words of R. Aqiva.

C. Said to him R. Eleazar b. Azariah, "Aqiva, Why do you involve yourself with (*mh lk ʾṣl*) *aggada*? Cease your speaking and go [expound the laws of] Negaim and Ohalot.

D. "Rather [interpret the matter as follows]: One for the throne [and] one for the camp stool.

E. "A throne to sit upon and a camp stool for his footstool, as it is written, 'Heaven is my throne and the earth is my footstool (Isa. 66:1).'"

b. Ḥag. 14a (b. San. 38b)

Comment: The pericope gives conflicting exegeses of Dan. 7:9: "Thrones were placed and one that was ancient of days days took his place." In C Eleazar is portrayed as ridiculing Aqiva's interpretation. He cynically tells Aqiva to stay clear of the *aggada*. He would be better off expounding the laws of Negaim and Ohalot, Eleazar says. Several other traditions indicate antagonism between Eleazar and Aqiva (cf., e.g., y. Ber. 4:1, b. Ber. 27b-28a).

87. A. ["And the frogs (lit.: frog) came up and covered the land of Egypt (Ex. 8:6)]." R. Aqiva says, "There was one frog and it filled all the land of Egypt."

B. Said to him R. Eleazar b. Azariah, "Aqiva, Why do you involve yourself with *aggada*? Cease your speaking and go [expound the laws of] Negaim and Ohalot.

C. "[Rather] there was one frog and it croaked for them [the other frogs] and they came."

b. San. 67b; (Yalqut Ex. 183;
Ex. Rab. 10:5)

Comment: As in the previous pericope, Aqiva is chastised for trespassing on the ground of *aggada*. Here, however, his exegesis indeed seems ridiculous. B may have originated with this pericope and then been transposed to preceding one intact as Eleazar's standard retort to Aqiva.

88. A. *tny'*: R. Eliezer says, "Anyone who does not engage in [fulfilling the commandment of] procreation --it is as if he sheds blood, as it is written, 'Whoever sheds the blood of man, by man shall his blood be shed (Gen. 9:6).' *And after it is written*, 'And you shall be fruitful and multiply (Gen. 9:7).'"

B. R. Jacob [= Aqiva] says, "It is as if he diminishes the image [of God]. As it is written, 'For God made man in his own image (Gen. 9:6).' *And after it is written*, 'And you shall be fruitful and multiply.'"

C. Ben Azzai says, "It is as if he sheds blood and diminishes the image. As it is written, 'And you...'"

D. They said to Ben Azzai, "There are those who expound well and practice well and those who practice well and do not expound well. And you expound well and do not practice well."

E. Said to them Ben Azzai, "And what shall I do? My soul is infatuated with Torah. The world can [continue to] exist through [the children of] others."

F. *tny' 'ydk*: R. Eliezer says, "Anyone who does not engage in procreation--it is as if he sheds blood. As it is written, 'Whoever sheds the blood of man...' And after it is written, 'And you shall be fruitful...'"

G. R. Eleazar b. Azariah says, "It is as if he diminishes the image..."

H. Ben Azzai says,...

I. They said to Ben Azzai, "There are those who expound well..."

b. Yeb. 63b

A. Expounded R. Aqiva, "[Concerning] anyone who spills blood, he is considered as if he diminished the image [of God]. What is the reason? [The verse says,] 'Whoever sheds the blood of man (Gen. 9:6).'

B. "What is the reason? [It says] 'For God made man in his own image.'"

C. Expounded R. Eleazar b. Azariah, "Anyone who neglects [the commandment of] procreation diminishes the image [of God]. What is the reason? [The verse says] 'For God made man in his own image.' And after it is written, 'And you shall be fruitful and multiply.'"

D. Expounded Ben Azzai, "Anyone who neglects procreation it is as if he spills blood and diminishes the image [of God]..."

B.R. 34, ed. Theodor-Albeck, p. 326, ls. 2ff.

Comment: A-C in b. give three statements on the status of one who does not have children. A contains the protasis for B and C as well. According to Eliezer, who bases his reasoning on the proximity of the verses, one who does not have children is like a murderer. Aqiva says he diminishes the image of God. Ben Azzai combines the characterizations of A and B. D-E may be an independent tradition about Ben Azzai. F-I has a second version of the pericope. It is the same as A-E except for the replacement of Aqiva's name with Eleazar b. Azariah.

B.R. has a different version of the pericope. A and C focus on the question of what diminishes the image of God. Aqiva in A says that it is murder which does so. Eliezer's equation of the murderer and childless person in b. is absent in B.R. C here equates one who neglects procreation with one who diminishes the image of God. It is attributed to Eleazar as in the second version of the pericope in b. Ben Azzai in D attributes two evils to the neglecter of procreation. A, C, and D use the attributive formula "Expounded x" instead of the "x says" of b.

T. Yeb. 8:4 (ed. Zuckermandel, p. 250) has a version of the pericope similar to that of B.R. Eleazar's name is absent and the opinion attributed to him in B.R. (C) is instead attributed to Ben Azzai. The following chart summarizes the versions:

b. (1)	b. (2)	B.R.	T.
A. Eliezer: procreation/murder	F. " "	A. Aqiva: murder/image	Aqiva: murder/image
B. Aqiva: procreation/image	G. Eleazar b. Azariah: " "	C. Eleazar: procreation/image	Ben Azzai: procreation/image
C. Ben Azzai: procreation/both	H. " "	D. Ben Azzai: procreation/both	- - - -

B.R. is closer to T. in its presentation of the material. b. has a more refined pericope as all three opinions direct themselves to the question of one who neglects the commandment of procreation. In any event, the attribution to Eleazar is not certain.

89. A. *The wife of R. Yosé the Galilean used to trouble him greatly.*

B. *R. Eleazar b. Azariah went to him. He said to him, "Rabbi, divorce her for she does you no honor."*

C. *He said to him, "Her endowment is too large for me [and I cannot afford to divorce her]."*

D. *He said to him, "I will give you her endowment and [you may then] divorce her."*

E. *He gave him her endowment and he divorced her.*

F. *She went and married the guardsman of the town. He lost his property and went blind and sent her out around the town to speak for him [and collect alms].*

G. *Once she went around the whole city and nothing was given to her.*

H. *He said to her, "Is there not another neighborhood [in which you might collect something]?"*

I. *She said to him, "There is another neighborhood which I have left out [for my first husband lives there] but I have not the strength to enter there [because I am ashamed]."*

J. *He began to strike her.*

K. *R. Yosé the Galilean passed by there and heard the sound of her being despised in the market.*

L. *He took them [his wife and her husband] and put them in one of his houses and gave them sustenance for the rest of their lives on the basis of [the verse], "And from your flesh you shall not turn away," [which he interpreted as meaning] his divorced wife.*

M. *Even so they turned their ears to her at night and heard her say, "Was it not enough that I suffered externally and not internally [too, from shame]?"*

y. Ket. 11:3

A. *Said R. Joshua bar Naḥmani, "If one is worthy [his wife will be] like the wife of Ḥananiah b. Ḥakinai. If not [she will be] like the wife of R. Yosé the Galilean."*

B. *R. Yosé the Galilean had an evil wife; and she was the daughter of his sister; and she used to embarrass him.*

C. *His students said to him, "Rabbi, divorce this woman for she does you no honor."*

D. *He said to them, "She has a large endowment and I have not the means to divorce her."*

E. *One time he and R. Eleazar Azariah were sitting and explaining [the Torah].*

F. *When they concluded he [Eleazar] said, "If Rabbi permits, I will accompany him home."*

G. *He said to him, "Yes [you may]."*

H. *When they arrived [his wife] looked down [in anger] and went out.*

I. *He saw a pot on the oven and said to her, "Is there anything in this pot?"*

J. *She said to him, "There is an appetizer [prpryyn] in it."*

K. *He went and uncovered it and found in it a young bird [prgyyn].*

L. *R. Eleazar b. Azariah knew what he heard [that Yosé's wife did not act with honor towards him].*

M. *They sat down to eat and he [Eleazar] said to him, "Rabbi, did she not say an appetizer [was in the pot] and lo, we have found a young bird in it!"*

N. *He said to him, "It is a miracle."*

O. *When they finished he [Eleazar] said to him, "Rabbi, divorce her for she does you no honor."*

P. *He said to him, "Rabbi, she has a large endowment and I have not the means to divorce her."*

Q. *They said to him, "We will give you the endowment so that you may divorce her."*

R. *They did so. They gave him the endowment and he divorced her...*

B.R. 17, ed. Theodor-Albeck, pp. 152-54; Lev. R. 34:14, pp. 802-4

Comment: The pericope in y. forms a continuous narrative about R. Yosé's evil wife. Eleazar is involved only from B-E. In that section, we see two elements of Eleazar's tradition. First, that Eleazar was close to Yosé. This may emerge from their appearance together in several pericopae.[7] Second, that he had the money to give Yosé so that he might divorce his wife. The tradition attributing riches to Eleazar appears in several places.[8]

Turning to the version in B.R. and Lev. R, we see that the story from B-D which continues at Q is basically the same as y.'s. Eleazar, however, is replaced in it by Yosé's students. E-P forms a separate account, describing in detail why Eleazar offers to help Yosé out. Here Yosé and Eleazar appear studying together and later eating together. It is possible that the y. editor combined the two stories and shortened the account. It is equally likely that independent and different versions were circulating and that he did not have the story given in B.R. E-P.

90. A. R. Aqiva expounded, "'Then Elihu the son of Barachel the Buzite, of the family of Ram, became angry (Job 32:2).'

B. "'Elihu'--this is Balaam;

C. "'Son of Barachel'--who came to curse Israel and who blessed them 'and nevertheless the Lord your God would not hearken to Balaam (Deut. 23:6).'

D. "'The Buzite'--whose prophecy was contemptible [as the verse says] 'falling down but having his eyes uncovered (Num. 24:4).'

E. "'From the family of Ram'--[as the verse says] 'From Aram Balak has brought me (Num. 23:7).'"

F. Said to him R. Eleazar b. Azariah, "*If this is so* [that Elihu is Balaam] then God has already covered [his anger] for him [and forgiven him].

G. "*And if this is not so*, you will have to answer to him [Elihu, for identifying him with Balaam]."

H. Rather [expound in the following manner]: "'Elihu'--is Isaac.

I. "'Son of Barachel'--the son whom God has blessed as it says, 'The Lord blessed him (Gen. 26: 12).'

J. "'The Buzite'--who made the idolators contemptible when he was bound on the altar [by his willingness to be sacrificed to the Lord].

K. "'From the family of Ram'--son of Abram."

y. Soṭ. 5:6

Comment: The pericope contains two different exegeses of Job 32:2, Aqiva's (A-E) and Eleazar's (H-K). Each could stand independently but they are joined by F-G. Eleazar shows that Aqiva's explanation is problematical. The presumption is that Balaam was identified at this time as an evil personality. If so, then Aqiva either teaches that Balaam was forgiven since he is identified with Elihu who seems to be above reproach in the book of Job, or if Aqiva is incorrect in his identification then he has done Elihu a disservice by comparing him to Balaam. Thus Eleazar says that Elihu was in fact Isaac as he shows in H-K. This pericope may be an allusion to the issue of the interpretation of Balaam's nature.

Eleazar emerges as an opponent of Aqiva's teaching as he does elsewhere (cf. b. Ḥag. 14a and b. San. 67b and the deposition story in y. Ber. 4:1).

91. A. In like manner R. Judah the prince used to list the praise of the sages: of R. Tarfon, R. Aqiva, R. Eleazar b. Azariah, R. Yoḥanan b. Nuri and R. Yosé the Galilean.

B. R. Tarfon he called a heap of stones.

C. Or some say--a heap of nuts.

D. When a person removes one from the pile, they all go tumbling over each other. This is what R. Tarfon was like. When a student came to him and said, "Teach me," R. Tarfon would cite for him

Scripture and Mishnah, Midrash, *Halakhah* and *Aggada*. When the student parted from him, he went away filled with blessing and good.

E. R. Aqiva he called a well stocked storehouse.

F. To what might R. Aqiva be likened? To a laborer who took his basket and went forth. When he found wheat, he put some in [the basket]; when he found barley, he put some in; spelt, he put some in; lentils, he put some in. When he returned home he sorted out the wheat by itself, the barley by itself, the beans by themselves, the lentils by themselves. This is how R. Aqiva acted, and he arranged the whole Torah by rings.

G. R. Eleazar b. Azariah he called a spice peddler's basket.

H. For to what might R. Eleazar be likened? To a spice peddler who takes up his basket and comes into a city; when the people of the city come up and ask him, Have you good oil with you? Have you ointment with you? Have you balsam with you? They find he has everything with him. Such was R. Eleazar b. Azariah when students came to him. If questioned on Scripture, he answered; on Mishnah, he answered; on Midrash, he answered; on *Halakhah*, he answered; on *Aggada*, he answered. When one parted from him, he was filled with good and blessing.

ARN A 18, ed. Schechter, p. 65

A. Isi b. Judah used to list the praise of the sages:

B. R. Meir: A sage and a scribe.

C. R. Judah: A sage when he wished to be so.

D. R. Tarfon: A heap of nuts.

E. R. Ishmael: A prepared [stocked] store.

F. R. Aqiva: A well-stocked storehouse.

G. R. Yoḥanan b. Nuri: The box of the travelling salesman.

H. R. Eleazar b. Azariah: A spice peddler's basket.

I. The teaching of R. Eliezer b. Jacob: A *qab* and clean.

J. R. Yosé: His depth is with him.

K. R. Simeon: He grinds much and brings forth a little.

b. Giṭ. 67a

Comment: A of ARN lists five names. All of them except Yosé the Galilean appear in the list of ten sages in b. Giṭ. 67a. Of the five only Yosé and Yoḥanan appear in a third list at the end of ARN A 18. The latter two lists are clearly composite, consisting of both Yavneans and Ushans. ARN lists five Yavneans. Although the lists are clearly related we cannot say that one is primary to the other two.

B-H spells out the characterizations of three of the sages: Tarfon, Aqiva, and Eleazar (the third, fifth, and seventh names in b.). ARN explains the similes by introducing its own concern: the relation of the oral and written Torah. D tells us that Tarfon had great knowledge but that it was not well organized. It says Tarfon was master of five areas of Torah. Aqiva is credited with the collection and arrangement of the Torah into the five separate areas, referred to here as five types of produce. Again ARN introduces its own agendum into the interpretation of the metaphor.

Eleazar is portrayed as a methodical sage, knowledgable in all five fields of learning. If questioned in any one of them he can answer. b. Ber. 28a describes Eleazar as a sage "for if one questions him, he can answer," a related tradition.

Aqiva seems to play the primary role in this pericope. The other two Rabbis make use of the several types of Torah teaching, but Aqiva is represented as the organizer of the material. Eleazar's inclusion in ARN and b. is added evidence that his name was associated with standard lists of the sages (cf. M. Soṭ. 9:15 and T. Soṭ. 15:3).

91a. A. R. Huna said, "In the days of R. Eleazar b. Azariah they sought to bring them [the *ntynym*] closer [i.e., allow them to marry Jews]."

B. R. Abahu changed the version [to read], "In the days of R. Eleazar."

y. Qid. 4:1 (43a)

Comment: There is no other evidence linking Eleazar to this issue.

92. A. *tny'*: R. Eliezer says, "The days of the messiah [will last] forty years as it says, 'For forty years I loathed that generation (Ps. 95:10).'"

B. R. Eleazar b. Azariah says, "[They will last] seventy years as it says, 'In that day Tyre will be forgotten for seventy years like the days of one king (Isa. 23:15).'

C. "Who is the singular king? Say then he is the messiah."

D. Rabbi says, "[They will last] three generations as it says, 'May he live while the sun endures, and as long as the moon throughout all generations (Ps. 72:5) (*dwr dwrym*).'"

E. R. Hillel says, "There is no messiah for Israel.

F. "For he was already consumed (*'klwhw*) in the days of Hezekiah."

b. San. 99a

Comment: The pericope contains four traditions concerning the days of the messiah, a central issue in post-seventy Palestine. The first three discuss the time of the messianic age. The fourth denies that a messiah will come to save Israel. Presumably God alone will provide salvation. C glosses B and explains the relationship between the verse and its interpretation as relating to the messiah. This is the only explicit tradition we have associating Eleazar with the idea of the messiah.

iii. *The Tannaitic Midrashim*

93. A. *tnw rbnn*: When R. Eliezer fell sick four elders went to visit him: R. Tarfon, R. Joshua, R. Eleazar b. Azariah, and R. Aqiva.

B. Answered R. Tarfon and said, "You are better for Israel than rain drops; for rain drops are in this world and our rabbi is in this world and in the world to come."

C. Answered R. Joshua and said, "You are better for Israel than the disc of the sun; for the disc of the sun is in this world and our rabbi is in this world and in the world to come."

D. Answered R. Eleazar b. Azariah and said, "You are better for Israel than a father and a mother; for a father and a mother are in this world and our rabbi is in this world and in the world to come."

E. Answered R. Aqiva and said, "Beloved is suffering."

E. Said to them [R. Eliezer], "Support me and I will listen to the words of Aqiva my student who said, 'Beloved is suffering.'"

G. He [Eliezer] said to him, "Aqiva, from whence do you know this?"

H. He said, "I expound a verse: 'Manasseh was twelve years old when he began to reign, and he reigned fifty and five years in Jerusalem...and he did that which is evil in the sight of the Lord (II Kings 21:1).' And it is written, 'These are also the proverbs of Solomon, which the men of Hezekiah king of Judah copied out (Prov. 25:1).' And would Hezekiah king of Judah have taught Torah to the whole world and not have taught it to his son Menasseh? But all the pains he spent on him and all the labors he lavished on him did not bring him up to the good [path]. Rather suffering [alone did].

I. "As it says, 'And the Lord spoke to Menasseh and to his people but they would not hearken unto him. Wherefor the Lord brought upon them the captains of the host of the king of Assyria, which took Menasseh among the thorns, and bound him with fetters and carried him to Babylonia (II Chron. 33:10).' And it is written, 'And when he was in affliction, he besought the Lord his God and humbled himself greatly before the God of his fathers and prayed unto him, and he was entreated of him, and heard his supplication, and brought him again to Jerusalem unto kingdom, and Menasseh knew that the Lord he was God (II Chron. 33:12).'

J. "Thus you have learned that beloved is suffering."

b. San. 101a-b; cf. Sifré Deut. 32, ed. Finkelstein, pp. 57-58, ls. 12-16, 1-12

Comment: A is a standard protasis for this type of story which is commonly prefaced by *m'śh b*. The occasion is noted and the names of the rabbis are listed. In B, C, and D the masters praise Eliezer. In E Aqiva extols suffering. He and Eliezer are the protagonists of the narrative. The other rabbis serve merely as names. Each tells Eliezer that he is better than either rain or the sun or parents since he will provide for them in the world to come as well as in this world. Aqiva comforts Eliezer by praising the merits of suffering. H-J gives proof texts for his assertion.

This is another instance in which Eleazar is listed as one of four sages in a highly stylized account (but cf. ARN A 25).

94. A. *wkbr*: Rabban Gamaliel and R. Joshua and R. Eleazar b. Azariah and R. Aqiva were entering Rome and they heard the din of the city of Puteoli for a hundred and twenty miles [around].

B. They began to cry and R. Aqiva to laugh.

C. They said to him, "Why are we crying and you laughing?"

D. He said to them, "Why are you crying?"

E. They said, "Shall we not cry? For the gentile idolators who sacrifice to their gods and bow down to idols dwell securely in peace and undisturbed and the house of the footstool of our God was burned by fire and wild animals dwell there."

F. He said to them, "Even I laughed for this very reason. For if this is how He has acted towards those who anger him, *qal veḥomer* [will he reward with peace, etc.] those who do his will."

Sifré Deut. 43, ed. Finkelstein, pp. 94-95, ls. 9-14, 1

A. Once (*wkbr*): R. Gamaliel and R. Eleazar b. Azariah and R. Joshua and R. Aqiva were walking in the way and they heard the sound of the multitudes of Rome [Jastrow: the din of the city of Rome] emerging 120 miles away and they began to cry.

B. And R. Aqiva laughed.

C. They said to him, "Why are you laughing?"

D. He said to them, "And you, why are you crying?"

E. They said to him, "They (*kwšyym*) who bow down to idols and offer incense to celestial bodies, dwell securely and in peace. And we? The house of the footstool of our God is burnt by fire, shall we not cry?"

F. He said to them, "I laugh [for I reason that] if this is [the manner in which] those who transgress His will [dwell], so those who do his will how much more so [will they be rewarded in the future]."

b. Mak. 24a-b

Comment: A is a standard protasis listing the four rabbis and the occasion. The gloss B and the subsequent exchange distinguish Aqiva's attitude towards Rome from that of the rabbis. They bemoan its power and size, offering a simple assessment of the contrast between Rome and Israel. He injects a note of hope into the situation.

Eleazar is merely cast as one of the rabbis in this pericope, as in several others.

95. A1. *tny'*: Said R. Tarfon, "I would be surprised if there is in this generation one who receives reproof [properly].

A2. "If one says to a person, 'Take the chip (*kysm*) [MSS. O: *qyṣ*'-thorn] out of your eye [MSS. H: from between your teeth],' he answers, 'Take the beam out of your eye [H: from between your teeth].'"

B. Said R. Eleazar b. Azariah, "I would be surprised if there is in this generation one who knows how to give reproof."

[Mu.: Said R. Aqiva, "I would be surprised if there is in this generation one who receives reproof."]

C. Said R. Yoḥanan b. Nuri, "I call the heaven and earth to be my witnesses--many times Aqiva was smitten, for I used to bring charges against him before R. Simeon b. Rabbi [Mu.: b. Gamaliel]. And surely he loved me more [for it].

D. "To fulfill what is said, 'Do not reprove a scoffer, or he will hate you; reprove a wise man and he will love you (Prov. 9:8).'"

b. Arak. 16b

A. Another matter: "To all Israel (Deut. 1:1)." It teaches that all of them were admonishers and were capable of standing up to admonishment.

B. Said R. Tarfon, "By the worship! [*h'bwdh*] [I doubt] if there is [anyone] in this generation who can give admonishment [properly]."

C. Said R. Eleazar b. Azariah, "By the worship! [I doubt] if there is in this generation [one] that knows how one admonishes."

E. Said R. Yoḥanan b. Nuri, "I call the heaven and earth to be my witnesses that more than five times was R. Aqiva rebuked on my account before R.

Gamaliel at Yavneh for I used to bring charges against him and [Gamaliel] used to rebuke him. And even so [*kl kk*] I know of him that his love for me grew each time.

F. "To fulfill what is said, 'Do not reprove a scoffer, or he will hate you; reprove a wise man and he will love you (Prov. 9:8).'"

Sifré Deut. 1, ed. Finkelstein, pp. 3-4, ls. 8-11, 1-3; B-E: cf. Sifra, *Qedošim*, 84, ed. Weiss, p. 89a

Comment: A1 and B of b. are balanced and present contrasting opinions. A2 is an interpolation which explains why there is no one who receives admonishment. It is likely that its meaning is that since no one is free of sin no one will wish to receive reproof from another sinner. In C Yoḥanan responds to B by giving an example of one who knows how to give admonishment. He has done so by bringing charges against Aqiva, and he did so properly. C-D may, however, be independent of A-B--a separate tradition about Yoḥanan, Aqiva, and Gamaliel. On A2 of b., cf. Matthew 7:3-5.

Turning now to Sifré, we see that it reverses the opinions of Eleazar and Tarfon in B-C. Sifré adds D, an opinion attributed to Aqiva. Although he merely repeats Tarfon's view, D serves as a link between the dispute of B-C and the story in E-F. Since Aqiva gives an opinion, an appropriate story is brought to contradict it.

It is unlikely that there is any connection between this pericope and the deposition story in which Gamaliel is reproved by the assembly.

95a. Said R. Eleazar b. Azariah, "Disciples of the sages increase peace in the world, as it says, 'All your sons shall be taught by the Lord and great shall be the prosperity [lit.: peace] of your sons (Isa. 54:13).'"

b. Tam. 32b

Comment: It is probable that this is not correctly attributed to our Eleazar since in four other places (b. Ber. 64a; b. Naz. 66b; b. Yeb. 122b; b. Ker. 28b), it is prefaced by the formula, "Said R. Eleazar, Said R. Ḥaninah..."

96. A. R. Eleazar b. Azariah says, "Through the merit of Abraham our father he brought them out of Egypt.

B. "As it says, 'For he remembered his holy promise, and Abraham his servant. So he led forth his people with joy, his chosen ones with singing (Ps. 105:42-43).'"

Mekh. *Pis*. 16, ed. Horowitz-Rabin, p. 62, ls. 10-12

A. R. Eleazar b. Azariah says, "Through the merit of Abraham their father I will split the sea for them.

B. "As it says, 'For he remembered... (Ps. 105: 42-43).'"

Mekh., *Vayehi* 3, ed. Horowitz-Rabin, p. 98, ls. 16-18

Comment: Another tradition attributed to Eleazar concerning the exodus from Egypt appears in M. Ber. 1:5 and its parallels. On the splitting of the sea, see b. Pes. 118a where Eleazar extolls the greatness of the miracle. The question of merit or the basis for salvation was an important issue in post-seventy Palestine.

97. A. R. Eleazar b. Azariah says, "Great is labor,

B. "for the Divine Presence did not dwell in the midst of Israel until they performed labor.

C. "As it says, 'And let them make me a sanctuary, that I might dwell in their midst (Ex. 25:8).'"

Mekh. DeR. Simeon, ed. Epstein-Melamed, p. 149, ls. 9-10

R. Eleazar b. Azariah says, "Great is labor, for each and every craftsman is praised for his craftsmanship."

ARN B 21, ed. Schechter, p. 23

Comment: The pericope appears in a group of sayings with similar protases: "X says, Great is labor..." (five in ARN; four in Mekh.). The tradition does not seem to be drawn from or developed upon in any other pericope attributed to Eleazar.

98. A. R. Simeon b. Gamaliel says in the name of R. Eleazar b. Azariah, "Behold it says, 'And Nadab and Abihu died before the Lord when they offered an unholy fire before the Lord (Num. 3:4).'

B. "And they had no sons. For if they had sons, they would have taken precedence over Eleazar and Ithamar.

C. "For all who take precedence in inheritance take precedence in honor."

D. If so why does it say, [concerning Eleazar and Ithamar] "The sons that were left (Lev. 10:12)"?

E. He [Moses] said to them, "It was not right for you to watch those who performed an uncounseled act and were carried off (*nštpw*)."

F. R. Eleazar says, "They were close to being carried off (*štp*), but God had mercy on Aaron."

Sifra *Šemini*, *pereq* 1:2, ed. Weiss, p. 47a

Comment: A-B tells us nothing new, since the verse continues: "and they had no children; so Eleazar and Ithamar served as priests in the lifetime of Aaron their father." C makes Eleazar's point. It introduces a general rule based on the verse in Numbers: the priesthood is passed along to heirs in the same order as inheritance. It is interesting that the order of the succession to the office of Patriarch is a major theme in Eleazar's traditions.

D-E is a comment on Lev. 10:12 explaining that the phrase, "The sons that were left" serves as a warning to the other sons of Aaron. It is probably independent of A-C. There is no indication that Eleazar in F is our man. On this verse, see below, next comment. On the Patriarchal succession theme, see above, comment to b. Ber. 28a.

99. A. ["And the Lord spoke to Moses, after the death of the two sons of Aaron,] when they drew near before the Lord and died (Lev. 16:1)."

R. Yosé the Galilean says, "They died on account of drawing near [the Lord] and they did not die on account of the offering [of the unholy fire]."

B. R. Aqiva says, "One verse says, 'When they drew near before the Lord and died' (*ibid.*), and one verse says, 'And [they] offered unholy fire before the Lord (Lev. 10:1).'

C. "[A third verse] decides [the matter:] 'When they offered an unholy fire before the Lord (Num. 3:4).' It was on account of the drawing near that they died, but they did not die on account of the offering [of the unholy fire]."

D. R. Eleazar b. Azariah says, "Offering [an unholy fire] was sufficient [for them to die] and drawing near [before the Lord] was sufficient [for them to die]."

Sifra *Aḥare*, *par*. 1:2, ed. Weiss, p. 79b

Comment: A and D could stand as a complete pericope with Eleazar's lemma dependent on Yosé's view for its context. In B-C Aqiva repeats Yosé's opinion providing a scriptural basis for it.

The question is which sin made Nadab and Abihu liable to death. Yosé and Aqiva say it was the act of drawing near the Lord, not the sacrifice. Eleazar says either of the two acts was enough of a sin to bring sudden death upon them. See the preceding pericope for another tradition linking Eleazar with a teaching about the episode.

The theme of infringing on the legitimacy of the hereditary priesthood is the issue of the pericope.

100. A. ["And the Lord said to Moses, 'Tell Aaron your brother not to come at all times into the holy place (Lev. 16:2).'"]

R. Eleazar b. Azariah used to say, "One may draw a parable. To what may the matter be compared? To a physician who came to a sick person [and] says to him, 'Do not drink cold liquids and do not sleep on moist grass (*tḥb*; Arukh: cold).'

B. "Another comes and says to him, 'Do not drink cold liquids and do not sleep on moist grass so that you will not die as so and so did.'

C. "This one [made him heed the advice more] vigorously than all of them.

D. "Therefore it says, 'After the death of the two sons of Aaron, [when they drew near before the Lord and died] and the Lord said to Moses, Tell your brother Aaron not to come at all times into the holy place.'"

Sifra *Aḥare*, *par*. 1:3, ed. Weiss, p̣. 79b

Comment: The pericope is a unitary account. Eleazar offers a parable explaining why the incident of the death of Nadab and Abihu is mentioned immediately before the injunction against entering the holy of holies throughout the year. The account of the ritual for the Day of Atonement follows in the chapter in Lev.

101. A. "And I have separated you from the peoples, that you should be mine (Lev. 20:26)."

B. If you are separated from the nations, you are mine (*lšmy*). If not, lo, you [belong] to Nebuchadnezzar the king of Babylonia and his associates.

C. R. Eleazar b. Azariah says,

D. "From whence do we know that

E. "one should not say, 'I do not wish to wear *š'ṭnz*; I do not wish to eat meat of a swine; I do not wish to have relations with a forbidden relation (*'rwh*)'?

F. "But [he should say rather], 'I wish to [perform all these forbidden acts but] what can I do, for my father in heaven so decreed on me [that I cannot do so].'

G. "It comes to teach, 'And I have separated you from the peoples, that you should be mine.'

H. "We find that one separates himself from transgression and takes upon himself the yoke of heaven."

Sifra *Qedošim*, *pereq* 11:22,
ed. Weiss, p. 93b

Comment: C, E, and F are Eleazar's statement. D and G provide the exegetical language and verse as a context for the statement. The comment in H provides an appropriate gloss for the unit C-G, linking it back to A-B.

Eleazar's saying is related to the issue of one's intention. Here the question is not intention in the performance of a commandment but in the abstention from sin. Intention in general is not a common concern of Eleazar's rulings. The question of proper attitudes is a central concern in the era following the destruction of the Temple.

102. A. R. Eleazar b. Azariah says, "We have found that you recite part of a man's praise in his presence. For so we have found concerning Noah.

B. "As it says, 'For I have seen that you are righteous before me in this generation (Gen. 7:1).'

C. "And not in his presence [one may recite his full praise as] he says, 'Noah was a righteous man, blameless in his generation (Gen. 6:9).'"

D. R. Eliezer the son of R. Yosé the Galilean says, "We have found that you recite part of the praise of God (*my š'mr whyh h'wlm*).

E. "As it says, 'Say to God, How awesome are thy deeds (Ps. 66:3)'!

F. "If you [only] recite part of the praise of God, *qal veḥomer* [that you only say part of the praise of one who is but] flesh and blood."

Sifré Num. 103, ed. Horowitz-Rabin, p. 101, ls. 1-6; B.R. 32, ed. Theodor-Albeck, pp. 290-91, ls. 10, 1-4

Comment: A-C and D-E are independent traditions related only by a common phrase (*mqṣt šbḥ*). b. Erub. 18b gives a tradition similar to A-C in the name of Jeremiah b. Eleazar. All manuscripts of B.R. and Sifré have Eleazar b. Azariah or Eleazar. None preserve b.'s attribution.

103. A. R. Eleazar b. Azariah says: In four places Moses made requests before the Holy One:

B. Similarly you say (*kywṣ' bw 'th 'wmr*) [this is one instance]: "But Moses said to the Lord *l'mr*, 'Behold the people Israel have not listened to me (Ex. 6:12)." *l'mr* teaches only that he said to Him (to God), "Answer me [as to] whether you are going to redeem them or not."

C. Until God answered him, "Now you shall see what I will do to Pharaoh (Ex. 6:1)."

D. [Another instance:] (*kywṣ' bw 't' 'wmr*) "Moses said to the Lord, *l'mr* 'Let the Lord, the God of the spirits of all flesh, [appoint a man over the congregation] (Num. 27:15-16).'" *l'mr* comes to teach only that he said to Him, "Answer me [as to] whether you are going to appoint officials over them or not."

E. Until God answered him as it says, "And the Lord said to Moses, 'Take Joshua the son of Nun (Num. 27:18).'"

F. [Another instance:] (*kywṣ' bw 't' 'wmr*) "And I besought the Lord at that time saying *l'mr*... [Let me go over, I pray, and see the good Land beyond the Jordan.] (Deut. 3:23-25)." *l'mr* comes to teach only that he said to Him, "Answer me [as to] whether I will enter the Land or not."

G. Until God answered him, "Let it suffice you; speak no more to me of this matter (Deut. 3:26)."

H. Even here [with regard to the verse] "And Moses cried to the Lord *l'mr*, 'Heal her, O God, I beseech thee (Num. 12:13).'" *l'mr* comes only to teach that he said to Him, "Answer me [as to] whether you are going to heal her or not."

I. Until God said to him, "If her father had but spit in her face, should she not be shamed for seven days (Num. 12:14)"?

Sifré Num. 105, ed. Horowitz-Rabin, p. 104, ls. 1-14 (Sifré Num. 138, ed. Horowitz-Rabin, pp. 184-85, ls. 14-25, 1-4)

Comment: The pericope uses stylized formularies. In B, D, F, and H a question is deduced from the use of the word *l'mr* in the verse. C, E, G, and I give God's answers to Moses. The order of the pericope seems to be adjusted to fit the context in Sifré. If the tradition followed the order of the appearance of the verses in the Pentateuch the last question and answer (H-I) would follow the first (B-C). Such reorganization is standard. Of the four themes of the pericope--the redemption of Israel from Egypt, the healing of Miriam, the appointing of officials, Moses' entry into the Land of Israel--the last three are not found elsewhere in Eleazar's traditions.

104. A. R. Eleazar b. Azariah says: In three places Moses became angry (*lkll k's*) and erred:

B. Similarly you say (*kywṣ' bw 'th 'wmr*): "And he became angry with Eleazar and Ithamar the sons of Aaron who were left, saying." What does it say?

"Why have you not eaten the Sin-offering in the place of the sanctuary (Lev. 10:16-17)"?

C. Similarly you say: "And he said to them, 'Hear now, you rebels; shall we bring forth water for you out of this rock'"? What does it say? "And Moses lifted up his hand and struck the rock with his rod twice (Num. 20:10-11)."

D. Also here [this verse is an illustration]: "And Moses was angry with the officers of the army, the commanders of thousands and the commanders of hundreds who had come from service in the war (Num. 31:14)." What does it say? "And Eleazar the priest said to the men of war who had gone into battle: 'This is the statute of the law which the Lord has commanded Moses (Num. 31:21).'"

E. Since Moses our Rabbi became angry, he erred.

Sifré Num. 157, ed. Horowitz-Rabin, p. 213, ls. 10-18

Comment: A introduces the pericope. B-D list three instances in which Moses erred in judgment or action and attributes the cause of his mistake to anger. B relates Moses' anger over the burning of the Sin-offering by Eleazar and Ithamar. The incident is related shortly after the death of Nadab and Abihu. Moses may have erred in thinking that the other sons of Aaron also brought an unholy fire into the sanctuary as the verse says, "Behold, it was burned (Lev. 10:16)" [cf. commentary of Solomon Ephraim of Prague (*kly yqr*) to the verse].

The other two cases are clearer cases of anger and error. In C he becomes angry over the rebellious people and strikes the rock. In D Moses' anger causes him to forget the laws of purifying the utensils of gentiles. Eleazar the priest announces the laws to the people [cf. commentary of Rashi to the verse].

This pericope uses formulary language similar to the tradition in Sifré Num. 105 ("In four places Moses made requests before the Holy One..."). The joining language in B and C is unusual. "Similarly you say (*kywṣ 'bw 'th 'wmr*)" normally indicates that what is given is the second or third illustration of a point. Here B, the first example, is introduced by the phrase. The pericope thus may be defective or reorganized.

105. A. "But if the manslayer shall at any time go beyond the bounds of his city of refuge to which he has fled... (Num. 35:26)."

B. Said R. Eleazar b. Azariah, "Just as the divine attribute of punishment is small [i.e., strict], for if one steps a step he is liable to be killed, *qal veḥomer* that the divine attribute of mercy is great [i.e., lenient]."

Sifré Num. 140, ed. Horowitz-Rabin, p. 220, ls. 15-16

Comment: In the case of an accidental death the city of refuge provides protection for the killer as long as he stays within the city limits. Eleazar's statement makes sense only as a comment to the verse cited. We have no other tradition in which he discusses the divine attributes, but they are a common theme at Yavneh.

106. A. "Then God will drive out... (Deut. 11:23)." God will drive out [the nations] but man will not drive them out.

B. "...all these nations..." Should I understand it literally? [No, for] it comes to teach, "These" [only the nations in the Land].

C. From whence do we know that their allies are included? It comes to teach, "All these nations before you." For you will become greater and greater and they will become fewer and fewer.

D. And likewise it says, "Little by little I will drive them out from before you (Ex. 23:20)" and it says, "I will not drive them out from before you in one year, lest the Land become desolate and the wild beasts multiply against you (Ex. 23:29),"

E. the words of R. Jacob.

F. Said to him R. Eleazar b. Azariah, "If the Israelites were righteous why did they fear the wild beasts?

G. "For lo, if they are righteous, they need not fear wild beasts.

H. "For so it says, 'For you shall be in league with the stones of the field, [and the wild beasts of the field shall be at peace with you] (Job 5:23).'

I. "If you will ask, Why did Joshua have to exert so much effort [to conquer the Land]?

J. "Because Israel sinned it was decreed against them that, 'Little by little I will drive them out from before you.'"

Sifré Deut. 50, ed. Finkelstein, p. 115, ls. 6-14

Comment: A-C is an independent tradition, unrelated to D-J, telling that God will drive the nations out of the Land of Israel. The joining language in O ("and likewise it says") is the only link between A-C + D-J. D-J presents two differing explanations of the gradual process forecast here for driving the nations out of the Land of Israel. D merely explains the verse by citing the previous verse. Jacob may be Aqiva although there is no MSS evidence to so indicate (see Finkelstein's note *ad. loc.*). F responds to D. G-H explains Eleazar's question in F by citing an appropriate verse. I-J suggests an alternative explanation for the painstaking process of driving the nations out of the Land. Eleazar suggests that it was the sin of the people that made God punish them. They therefore could not defeat their enemies quickly but, "Little by little" through much struggling.

The idea that Israel suffers because of sin is not common in Eleazar's traditions. As in the previous pericope, the theme is punishment for sin, the Deuteronomic principle, part of the theodicy of Yavneh.

107. A. "You shall not abhor an Egyptian because you were a sojourner in his land (Deut. 23:7)."

B. Said R. Eleazar b. Azariah, "The Egyptians only accepted Israel [into their land] for their own sake, and God set reward aside for them.

C. "Are not the matters a *qal veḥomer*? If one who does not intend [to act in order] to receive merit, received merit [for his act and]--Scripture bestows upon him [reward] as if he merited it.

D. "[Concerning] one who intends to receive merit--how much more so [will he receive reward]."

Sifré Deut. 252, ed. Finkelstein, p. 279, ls. 1-4

A. Said R. Eleazar b. Azariah, "From whence do we know that if one lost a *sela'* and a poorman found it and sustained himself with it, that Scripture speaks of him [the one who lost it] as if he received merit?

B. "It comes to teach, 'It shall be for the sojourner, the fatherless and the widow (Deut. 24:19).'"

C-D = C-D above.

Sifré Deut. 283, ed. Finkelstein, pp. 300-1, ls. 12-13, 1-2

A. R. Eleazar b. Azariah says, "Behold it says, 'When you reap your harvest in your field, and have forgotten a sheaf in the field, you shall not go back to get it: it shall be for the sojourner, the fatherless and the widow; that the Lord your God may bless you in all the work of your hands (Deut. 24:19).' Scripture established a blessing for one to whom a *miṣwah* came without his knowledge.

B. "Say now, If a *sela'* was wrapped in his garment and fell from him [and] a poorman found it and sustained himself with it,

C. "behold, Scripture establishes for him a blessing as [it does] for one who forgets a sheaf in his field."

Sifra, *Vayiqra*, *par*. 12:3,
ed. Weiss, p. 27a

Comment: The three pericopae treat related themes: One receives reward for an act even though his original intention was not directed towards the performance of a good deed. Sifré 252A-B could stand alone. Eleazar points out that the Egyptians received the Israelites into their land only so that they might benefit from Joseph's counsel. Yet they were rewarded and survived the famine.

C-D introduces the idea of the intention of an act. If one who did not intend to act out of proper motivation is rewarded, one who does will surely be rewarded. C-D could be an independent tradition, although it makes more sense within a given context. Sifré 282 cites C-D verbatim. A-B there, however, speaks not of the Egyptians but of one whose unintentional loss results in the sustenance of a poorman. B compares the case of unintentional charity to the law of the forgotten sheaf. C-D's original context may have been either Sifré 252 or 283 or it may have been an entirely separate tradition circulating in Eleazar's name.

Sifra presents an alternative version of A-B of Sifré 283. It knows nothing of C-D of Sifré. The comparison between unintentional charity and the forgotten sheaf is spelled out in B-C of Sifra. The issue of the pericope had contemporary relevance to Eleazar's era. See comment to Sifra *Qedošim*, *pereq* 11:22.

iv. *Later Compilations*

108. A. Resh Laqish in the name of R. Eleazar b. Azariah, "'Ah Lord God! It is thou who hast made the heavens and the earth... (Jer. 32:17).'

B. "From that time onward, 'Nothing is too hard for thee (*ibid*.).'"

B.R. 9, ed. Theodor-Albeck,
pp. 68-69, ls. 10-11, 1

Comment: The exegetical remark is cited by the editor of B.R. after Gen. 1:31: "And God saw everything that he had made, and behold it was very good." In the book of Jeremiah the verse precedes a section praising God's omnipotence, omniscience and his wondrous deeds on Israel's behalf. The teaching merely points out that the miracle of the creation is to be seen as God's greatest act in history. Resh Laqish also appears as a tradent of Eleazar's traditions in B.R. 84.

109. A. "And she conceived and bore Cain... (Gen. 4:1)." Said R. Eleazar b. Azariah, "Three wonders occurred on that day.

B. "On that day they were created; on that day they had intercourse; on that day they bore offspring."

B.R. 22, ed. Theodor-Albeck,
p. 205, ls. 3-5

110. A. "His eyes were dim so that he could not see (Gen. 27:1)." R. Eleazar b. Azariah said, "'He could not see' the evil of the wicked one."

B. God said, *Isaac will go out to the market place and people will say, "There is the father of that wicked one."*

C. *Thus ('l') I will dim his eyes and he will not go out.*

D. The same [may be said on the basis of the verse] (*hw' hdyn*) "When the wicked rise, men hide themselves (Prov. 28:28)."

E. From here they said, All those who raise up a wicked man or a wicked student, his eyes will grow dim.

B.R. 65, ed. Theodor-Albeck,
pp. 718-19, ls. 10-11, 1-2

Comment: A and possibly D are attributed to Eleazar. B-C is clearly an interpolation and E a gloss. If A and D comprise the tradition then Eleazar interprets the verse in Genesis by citing a verse in Proverbs. In all probability, however, only A is Eleazar's.

Some manuscripts attribute the saying to Eleazar b. Azariah *hqyrḥ* (the bald one). Others have just Eleazar. This evidence calls the attribution into question.

111. A. "And he made him a long robe with sleeves (Gen. 37:3)." Resh Laqish in the name of R. Eleazar b. Azariah, "A man must not differentiate between his sons.

B. "For on account of the robe with sleeves that our father Jacob made for Joseph 'they hated him... (Gen. 37:4).'"

B.R. 84, ed. Theodor-Albeck,
p. 1010, ls. 5-7

A. Resh Laqish in the name of R. Eleazar b. Azariah, "'Come and see what God has done: he is terrible in his deeds among men (Ps. 66:5).' Why [does it say] 'they hated him'? Because he split the sea before them.

B. "'With many sleeves' (*psym*): he split the sea (*ps ym*) [a play on the word]."

B.R. 84, ed. Theodor-Albeck,
p. 1011, ls. 1-3

Comment: Resh Laqish serves as tradent for two exegeses of Eleazar on the same verse. In the first, Eleazar explains the verse literally. The brothers hated Joseph because of the favoritism which Jacob showed him. Therefore one should be careful not to favor one son over another. The second explanation first cites a verse from Psalms extolling God's deeds. The implication of the teaching is that the brothers were jealous of Joseph because on his account the Jews went down to Egypt and God subsequently performed the miracle of splitting the sea. On other references by Eleazar to the miracle of splitting the sea, cf., e.g., b. Pes. 118a.

112. A. "And Joseph said to his brothers, 'I am your brother Joseph; is my father still alive'? But his brothers could not answer him, for they were dismayed at his presence (Gen. 45:3)."

R. Simeon b. Eleazar in the name of R. Eleazar b. Azariah, who said the matter in the name of Abba Kohen b. Daliah, "Woe to us the day of judgment! Woe to us the day of reproof!

B. "Balaam was the sage of the gentiles and could not stand before the reproof of his ass. [As it says,] 'Was I ever accustomed to do so to you? And he said, No (Num. 22:30).'

C. "Joseph was the youngest among the tribes and his brothers could not stand before his reproof. As it says (*hw' hdyn*), 'But his brothers could not answer him.'

D. "And when God will come and reprove each and every person, [as it says,] 'But now I rebuke you and lay the charge before you (Ps. 50:21),' how much more so [will they not be able to stand before the reproof]."

B.R. 93, ed. Theodor-Albeck,
pp. 1159-60, ls. 5-6, 1-4

A. Said R. Eleazar b. Azariah, "Woe to us the day of judgment! Woe to us the day of reproof!

B. "Joseph the righteous one who is flesh and blood, when he reproved his brothers, they could not stand before his reproof.

C. "God, who is the judge and possessor of judgment and sits on the throne of judgment and judges each and every person, how much more so [must we say that] no one who is flesh and blood can stand before his reproof (*'tmh'*)!"

B.R. 93, ed. Theodor-Albeck,
p. 1170, ls. 2-6

A. "And Joseph said to his brothers, 'I am Joseph... (Gen. 45:3).'" When he said, "I am Joseph,"

"His brothers could not answer him, for they were dismayed at his presence."

B. R. Eleazar b. R. Simeon in the name of R. Eleazar b. Azariah said, "If they could not answer Joseph who said to his brothers, 'I am Joseph,' and they knew what they had done to him,

C. "when God comes to converse with each of his creatures and to tell him of his deeds, as it is written, 'For lo, he who forms the mountains and creates the wind, and declares to man what is his thought... (Amos 4:13),'

D. "how much more so will no creature be able to stand [before God]."

Tanḥ. *Vayigaš* 7, ed. Buber, p. 104a

Comment: We have three versions of a pericope in which Eleazar compares the reproof of the brothers by Joseph to the reproof of man by God. The following chart compares the versions.

B.R. (1)	B.R. (2)	Tanḥ.
A. Gen. 45:3 + Simeon b. Eleazar/Eleazar b. Azariah/Abba Kohen: Woe!	A. Eleazar b. Azariah: Woe!	A. Gen. 45:3
B. Balaam + Num. 22:30	- - - -	B. Eleazar b. Simeon/Eleazar b. Azariah: could not answer.
C. Joseph: youngest	B. Joseph: righteous/ flesh and blood	- - - -
D. God + Ps. 50:21	C. God: judge	C. God + Amos 4:13

The attribution in each version is different. The first version in B.R. gives a chain of tradition which appears nowhere else: Simeon, Eleazar b. Azariah, and Abba Kohen. The reference to Balaam (B) and the verse cited in D do not appear in the two parallels. Tanḥ. has Eleazar b.

Simeon as the tradent of the tradition and omits the reference to Abba Kohen. It also gives a shorter version of the pericope, omitting the reference to Balaam, combining A and C of B.R. (1), and finally giving a different verse in C.

The second version in B.R. is the shortest. It simply attributes the tradition to Eleazar b. Azariah, omits reference to any verse but adds the contrast between God the judge and man who is flesh and blood. It is difficult to say which version is primary. It seems that the shorter versions are derivative since the likelihood is greater that the chain of tradition and the verses were omitted rather than added to a more concise version.

b. Hag. 4b attributes a similar tradition to Eleazar the amora:

> A. *When R. Eleazar came to this verse he cried*: "'His brothers could not answer him, for they were dismayed at his presence.'
> B. "If such is the reproof of flesh and blood, how much more so the reproof of God."

Our Eleazar does appear in other traditions discussing reproof, however. This fact increases the likelihood that the attribution of b. is not accurate (cf. Sifré Deut. 1, etc.).

112a. A. When Rabban Yoḥanan b. Zakkai's son died, his students came in to comfort him...

B. R. Eleazar b. Arakh [printed versions and MSS have: b. Azariah] entered. When [Yoḥanan] saw him he said to his servant, "Take my clothing and follow me to the bathhouse, for he is a great man and I will not be able to stand before him..."

ARN A, 14, ed. Schechter, p. 30

Comment: b. Arakh is surely the correct reading.

113. A. R. Eleazar b. Azariah says, "Moses only broke the tablets because God told him to do so.

B. "As it says, 'Which Moses wrought in the sight of all Israel (Deut. 34:12).'

C. "Just as there he was commanded and acted, even here he was commanded and acted."

ARN A 2, ed. Schechter, p. 6

Comment: The tradition appears in a sequence of six similar statements each preceded by, "x says, Moses only broke the tablets..." There are no other traditions associated with Eleazar on this theme. It would seem that Eleazar is merely a name on a list here. On Moses, see Sifré Num. 105, 157.

Deut. 34:12 is the last verse in the Pentateuch which speaks of, "all the mighty power and all the great and terrible deeds...which Moses wrought in the sight of all Israel." Just as the performance of those acts was commanded by God, so too the shattering of the tablets (one of the "deeds") was done at God's command.

114. A. *m'śh b*: A woman, married to a scholar; she used to bind *tefillin* around his arm. The scholar died and she married a tax collector and used to attach the tax seals for him.

B. R. Eleazar b. Azariah made a public proclamation.

Kallah Rabbati 1:5 (51b), trans. Rabbinowitz, p. 418

Comment: The story names Simeon b. Eleazar instead in b. A.Z. 39a.

115. A. *m'śh b*: Four elders: Rabban Gamaliel, R. Joshua, R. Eleazar b. Azariah and R. Aqiva, who journeyed to a kingdom in the interior where they had a friend who was a philosopher.

B. Said R. Joshua to Rabban Gamaliel, "Rabbi, if it be thy wish, let us go and pay respects to our friend the philosopher."

C. He said to him, "No."

D. In the morning he said to him, "Shall we go to pay respects to our friend the philosopher?"

E. He said to him, "Yes."

F. They went and stood by the door of the philosopher's [house]. Rabban Gamaliel knocked at the door and the philosopher thought to himself, "This can only be the manners of the sages." [He knocked] a second time and the philosopher arose and washed his hands and feet. [He knocked] a third time [and the philosopher] opened the door and saw the sages of Israel, some coming on one side and some coming on the other--Rabban Gamaliel in the center, R. Joshua and R. Eleazar b. Azariah on his right and R. Aqiva on his left.

G. The philosopher thought to himself and said, "How shall I greet the wise men of Israel? If I say, 'Peace be upon you Rabban Gamaliel,' I will offend the sages of Israel. If I say, 'Peace be upon you sages of Israel,' I will offend Rabban Gamaliel. When he reached them, he said to them, 'Peace be upon you sages of Israel, and to Rabban Gamaliel at the head.'"

Kallah Rabbati, 7:1 (54a),
ed. Higger, pp. 316-17; Derekh
Ereṣ Rabbah 5:2

Comment: As is common Eleazar is one of the sages travelling with Gamaliel. It would have seemed more appropriate for Eliezer to appear here, though, as he is commonly paired with Joshua.

116. A. R. Eleazar b. Azariah and R. Eleazar HaModai: One says, "Could the mountain [Sinai] hold them? Rather God said to it, Lengthen, widen, and accept the sons of your master."

B. And one says, "When God returns to Jerusalem, he will return the dispersed [peoples] to its midst. As it says, 'Lo, these shall come from afar, and lo, these from the north and from the west (Isa. 49:12).'

C. "And can [Jerusalem] hold them [all]? But God will say to her, 'Enlarge the place of your tent (Isa. 54:2).'"

Pesikta deRav Kahana, ed. Mandelbaum, p. 221 (Tanḥ. *Yitro* 14, ed. Buber, p. 39a, Pesikta Rab., ed. Ish Shalom, p. 103b)

A. *dylmh*: R. Leazar b. Azariah and R. Leazar HaModai *were sitting involved in* [*expounding*] *this verse*, "At that time Jerusalem shall be called the throne of the Lord (Jer. 3:17)."

B. Said R. Eleazar b. Azariah to R. Eleazar HaModai, "Will Jerusalem hold them? [i.e., the nations, as the verse continues, 'And all the nations shall gather to it.']."

C. He said to him, "In the future God will say to her, '[Jerusalem] be lengthened, be widened, accept your population. Enlarge the place of your tent... (Isa. 54:2).'"

Pesikta deRav Kahana, ed. Mandelbaum, p. 316

Comment: The two related pericopae both refer to the ingathering of the exiles. As such they have a distinctive messianic character. Both cite Isa. 54:2. In A of the first it is presumably Eleazar b. Azariah who speaks of the Israelites at Sinai. Through a miracle God enlarged the space before the mountain to hold all the Israelites. B-C speaks of the ingathering of the exiles referred to in Isa. Jerusalem will be enlarged at that time to accommodate all the returning exiles.

The second tradition seems to be based on the first, referring only to the problem of Jerusalem. A cites another verse as the focus of the pericope (Jer. 3:17). B has Eleazar b. Azariah pose a question to Eleazar HaModai. C gives his answer which seems to draw upon the first tradition for its formulation. The following chart compares the two versions:

(1)	(2)
A. Eleazar b. Azariah and Eleazar HaModai/One says: Sinai	A. Eleazar b. Azariah and Eleazar HaModai/+ Jer. 3:17
B. One says: Jerusalem + Isa. 49:12	B. Eleazar b. Azariah: Will Jerusalem...?
C. Isa. 54:2	C. Isa. 54:2

The second version omits reference to Sinai. The first appears to be primary.

117. A. "And he dreamed that there was a ladder set up on the earth... (Gen. 28:12)." Said R. Eleazar b. Azariah, "He [God] showed him Jonah, as it says, 'At the roots of the mountains I went down to the land (Jonah 2:6).'"

B. "And the top of it reached to heaven." He showed him Elijah, as it says, "And Elijah went up by a whirlwind to heaven (II Kings 2:11)."

Tanh. *Vayeṣe* 7, ed. Buber, p. 75a

Comment: We have no other tradition linking Eleazar to traditions about Jacob, Jonah, or Elijah.

118. A. Said R. Aqiva, "All the world and its contents are not equal to (*kd'y*) the day that the teaching of the Song of Songs was given to Israel.

B. "For all the writings are holy but the Song of Songs is the holy of holies."

C. Said R. Eleazar b. Azariah, "To what may the matter be compared? To a king who took a *se'ah* of wheat and gave it to the baker and said to him, 'Produce for me so much flour, so much coarse bran, so much bran flour [printed eds. add: *and make for me one fine quality cake*].'

D. "So too all the writings are holy but the Song of Songs is holy of holies."

Tanḥ. *Teṣaveh* 1, ed. Buber, p. 48a

Comment: Our pericope was probably generated by M. Yad. 3:5 ("Said Simeon b. Azzai, I have a tradition from seventy two elders that on the day they seated R. Eleazar b. Azariah in the assembly that Song of Songs and Qoheleth render the hands unclean. Said R. Aqiva, etc."). A-B refer to Aqiva's statement there. C is likely attributed to Eleazar because of the reference to him in M. D repeats B. The writings are compared to wheat in the parable in C. The finest product of the inspiration (wheat) given to man (baker) by God (king) is the Song of Songs (cake, supplied by the printed versions). There are no other traditions attributed directly to Eleazar concerning the Song of Songs.

119. A. *m'śh b*: Rabban Gamaliel and R. Joshua and R. Eleazar Azariah and R. Aqiva who went to Rome and expounded there:

B. "The ways of God are not like the ways of man; for he [man] decrees a decree and he tells others to act and he does nothing. But God is not like that."

Ex. R. 30:6, p. 164a

Comment: The four rabbis commonly appear together in Rome.

120. A. "[God gives the desolate a home to dwell in; he leads out the prisoners] to prosperity (Ps. 68:6)." Said R. Eleazar b. Azariah, "Here there is weeping and song.

B. "The Egyptians weep because they were despoiled, for Israel had despoiled them and emptied their houses. And the Israelites sang for they carried the spoil of their enemies.

C. "That is, 'to prosperity.'"

Num. R. 3:4, p. 64b

Comment: The exodus from Egypt is a common theme in traditions attributed to Eleazar.

NOTES

CHAPTER III

[1] His exegesis contradicts the pausal stops indicated by the accents for the cantillation of Scripture and by the interpretation of Targum Pseudo-Jonathan.

[2] On the early Christian attitudes towards circumcision as reflected in the letters of Paul, see Galatians, Chs. 2, 5, 6; Romans, Chs. 2, 4; Philippians 3:3, and, from the Pauline circle, Ephesians 2:11.

[3] See David M. Goodblatt, *Rabbinic Instruction in Sassanian Babylonia*, Leiden, 1975, pp. 65ff., esp. p. 65, n. 5.

[4] *Ibid.*, p. 255.

[5] See Robert Goldenberg, "The Deposition of Rabban Gamaliel II: An Examination of the Sources," *Journal of Jewish Studies*, Vol. 23, no. 2, 1972, pp. 167-90.

[6] See Goodblatt, *op. cit.*, p. 86.

[7] M. Kel. 3:8, b. Giṭ. 67a.

[8] M. Soṭ. 9:15, T. Soṭ. 15:3.

CHAPTER IV

THE TRADITION AS A WHOLE: THE ATTESTATIONS

All of the one hundred and twenty traditions examined in the preceding chapters are either attributed to R. Eleazar b. Azariah or mention his name. We therefore should assume that we have sufficient evidence to reconstruct the life or worldview of Eleazar. However, none of the traditions before us derives from primary evidence of the period of Eleazar's lifetime, the late first and early second century. Of the documents in which Eleazar's traditions appear, Mishnah and Tosefta are acknowledged to be the oldest. Even these were edited approximately 100 years after Eleazar's lifetime, at the beginning of the third century.[1] Our earliest manuscript of Mishnah is dated at almost a millennium after Eleazar's death.[2] The Talmudim, Midrashim, and later compilations which serve as the repository for more than half of the traditions concerning Eleazar reached their final forms centuries later than Mishnah.[3]

We shall base this and succeeding chapters on the assumption that those traditions which can be dated the earliest preserve the most reliable information about Eleazar the man. Moreover, if a certain saying appears in a compilation which reached its final form in the third century we may safely assume, barring later interpolation or error in transmission, that in its present form it accurately represents the state of the traditions contained therein of the period no later than the era of its redaction, and perhaps contains material which can be shown to derive in substance from earlier generations.

The chart which follows lists the traditions, giving in parallel columns a notation of the documents in which they appear. Column I lists references to M.-T., II to the so-called Tannaitic Midrashim, III to the *beraita*-stratum of *gemara*, IV to materials in b. and y. not designated as Tannaitic, and V to later compilations.

THE TRADITION AS A WHOLE

		I	II	III	IV	V
1.	Mention Exodus at night	M. Ber. 1:5 T. Ber. 1:12	Sifré Deut. 130			
2.	The additional service	M. Ber. 4:7				
3.	Time for reciting *shema'*	T. Ber. 1:2		y. Ber. 1:3		
4.	Reclining/sitting for *shema'*	T. Ber. 1:4	Sifré Deut. 34	y. Ber. 1:3 b. Ber. 11a		
5.	Recites *shema'* must hear his words			b. Ber. 15a		
6.	Houses' dispute *re*: sheaves	T. Peah 3:2		y. Peah 6:2		
7.	Saplings *re*: Seventh year	M. Sheb. 1:8				
8.	Storing dung in field	M. Sheb. 3:3				
9.	Seedlings *re*: tithes	M. Maas. 5:1				
10.	Seedling, etc. *re*: tithe *wdyy/demai*	T. Maas. 3:8		y. Maas 5:1		
11.	Tithe to Eleazar	M. M.S. 5:9		b. Qid. 26b b. B.M. 11a		
12.	Tithe to priest			b. Yeb. 86a-b	y. M.S. 5:5	
13.	Houses' dispute *re*: Dough offering of Nazirite	T. Ḥal. 1:6		b. Pes. 38b		

		I	II	III	IV	V
14.	Removing food from insulation	M. Shab. 4:2				
15.	Eleazar's cow went out with strap	M. Shab. 5:4 (M. Beṣ. 2:8; M. Ed. 3:11)				
16.	Washing child on Sabbath	M. Shab. 19:3				
17.	Eleazar entered bathhouse on festival	T. Shab. 3:3		b. Shab. 40a		
18.	Mortal danger overrides Sabbath		Mekh. *Shab*. I	b. Yoma 85a-b b. Shab. 132a		Tanḥ. *Vayešeb* 8
19.	Sabbath limit, ship	M. Erub. 4:1				
20.	Passover eaten until midnight		Mekh. de R. Simeon, pp. 13, 15	b. Pes. 120b; b. Ber. 9a; b. Meg. 21a; b. Zeb. 57b		
21.	*Lulav* on boat		Sifra *Emor*, *pereq* 16:2	b. Suk. 41b		
22.	Strap on cow, curry cattle, grind pepper on Sabbath	M. Beṣ. 2:8 (M. Ed. 3:12)				
23.	Dig water channel on festival, Seventh year	M. M.Q. 1:2				

		I	II	III	IV	V
24.	Watering from newly flowing spring	T. Moed 1:1		b. M.Q. 2a		
25.	Funeral of infant				b. M.Q. 24b	M. Sem. 3:3-4
26.	Maintenance of daughters	M. Ket. 4:6		y. Yeb. 15:3 y. Ket. 4:8		
27.	Amount of *ketubah*	M. Ket. 5:1				Num. Rab. 10:9
28.	Liability of Nazirite	M. Naz. 6:2 T. Nez. 4:1	Sifré Num., p. 29			
(28a.	Cutting hair of Nazirite			y. Naz. 6:3)		
29.	Time for intercourse	T. Soṭ. 1:2				
30.	Conditional divorce	T. Giṭ. 9:1-5	Sifré Deut. 269	y. Giṭ. 9:1 b. Giṭ. 83a-b		
31.	Remarriage to former wife		Sifré Deut. 270	b. Yeb. 11a		
32.	Gentiles judge by laws of Israel		Mekh. *Neziqin* 1			
33.	Furnishing a slave (Deut. 15:12-14)			b. Qid. 17b b. B.M. 31b		M. Abadim 2:4
34.	Slave or master took sick		Mekh. de R. Simeon, p. 163			
35.	Drinking from *kallah*					Kallah 1:3 Kal. Rab. 1:5

		I	II	III	IV	V
36.	Spread of fire *re*: liability	M. B.Q. 6:4	Mekh. *Nez*. 14	y. B.Q. 6:6 b. B.Q. 61a-b		
37.	Liability of owner of ox (Ex. 21:28)		Mekh. de R. Simeon, p. 179			
38.	Sale of field	T. B.M. 4:2		b. Meg. 27b	b. B.M. 63a b. Arak. 31a	
39.	Attaching scrolls together			b. B.B. 13b		Soferim 3:5
40.	Sanhedrin which executes	M. Mak. 1:10				
41.	Strap for lashes (Deut. 25:3-4)				b. Mak. 23a	
42.	Levir with boils				b. Yeb. 4a; b. Mak. 23a	
43.	Divine names sacred				b. Shabuot 35b	
44.	Eleazar dealt in wine and oil	T. A.Z. 4:1		b. B.B. 91a		
45.	Pledge of Burnt-offering	M. Men. 13:6				
46.	Oil with thanksgiving (Lev. 7:12), Nazirite's offering, days between menstrual periods		Sifra *Ṣav*, *pereq* 11:4-6	b. Men. 89a; b. Nid. 72b		
47.	Dedicate only part of property	M. Arak. 8:4 T. Arak. 4:23	Sifra *Behar*, 5:1			

		I	II	III	IV	V
48.	Eating meat (Deut. 12:20)	T. Arak. 4:26	Sifré Deut. 75	b. Ḥul. 84a		
49.	Daily diet	T. Arak. 4:27		b. Ḥul. 84a		
50.	Half bondwoman, half freedwoman (Lev. 19:20)	M. Ker. 2:5	Sifra *Qed.*, *par.* 5	b. Ker. 11a		
51.	Reviling the Lord (Num. 15:30)		Sifré Num., 112	b. Ker. 7b		
52.	Funnel stopped with pitch	M. Kel. 3:8				
53.	Elders sitting in store of Eleazar	T. Kel. B.B. 2:2				
54.	Five things torn, immerse them as they are	T. Kel. B.B. 2:6				
55.	Shoe attached to shoelast					ARN A 25
56.	Appearance of bright spot changed	M. Neg. 7:2	Sifra *Neg.*, *pereq* 1:1			
57.	Quickflesh spread over limb tips, reappear	M. Neg. 8:9				
58.	House/tree shades house with plague	M. Neg. 13:6				
59.	Put hand into house with plague	T. Neg. 7:3				

		I	II	III	IV	V
60.	Clothes in wall niche	M. Ṭoh. 7:7; T. Ṭoh. 8:7				
61.	Cistern in courtyard	M. Miq. 3:2				
62.	Woman discharges semen on third day	M. Miq. 8:3; T. Miq. 6:6	Mekh. *Baḥodesh* 3, Mekh. de R. Simeon, p. 142			
63.	Definition of a period			y. Shab. 9:3		
64.	Blood of menstruant does not render susceptible	M. Maksh. 6:6				
65.	On the day/Song of Songs	M. Yad. 3:5				
66.	On the day/sacrifices slaughtered not for their own sake	M. Yad. 4:2; M. Zeb. 1:3				
67.	Ammon and Moab in Seventh year	M. Yad. 4:3 T. Yad. 2:15-16		b. Ḥag. 3b		
68.	Declares clean fruit-stalks of beans	M. Uqṣ. 1:5		b. Ḥul. 119b		
69.	Atonement	M. Yoma 8:9	Sifra *Aḥare*, *pereq* 8:1-2			
(69a.	Four types of atonement			b. Yoma 86a etc.)		
70.	Uncircumcision (Jer. 9:26)	M. Ned. 3:11	Mekh. *Amaleq* 1			

		I	II	III	IV	V
71.	When Eleazar died riches departed	M. Soṭ. 9:15 T. Soṭ. 15:3				
72.	Eleazar in dream = wealth				b. Ber. 57b	ARN A 40
73.	Eleazar tithed, 12,000 calves				b. Shab. 54b b. Beṣ. 23a	
74.	What new teaching? (Deut. 31:12, Qoh. 12:11)	T. Soṭ. 7:9-10	Mekh. *Pisḥa* 16	b. Ḥag. 3a-b y. Ḥag. 1:1		ARN A 18 Sof. 18:8
75.	Manna	T. Soṭ. 11:2-3				
76.	Torah/seemly behavior, etc., wisdom/deeds (Jer. 17:6,8)	M. Abot 3:17				
77.	Deposition of Gamaliel: hair turned grey, tenth to Ezra, benches, sprinkler, etc.				y. Ber. 4:1 b. Ber. 27b-28a	
78.	Eleazar relinquished crown				y. Pes. 6:1	
79.	Tenth to Ezra				y. Yeb. 1:6 b. Yeb. 16a b. Men. 53a	Song Rab., p. 36
80.	Exegesis of Prov. 12:27				b. Erub. 54b b. A.Z. 19a	

	I	II	III	IV	V
81. Free the world from judgment (Isa. 51:21)				b. Erub. 64b-65a	
82. Hallel: Who said it?				b. Pes. 117a	
83. a. Sustenance of man (Ps. 136:25,13) b. Splitting of sea (Ps. 51:14-15) c. Mock festival = worship idols (Ex. 34:17-18) d. Speak maliciously--cast to dogs (Ex. 22:31, 23:1)				b. Pes. 118a	
84. Aqiva's *sukkah* on ship			y. Suk. 2:4 y. Erub. 1:7		
85. Consoles Ishmael (Jer. 34:5)			b. M.Q. 28b		
86. God's throne (Isa. 66:1) *vs*. Aqiva				b. Ḥag. 14a b. San. 38b	
87. Frog (Ex. 8:6) *vs*. Aqiva				b. San. 67b	Ex. Rab. 10:5
88. Procreation (Gen. 9:6-7)			b. Yeb. 63b		B.R. 34
89. Eleazar and Yosé the Galilean's wife				y. Ket. 11:3	B.R. 17
90. Exegeses of Job 32:2				y. Soṭ. 5:6	

	I	II	III	IV	V
91. Eleazar: a spice peddler's basket				b. Giṭ. 67a	ARN A 18
(91a. Bring *ntynyn* closer				y. Qid. 4:1)	
92. Days of Messiah 70 years (Isa. 23:15)			b. San. 99a		
93. Eliezer sick		Sifré Deut. 32	b. San 101a-b		
94. Din of Rome		Sifré Deut. 43		b. Mak. 24a-b	
95. Give reproof/receive		Sifré Deut. 1 Sifra *Qedošim* 84		b. Arak. 16b	
(95a. Disciples and peace				b. Tam. 32b)	
96. Merit of Abraham (Ps. 105:42-43)		Mekh. *Pisḥa* 16; Mekh. *Vayeḥi* 3			
97. Great is labor (Ex. 25:8)		Mekh. de R. Simeon, p. 149			ARN B 21
98. Nadab and Abihu: precedence in honor (Num. 3:4)		Sifra *Šemini*, *pereq* 1:2			
99. Sons of Aaron died for drawing near/offering (Lev. 16:1)		Sifra *Aḥare*, *par*. 1:2			
100. Parable of physician (Lev. 16:1)		Sifra *Aḥare*, *par*. 1:3			

	I	II	III	IV	V
101. Should not say, I do not wish to sin		Sifra *Qedošim, pereq* 11:22			
102. Recite part of man's praise in his presence (Gen. 7:1)		Sifré Num. 103			B.R. 32
103. In four places Moses requests		Sifré Num. 105, 138			
104. In three places Moses became angry and erred		Sifré Num. 157			
105. Divine attribute of punishment and mercy (Num. 35:26)		Sifré Num. 140			
106. Israelites feared beasts because of sin (Ex. 23:29, Job 5:23)		Sifré Deut. 50			
107. Intention for merit		Sifré Deut. 252, 283; Sifra *Vayiqra, par.* 12:13			
108. Jer. 32:17					B.R. 9
109. Three wonders: Gen. 4:1					B.R. 22
110. Raise up wicked, eyes grow dim (Gen. 27:1, Prov. 28:28)					B.R. 65
111. Joseph's robe, split sea (Gen. 37:3-4)					B.R. 84

	I	II	III	IV	V
112. Woe day of judgment/reproof (Gen. 45:3, Num. 22:30)					B.R. 93 Tanḥ. *Vayigaš* 7
(112a. When Yoḥanan b. Zakkai died					ARN A 14)
113. Moses broke the tablets (Deut. 34:12)					ARN A 2
114. Eleazar made a proclamation					Kal. Rab. 1:5
115. Four elders visit philosopher					Kal. Rab. 7:1
116. Jerusalem will expand (Jer. 3:17, Isa. 54:2, 49:12)					Pesikta deRav Kahana, pp. 221, 316
117. Ladder--Jonah and Elijah (Gen. 28:12, Jonah 2:6, II Kings 2:11)					Tanḥ. *Vayeṣe* 7
118. Parable of Baker to Song of Songs					Tanḥ. *Teṣaveh* 1
119. Way of God					Ex. R. 30:6
120. Ps. 68:6--exodus					Num. R. 3:4

i. *The Attestations: The Problem*

Before turning to an analysis of the above chart, we must make several observations about our method of "attesting" the various traditions to specific periods. First, as we said above, the appearance of a saying in a document attests to the fact that both its form and substance were known no later than the date of the redaction of that compilation. Thus items appearing in M. can be said to have reached their present form no later than approximately 200 C.E. A second method of attesting traditions is based on internal evidence within a given document. The theory behind it is as follows. If a named master other than Eleazar refers to a teaching of, or tradition about the man, we may say that the tradition is attested by the second master. If, for example, Judah refers to and modifies a saying of Eleazar which appears in M. or T. we have a warrant for assuming that the substance of the ruling was known in Judah's time. Of course, it seems that we are merely begging the question, for if we do not necessarily lend credence to the attributions which assign a teaching to Eleazar, we seem to be accepting the attribution of a saying to Judah as evidence for the reliability of attesting one of Eleazar's traditions to Judah's period at the latest. However, we may assume with some confidence that even if there was some sort of pseudepigraphic process of assigning Eleazar's name to later opinions, a tradition attested at Yavneh, for example, was known at that period and stems from the circle of Eleazar's tradents.

Thus within the various documents, we have a method of attesting some of the materials attributed to Eleazar, to a period preceding the ultimate redaction of each collection.[4] We may attest, for example, several of Eleazar's sayings in M.-T. to the periods of either Yavneh, Usha, or Bet Shearim depending on the named master who refers to those sayings. We may then claim with some certainty that the substance of that saying was known no later than the period to which we attest it. Before turning to those of Eleazar's sayings which can be attested, we must observe that there is yet a third method of attesting materials. If it can be shown that some source, *external* to the document in which a tradition has been preserved, refers to a tradition within that document, it attests a knowledge of the saying. Unfortunately, we have no references within compilations which can be dated before the redaction of M.-T. showing knowledge of either Eleazar or any of the traditions associated with him.

We first turn to the various documents and briefly sketch the types of materials attested within each. Then we discuss the further attestations within the documents, in our case mainly in M.-T.

M.-T. contain 54 separate items (45% of the total tradition). Of those, 48 deal with legal themes (92% of the total tradition in M.-T.). The Tannaitic Midrashim contain 24 traditions which appear there first (accounting for 19% of the total) of which 8 (33%) deal with legal themes. The *gemarot* contain the first mention of 27 items (23% of the total). Of the nine *beraitot* in the *gemarot*, 5 deal with legal themes (55%). Only four of the eighteen statements in the *gemarot* not designated as Tannaitic discuss legal issues (22%). Later compilations contain the first mention of 15 traditions (13% of the total traditions), two of them of a legal nature.[5]

It is evident that the materials attested by appearance in the earliest document are of a predominantly legal nature. In other words, the best traditions seem to be the legal traditions. If we examine the entire *legal* corpus we note that 71% of its items appear first in M.-T. Furthermore, six items in later compilations clearly are related in theme or form to traditions in M.-T. Of the *beraitot*, number 5 is related in theme to nos. 3 and 4; no. 12 is related in theme to no. 11; number 39 is related in form to no. 38; no. 63 is related in theme to no. 62. Of materials first appearing in the Tannaitic Midrashim, no. 18 may be related to no. 16 and no. 21 is just a list of four names as in no. 11. Thus 80% of all the legal items can be shown to either appear first in, or bear relationship to items in M.-T.[6] We shall defer our discussion of the non-legal materials and their attestations by document and first consider the further attestations of some of the legal sayings.

The second type of attestation, that is *within* a document, may take a number of forms. The best variety has a named master, standing outside the framework of the pericope, showing knowledge of one of Eleazar's traditions. Of lesser import, but still significant, is a master modifying, or commenting, on a position of Eleazar from within the structure of a pericope. The least valuable is the chain of tradition which is usually found as "x says in the name of y." As Neusner says, "Chains of tradition are different from attestations. The latter supply a general notion as to the time at which a given tradition attributed to Eliezer may have been known. The former give more precise information about the authorities responsible for the preservation and transmission of teachings attributed to Eliezer."[7] The same is of course true for traditions of Eleazar.

We have eight traditions bearing attestations to Ushan times, none to the Yavnean period. Eleven items bear chains of traditions. The following is a list of the attestations and chains:

ii. *The Attestations: The Legal Traditions*

A. *Yavneh*: There are no attestations by Yavnean masters.

B. *Usha*:

1. *Judah*: Judah attests four of Eleazar's traditions.

    a. No. 2: *M. Ber. 4:7.*

       Eleazar: The additional service only said with the congregation of the city.

> Sages: With the congregation of the city and not with the congregation of the city.
>
> Judah says in his name: Wherever there is a congregation of the city, the individual is free from the additional service.

Judah stands within the pericope but comments upon the dispute. He assigns Eleazar a different opinion and thereby indirectly attests Eleazar's ruling. His opinion is a compromise between Eleazar and the sages. Following Eleazar he says that the service is said by the individual only if the community has a congregation. As per sages' opinion, if there is no congregation the individual still must recite the service. Judah clarifies the rulings of the dispute with regard to obligations of the individual--an issue raised by neither Eleazar nor the sages but surely building on their rulings.

b. No. 10: *T. Maas. 3:8/M. Maas. 5:1.*

> T.: Judah says in the name of Eleazar: One who sends his fellow seedlings, etc., the recipient must tithe them *wdyy*.
>
> Sages say: *demai*.
>
> M.: If one gathered [produce] to send to his fellow--he is free [of the obligation to tithe].
>
> Eleazar: If their kind were being sold in the market, they are liable.

Judah in T. cites a ruling in Eleazar's name concerning produce not generally sold in the marketplace. According to the law of M., Eleazar would rule that they need not be tithed by the sender. Judah and sages dispute over the obligation of the recipient to tithe the produce. The dispute in T. clearly attests the ruling in M.

c. No. 22: *M. Beṣ. 2:8.*

Three things Eleazar permits and sages forbid...they may curry cattle on the festival day.

Judah: They may not curry cattle because it creates a wound, but they may comb.

Sages: May neither curry nor comb.

The dispute attests one of the three rulings given in Eleazar's name in the pericope. The attestation is not that compelling since the disputants stand within the framework of the pericope.

d. No. 60: *M. Ṭoh. 7:7/T. Ṭoh. 8:7.*

M.: One who leaves clothes in the wall niche Eleazar declares clean;

Sages say [unclean] until he gives the key etc.

T.: Said R. Judah: Eleazar admits to the sages that wall niches which open to one another...are unclean.

And sages say: In either case--unclean.

Judah modifies Eleazar's ruling giving a case wherein Eleazar would not rule that the clothes are unclean.

2. *Meir*: Meir attests two traditions.

a. No. 24: *T. Moʿed 1:1.*

A newly flowing spring: One may water a householder's field from it. Words of Meir.

Sages: One only waters an irrigated field whose ditches had collapsed.

Eleazar: One does not water from it [at all].

The three rulings in reverse order give progressively more lenient rulings. Meir's and sages' rulings presuppose Eleazar's prohibition. Again, however, we have the master who attests the tradition within the pericope. Not a strong attestation.

b. No. 8: *M. Sheb. 3:3.*

One may store his dung together [in a mound]. Meir prohibits unless he lowers or raises it three. If he had a small amount he may add on to it. Eleazar prohibits unless he lowers or raises it three.

The attestation here is weak since Meir's law is within the pericope and moreover may not presuppose Eleazar's. Similarly the formulation of the qualification "lower or raise" may be original to Eleazar's ruling, in which case Meir attests it, or it may be redactional.

3. *Eleazar*: Eleazar attests one pericope.

No. 58: *M. Neg. 13:6.*

A house which shades a house which bears the plague...he who enters the outer house is clean. Words of Eleazar b. Azariah. Eleazar: If a single stone from it renders it unclean by entering in, will the house not render unclean by entering in?

Eleazar's objection attests Eleazar b. Azariah's ruling.

4. *Yosé*: Yosé's single attestation is highly suspect.

No. 30: *T. Giṭ. 9:1-5/b. Giṭ. 83a.*

In b.'s version of a long pericope on conditional divorce, Eleazar says: Divorce, a thing which cuts the tie between him and her. Thus we have learned this is not divorce.

b. adds at the end of the unit: Said Rava, All [the opinions] are subject to except for Eleazar's...

tny' nmy hky: Said R. Yosé, I prefer the words of Eleazar over all the others.

Yosé's statement appears in T.'s version, attributed to Yosé the Galilean in the body of the unit.

iii. *Chains of Traditions*

A. *Yavneh*

Ilai: Ilai's two chains are not in the expected "x says in the name of y" pattern.

a. No. 6: *T. Peah 3:2.*
Ilai says he first asked Joshua and then Eliezer about which sheaves the Houses disputed. He then came and recited [Eliezer's teaching] before Eleazar who, as he reports, said, "These matters were spoken at Sinai."

It is surely not clear that Eleazar's lemma need apply to this situation. Indeed it is also applied to the next example below. We can certainly learn little about Eleazar's view from the tradition. All we know is that Ilai reports that Eleazar agreed with Eliezer.

b. No. 13: *T. Ḥal. 1:6.*
Ilai here says that he asked Joshua, then Eliezer, whether cakes of a Thank-offering and wafers of a Nazirite are subject to *ḥallah*. When he recited Eliezer's teaching before Eleazar he said, "The covenant! These matters were spoken from Mount Horeb."

See comment to a.

B. *Usha*

1. *Judah*: Judah appears in six chains.

a. No. 3: *T. Ber. 1:2.*
Judah says one time he was following Aqiva and Eleazar and the time for reciting the *shema'* arrived. They recited after the sun had appeared on the mountaintops.

The story serves as a precedent for allowing the recital of the *shema'* late in the morning.

b. No. 5: *b. Ber. 15a.*
Judah says in the name of Eleazar: One who recites the *shema'* must hear his own words + verse/*vs.* Meir.

c. No. 10: *T. Maas. 3:8.* See above under attestations.

d. No. 15: *T. Shab. 3:3.*
Said Judah, *m'śh b*: The bathhouse of *Benei Beraq*--they stopped up its openings on the eve of the festival and Aqiva and Eleazar would enter and sweat inside and go out and bathe in cold water.

The story serves as a precedent for the anonymous law which precedes it in the pericope.

e. No. 38: *T. B.M. 4:2.*
Judah cites the action of Boethus b. Zunin according to the words of Eleazar as a precedent for his ruling on how one may avoid usury in a case in which the borrower mortgages his land to the creditor.

f. No. 39: *b. B.B. 13b.*
Same as the preceding, but the action of Boethus here serves as a precedent for Judah's ruling that books of Scripture may be sewn together. (Here the statement is preceded by *m'śh b*.)

Note that in both cases Judah's opinion in the pericope is not given "in the name of Eleazar."

2. *Joshua b. Qorḥa*

a. No. 54: *T. Kel. B.B. 2:6.*
The ball, the shoe last...if they hold what is in them are unclean.
Joshua b. Qorḥa in the name of Eleazar, One immerses them as they are.

b. No. 59: *T. Neg. 7:3.*
He who puts his hand in a house afflicted with the plague...
Leazar b. R. Simeon declares clean...
And so did Joshua b. Qorḥa declare clean in the name of Eleazar.

3. *Yose b. Kefar*: one chain
No. 31: *Sifré Deut. 270.*
Yose b. Kefar says in the name of Eleazar, After betrothal [to another] she is permitted, after marriage she is forbidden/ *vs.* sages.

C. *Chains with Amoraim*: These serve only to tell us at what stage the materials were known in b. or y.
No. 12: *y. M.S. 5:5.*

No. 41, 42: Sheshet give two legal exegeses.

iv. *Summary*

If anything, I have been quite liberal in accepting several of the above instances as reliable attestations. Even so we have at most eight traditions bearing attestations to before the redaction of M. and eleven chains of tradition, attesting in all 28% of the legal traditions. This surely does not compare favorably with the percentages of attested materials attributed to Eliezer although it does seem to be on par with or slightly better than the preliminary figures available for Joshua and Ishmael.[8] Admittedly, establishing attestations can be a subjective endeavor. Each study of a man emphasizes different criteria for attestations, and this may account for some of the disparity in the fitures. It is more likely, however, that Eleazar's traditions are, by and large, not attested early because they were not accepted into the central redactional circles until the late Ushan period. On this we will have more to say later.

In Chapter VII we will discuss Eleazar's legal agendum in greater detail. Here, however, it is suggestive to note the topical concern of the best attested traditions. Of the eight, one deals with Sabbath law, two with purity laws, three with agricultural taboos, one with divorce law, and one with liturgy. Except for the last, the sample suggests a Pharisaic legal agendum.[9] The chains of traditions give a more diverse picture with three traditions dealing with liturgy or Scripture, one with usury laws, one with the Sabbath, two with purity, one with divorce, and three with agricultural laws. As we shall see later, the range of issues is even more diverse if one considers the entire legal corpus.

v. *The Non-Legal Traditions: Attestations and Chains*

We turn now to a consideration of the non-legal materials--52 items in all, 44% of the entire tradition. Appearance of the items in the various documents attests them as follows: Six appear first in M.-T. (12% of the *aggadic* traditions); 15 in the Tannaitic Midrashim (29%); 18 in the *gemarot*; 4 in the *beraita* stratum (8%), and 14 in the Amoraic stratum (27%); 13 appear first in later compilations (25%). Further attestations are as follows:

Attestations: The non-legal traditions.

Only one tradition can be attested in part:

No. 78: *y. Pes. 6:1.*

Three relinquished their crown...Said Rabbi... Eleazar. The tradition does not attest the deposition story (77) in detail. Rabbi alludes to Eleazar's stepping down from the Patriarchate, attesting at most the incident but not any of the legends connected with it.

One tradition can be attested to a specific Amora:

No. 79: *y. Yeb. 1:6.*

Jacob bar Idi in the name of Joshua b. Levi cites a *m'śh* in which Dosa alludes to the traditions about Eleazar's premature aging and his lineage from Ezra.

Chains of Traditions: There are three chains.

A. *Usha*

Simeon b. Gamaliel:

No. 98: *Sifra Šemini, pereq 1:2.*

All who take precedence in inheritance take precedence in honor. This tradition may be related to the deposition story.

B. *Bet Shearim*

Isi b. Judah or Judah the prince

No. 91: *b. Giṭ. 67a/ARN A 18.*

The pericope is merely a list of the praise of the sages.

Simeon b. Eleazar or Eleazar b. Simeon

No. 112: *B.R. 93/Tanḥ. Vayigaš 7.*

Woe to us the day of judgment/reproof.

C. Amoraim give six chains, all of exegetical traditions.

Sheshet, No. 81, No. 83

Shizbi, No. 80, No. 83

Resh Laqish, No. 108, No. 111

vi. *Summary and Conclusions*

The non-legal corpus as a whole is attested to a much later date than the legal traditions. Approximately 60% of the items are of an exegetical nature. Many are related, moreover, in some way to the deposition story. The points of contact between the *aggadic* sources and the legal items are few. As we shall demonstrate in a later chapter (pp. 279ff.), the legal and non-legal corpuses form two separate traditions about Eleazar.

The above examination of the attestations has shown that in spite of the fact that Eleazar was a Yavnean, very few of his traditions are attested even in the generation following Yavneh. The bulk of his corpus seems to have entered the stream of redaction at a later date. We turn now to the forms of the corpus.

NOTES

CHAPTER IV

[1]On the date of the redaction of M., see J. Neusner, ed., *The Modern Study of the Mishnah*, Leiden, 1973, and *Pharisees* III, p. 180. On Tosefta, see Y. N. Epstein, *Introduction to Tannitic Literature* (Hebrew), Tel Aviv, 1957, pp. 241-262.

[2]The earliest Mishnah manuscript is Kaufman, J. Beer, ed., *Faksimile-Ausgabe des Mischna Codex Kaufman A50*, reprinted Jerusalem, 1968, dating from the 11th century. For further discussion of the dating of M. MSS, see *EJ* s.v. manuscripts.

[3]On the redaction of b., see J. Neusner, ed., *The Formation of the Babylonian Talmud*, Leiden, 1970. On y., see Y. N. Epstein, *Introduction to Amoraic Literature* (Hebrew), Tel Aviv, 1962, pp. 271-334. On the Tannaitic Midrashim, see Epstein, *Introduction to Tannaitic Literature* (Hebrew), pp. 545-746.

[4]See Neusner, *Eliezer* II, pp. 92-94; *Pharisees* III, pp. 180-84; G. G. Porton, *The Legal Traditions of Rabbi Ishmael: A Form-Critical and Literary-Critical Approach*, Ph.D. dissertation, Brown, 1973, Chapter Eight; W. S. Green, *The Legal Traditions of Joshua ben Hananiah in Mishnah-Tosefta and Related Materials*, Ph.D. dissertation, Brown, 1974, Chapter Nine.

[5]For Eliezer, 67% of the materials appear first in M.-T.

[6]For Eliezer, 92% of the legal corpus relates to M.-T.

[7]*Eliezer* II, p. 73.

[8]For Eliezer, 50% of the traditions are attested; for Joshua, 21% of the legal traditions in M.-T.; for Ishmael, less than 10%.

[9]See below, p. 290.

CHAPTER V

THE FORMS

i. *Definitions: The Problem. The Charts*

In this chapter we first outline the linguistic composition of the forms associated with the legal materials attributed to Eleazar. Then we make some observations about the content of the traditions associated with the various forms: the legal agenda and the named masters. We also examine the relation of the forms of Eleazar's tradition to distinct redactional-tradental circles, comparing them to the forms of the traditions associated with Eliezer, Joshua, Ishmael, and Gamaliel. Of course before proceeding to an examination of these issues we ask whether the forms attested to a specific generation bear any distinctive traits. Finally, we examine the relationship between the forms and their redactional settings--an important and heretofore unexplored consideration in the study of traditions of an individual master.

Neusner defines a linguistic form as follows:

> A form is an arrangement of words in accord with an established, consistent, and disciplined pattern without regard to the substance or theme of the consequent sentence. If it can be shown that a single recurrent pattern is followed for many different rules, and that the literary traits of the pattern bear no intrinsic relationship to the content of the rules, then we have a form.[1]

The forms used for the expression of Eleazar's legal traditions fall into three main categories. First we have the standard *attributive form*. Dicta of Eleazar standing neither in dispute with a contrary opinion nor in close relationship to a ruling on a similar matter in the name of another master are introduced by the words *Eleazar says*, *expounded*, *decreed*, or *said Eleazar*, or followed by *the words of Eleazar*.[2] We call this form, form A. Naturally the standard attributive form also serves as a building block for the dispute form to which we turn next.

The majority of traditions are preserved in the *dispute form*. This form takes on a wide range of variations, all of which, however, adhere to the minimum requirement that the form presents Eleazar's view together with an opposing opinion. The best disputes consist of *x said* or *says + lemma vs. y said* or *says + contrary rule*. The unit may or may not include a protasis stating the problem. Several examples have *x declares clean* or *decreed x/decreed y*. Traditions in this form are grouped under the letter B below.

Closely related to the dispute form of B are those traditions giving Eleazar's ruling as a *gloss to an anonymous law*.[3] The form usually appears as *rule + Eleazar says + lemma* or *declares clean* or *invalid*. The examples of this form and several variations of it are listed under letter C.

Under D we have listed all of the traditions which make some attempt at using the dispute form but do so rather loosely. Based on our literary analysis in the chapters above (II and III), we have shown that most of the traditions included in this list show signs of artificial construction joining independent conflicting views together or merely place related rulings in juxtaposition without creating a dispute. While many attempt to follow the form characteristically associated with the dispute, we may be justified in referring to these traditions only as *combinations or juxtapositions of independent rulings*.

The last form (E) is *Stories*. Many of these serve as precedents for a ruling and are introduced by the word *m'śh*. The traditions are herewith listed according to the forms outlined above.

A

The standard attributive form:

We have three items consisting of a ruling with an attributive formula.

T. Arak. 4:27--*And so Eleazar would say* + rulings (*re*: proper conduct).

M. Neg. 13:6--Ruling + *words of Eleazar b. Azariah* + *said Eleazar* gloss (*re*: house which shades, etc.) of independent law preceding it.

y. Shab. 9:3--*Eleazar says* + ruling + *concerning the teaching of Eleazar* + gloss.

Five pericopae make use of the simple attributive form in the context of an exegetical legal ruling.

Mekh. *Nez*. 1--exegetical legal ruling; verse + *Eleazar says* + exegesis.

Mekh. De R. Simeon, p. 163--*Eleazar says* + ruling + verse; standard exegesis.

b. Mak. 23a--Standard exegetical form: *Said Sheshet in name of Eleazar* + question + two verses (*from whence/as it is written*) (*re*: strap for lashes).

b. Yeb. 4a--same as above (*re*: levir with boils).

T. Arak. 4:26--*Eleazar says* + verse + three exegetical remarks.

M. Ket. 4:6--Protasis + *Eleazar expounded* (*re*: *ketubah*).

We have one instance in which Eleazar cites the exegesis of another master.

M. Ber. 1:5--*Said Eleazar* + citation of Ben Zoma's legal exegesis (verse + exposition + sages say + exposition).

Finally there is one example of the form *Eleazar decreed* standing alone not in the context of a dispute.

Kallah 1:3--*Eleazar decreed* etc. + ruling.

B

Disputes: The following are the clearest examples of the use of the dispute form in the transmission of materials attributed to Eleazar.

Four pericopae use the form *Eleazar says* or *declares clean* + *sages say*, etc.

M. Ber. 4:7--*Eleazar says/and sages say/Judah says in his name*; Judah glosses the dispute with a compromise.

M. Shab. 4:2--Dispute: *Eleazar says* + gloss + *sages say* (*re*: removing food from insulation on Sabbath).

M. M.Q. 1:2--Dispute: *Eleazar/sages say*(*s*) (*re*: dig water channel on seventh year/festival).

M. Ṭoh. 7:7--Protasis + *Eleazar declares clean* + *sages say*, etc. The dispute is not balanced and may be a juxtaposition of two independent rulings (*re*: clothes in niche).

Four items are in the form *protasis* or *question* + *two opposing opinions*.

b. Yeb. 86a-b--Protasis + ruling + *words of Aqiva* + *Eleazar says* + lemma + gloss. Dispute followed by Amoraic discussion + story (*re*: tithes).

y. M.S. 5:5--*Abbahu said, Joshua and Leazar disputed* + *Joshua said* + *Leazar said* + debate (same issue as above, different attribution).

M. Neg. 8:9--Dispute: Protasis + *Ishmael/Eleazar says* balanced apodoses (*re*: comes all white).

M. Yad. 4:3--*On that day* + question + *decreed Tarfon* + *decreed Eleazar* + debate between Ishmael and Eleazar + debate between Tarfon and Eleazar + Joshua defends Tarfon + they were polled + story about Eliezer. Combination of a dispute (balanced), three debates and a story.

We have three examples of exegetical disputes.

Mekh. De R. Simeon, p. 13--Dispute: verse + *Eleazar says* + exegesis + *Said to him Aqiva* + contrary exegesis.

Mekh. De R. Simeon, p. 179--Verse + *Ben Azzai says* + ruling + *said to him Aqiva* + question. This seems to be a variation of an exegetical dispute although the attributions are highly questionable.

b. Ker. 7b--two exegetical disputes: Verse + *Isi* (!) *says* + lemma + gloss + *Eleazar says* + lemma + gloss; verse + Eleazar/sages on same matter (*re*: reviling the Lord).

C

The gloss to an anonymous ruling:

In six instances Eleazar's ruling serves as a gloss to the preceding anonymous law, presenting a differing opinion.

M. Maas. 5:1--Eleazar qualifies an anonymous law (liability to tithes).

M. Ket. 5:1--Anonymous ruling + *Eleazar says* + contrary ruling (*re*: sum of *ketubah*).

M. Naz. 6:2--Anonymous law + *mšnh r'šwnh* + Aqiva + anonymous law + Eleazar, *re*: liability of Nazirite. Combination of two disputes: Eleazar *vs.* first anonymous law + Aqiva *vs. mšnh r'šwnh*. In its appearance Eleazar seems to gloss the second anonymous law and disputes it (cf. T. and Sifré).

M. Men. 13:6--Anonymous rule + *Eleazar says* + contrary rule (*re*: pledge of Burnt offering).

M. Miq. 3:2--Anonymous rule + *Eleazar declares invalid until*, etc. Eleazar's gloss of the preceding law does not balance it.

M. Uqṣ. 1:5--Anonymous ruling + *Eleazar declares clean*, etc. Eleazar glosses the preceding law and adds an exception.

One item appears to be a gloss + verse following an anonymous ruling, but in actuality gives a ruling on a related issue, not contrary to the first law.

M. Shab. 19:3--Anonymous law + *Eleazar says* + lemma + verse (on related issue).

There is one example of a tradent citing Eleazar's ruling as a gloss to an anonymous law and one item in which a tradent cites Eleazar's rule as a gloss to a dispute. There are also two instances in which a tradent cites Eleazar's comment on a Houses' dispute.

T. Kel. B.B. 2:6--Anonymous law + *Joshua b. Qorḥa in name of Eleazar* + gloss to ruling.

T. Neg. 7:3--*Joshua b. Qorḥa declares clean in name of Eleazar.* Third person report as gloss to dispute (Rabbi Leazar b. Simeon).

T. Peah 3:2--Ilai asks Joshua and Eliezer about Houses' dispute. Ilai then recites before Eleazar, who comments.

T. Ḥal. 1:6--same as above.

Finally, in one pericope Eleazar appears with another master as a tradent of the ruling of a third party citing his ruling as a gloss to an anonymous law.

b. Shabuot 35b--ruling + verse + contrary gloss Ḥaninah and Eleazar in name of Eleazar the Modaite (*re*: divine names).

D

Combinations or juxtapositions of independent rulings:

Several rulings introduced by one protasis, question, or narrative introduction (*once* or *m'śh*) (twelve items):

M. Sheb. 1:8--Protasis (question) + *Eleazar/Joshua/Aqiva says.* Eleazar responds to the question. Aqiva and Joshua do not. Materials from two circles are redacted together here.

Mekh. *Shab.* 1--*Once* + *Ishmael, Aqiva, and Eleazar walking* + question + three separate answers (*Answered x and said...*) with interpolations (*re*: mortal danger on Sabbath)--an artificial unit.

M. Beṣ. 2:8--Protasis: *Three things Eleazar permits and sages forbid* + dispute between Judah and sages on the second item.

T. Mo'ed 1:1--Three rulings on newly flowing spring (Meir, sages, Eleazar) with common protasis + lemma + *words of Meir* + *sages say* + lemma + *Eleazar says* + lemma.

T. Soṭ. 1:2--Question + list of seven different answers.

T. Giṭ. 9:1-5--Protasis + ruling (Eliezer) + gloss + protasis (story) + four elders... + *Said Tarfon* + *Said Yosé* + *Eleazar says* + *Said Aqiva*, etc.--an artificial construction (*re*: divorce).

M. B.Q. 6:4--Question + four separate answers (Eleazar, Eliezer, Aqiva, Simeon). The second and third answers respond directly to the question and with it would have made a balanced dispute.

M. Mak. 1:10--Protasis + two independent rules + gloss (Eleazar, Tarfon, and Aqiva, Simeon b. Gamaliel, *re*: Sanhedrin).

M. Kel. 3:8--Protasis + *Eleazar declares unclean* + *Aqiva* + *Yosé*; two independent rulings and a gloss (*re*: funnel).

M. Neg. 7:2--Protasis + glosses + three independent rulings (Eleazar, Eleazar Ḥisma, Aqiva); Eleazar's ruling can stand alone with the protasis. The other two go together (*re*: color of spot).

M. Miq. 8:3--Law + *words of Eleazar* + *Ishmael says* + *lemma* + *Aqiva says* + lemma (as gloss to Ishmael). Eleazar stands independent of the rulings of the other two (*re*: discharge of semen).

M. Maksh. 6:6--Ruling + list + three independent rulings disputing items on the list (Eliezer, Eleazar, Simeon).

Rulings on related issues juxtaposed: (three items)

M. Sheb. 3:3--Rulings on three related issues combined together with common requirement (raising or lowering a heap): Simeon *vs*. sages/Meir/Eleazar.

b. M.Q. 24b--Three rulings on infant's funeral (Aqiva, Simeon b. Eleazar, Eleazar) independent but related thematically. (Sem. 3:4 gives two more related rulings.)

M. Arak. 8:4--Two independent, related traditions: Ruling + *words of Eliezer/said Eleazar* (*re*: dedicating property).

Exegesis *vs.* independent rule, or exegesis of the same verse redacted together (three items);

b. Qid. 17b--verse + two independent exegeses (anonymous/Eleazar).

Sifra *Ṣav. pereq* 11:4-6--*Aqiva says* + long exegetical discussion + *said to him Eleazar* etc. + *three laws are traditions from Sinai.* Eleazar agrees with Aqiva's ruling but attacks the use of exegesis.

M. Ker. 2:5--Question + answer + verse + *words of Aqiva* + *Ishmael says* + lemma + *Eleazar says* + lemma. Eleazar repeats Aqiva's view. Aqiva and Ishmael are cast in an artificial dispute (*re*: definition of bondwoman).

A tradent cites Eleazar's ruling *vs.* a contrary opinion (three items). (In form these are disputes, but the tradental attribution attests them at the earliest at Usha. Therefore we include them here.):

b. Ber. 15a--Judah cites Eleazar's ruling + verse. Meir's contrary opinion is attached by *Said to him R. Meir.*

T. Maas. 3:8--*Judah in the name of Eleazar vs.* sages. Judah modifies Eleazar's ruling of M. Maas. 5:1. Sages' opinion appended (cf. y. Maas. 5:1).

Sifré Deut. 270--*Yosé b. Kefar in name of Eleazar* + ruling + verse *vs. sages say* + ruling + question, answer + verse; a dispute using a tradition of Eleazar's.

E

Stories:

m'śh + story, generally serving as a precedent (seven examples):

T. Ber. 1:2--Judah gives a *m'śh* as a precedent (cf. y. Ber. 3a).

T. Ber. 1:4--*m'śh*: Ishmael and Eleazar: The pericope has a debate but no dispute. Eleazar gives a parable, Ishmael cites a Houses' dispute.

M. M.S. 5:9--General rule + *m'śh* (Gamaliel, Joshua, Aqiva) + gloss (Joshua speaks of Eleazar). Serves as precedent that tithes go to the priest.

T. Shab. 3:3--Anonymous law + *Said Judah*: *m'śh b* + narrative about Eleazar and Aqiva in bathhouse on Sabbath + gloss (harmonizing story with preceding law). A precedent.

M. Erub. 4:1--Protasis + *Gamaliel and Eleazar say* + lemma + *Joshua and Aqiva say* + lemma, followed by *m'śh š*: protasis + Gamaliel and Eleazar traversed + Joshua and Aqiva did not + gloss (note: Patriarchs together).

Sifra *'Emor, pereq* 16:2--*m'śh b*: Four rabbis on boat + narrative. A precedent.

T. B.M. 4:2--*Said Judah* + second person report of Eleazar's ruling serving as a precedent for Judah's ruling. (b. Meg. 27b gives it in *m'śh b* form.)

b. B.B. 13b--Judah + *m'śh b* as above.

No introductory formula but similar to above (three items):

b. Yeb. 86a-b--Story (Aqiva and Eleazar *re*: tithes) illustrates preceding dispute between the two.

y. M.S. 5:5--Story (Aqiva and Eleazar *re*: tithes). Variation of above.

M. Shab. 5:4--Anonymous ruling + statement about Eleazar to the contrary (his cow *went out with its strap on Sabbath*) + gloss (*against the will of the sages*).

T. A.Z. 4:1--ruling + third person report; Eleazar's action as precedent.

Narrative including direct discourse (one item):

ARN A 25--(In context of story of Eliezer's death) *Said to him Eleazar* + question + *he said, Clean* (*re*: shoe).

Mention of Eleazar's name (no apparent association to any ruling of Eleazar: three items):

T. Kel. B.B. 2:2--*m'śh b*: Four elders sitting in store of Eleazar.

M. Yad. 3:5--Simeon b. Azzai gives tradition from 72 elders on the day they place Eleazar in the academy, etc.

M. Yad. 4:2--same as above (cf. M. Zeb. 1:3).

The Forms of the Non-Legal Traditions

A

The standard attributive form:

We have one non-exegetical tradition in this form and eighteen exegetical traditions:

T. Soṭ. 11:2-3--*Eleazar says*, They drew a parable (*re*: manna).

M. Yoma 8:9--*Eleazar expounded* + verse + lemma (*re*: atonement).

(b. Yoma 86a--Question + answer *re*: atonement.)

M. Ned. 3:11--*Eleazar says* + verse; standard exegetical form.

M. Abot. 3:17--*Eleazar says* + balanced lemma + *he used to say* + lemma + verse + lemma + verse.

Mekh. *Pis*. 16--*Eleazar says* + lemma + verse.

Mekh. de R. Simeon, p. 149--*Eleazar says* + lemma + verse.

Sifra *Aḥare*, *par*. 1:3--Verse + *Eleazar used to say*, One may draw a parable, etc.

Sifra *Qedošim*, *pereq*. 11:22--*Eleazar says* + whence + lemma + verse + gloss.

Sifré Num. 103--*Eleazar says* + lemma + verse + lemma + verse.

Sifré Num. 105--*Eleazar says* + In four places, etc. + verse + lemma (four times).

Sifré Num. 157--*Eleazar says* + In three places, etc. + verse + what does it say? + verse (three times).

Sifré Num. 140--Verse + *Said Eleazar* + lemma (*qal veḥomer*).

Sifré Deut. 252--Verse + *Said Eleazar* + lemma (*qal veḥomer*). (Sifré Deut. 283--*Said Eleazar*, Whence +

lemma + verse + lemma; Sifra *Vayiqra par.* 12:13--*Eleazar says* + *behold it says* + verse + lemma.)

B.R. 22--Verse + *Said Eleazar* + lemma.

B.R. 65--Verse + *Eleazar said* + lemma + interpolation + verse + gloss.

ARN A 2--*Eleazar says* + lemma + verse + lemma (in context of similar forms).

Tanḥ. *Vayeṣé* 7--Verse + *Said Eleazar* + lemma + verse + verse + lemma + verse.

Num. R. 3:4--Verse + *Said Eleazar* + lemma.

Seven more traditions appear in the form *x said in the name of Eleazar*, all exegetical.

b. Erub. 54b--Shizbi in the name of Eleazar, Why is it written? + verse + answer.

b. Erub. 64a-65b--Sheshet in name of Eleazar + lemma + verse.

b. Pes. 118a--Shizbi in name of Eleazar + lemma + two verses + Eleazar said + lemma + two verses + and said Sheshet in name of Eleazar + lemma + two verses + said Sheshet in name of Eleazar + lemma + two verses.

Sifra *Šemini, pereq* 1:2--Simeon b. Gamaliel in name of Eleazar, Behold it says + verse + lemma + law + question, etc. (*re*: sons of Aaron).

B.R. 9--Resh Laqish in name of Eleazar + verse + verse.

B.R. 84--Verse + Resh Laqish in name of Eleazar + lemma + verse (also: Resh Laqish in name of Eleazar + verse + question + answer + gloss).

B.R. 93--Verse + Simeon b. Eleazar in name of Eleazar in name of Abba Kohen + Woe, etc. + lemma + verse (three times) (also: Said Eleazar + Woe + lemma).

B

Disputes:

There is one non-exegetical item and five exegetical:

Tanḥ. *Teṣaveh* 1--*Said Aqiva* + lemma + said *Eleazar* + parable.

b. Ḥag. 14a--lemma + *words of Aqiva* + *Said to him Eleazar* + objection + contrary exegesis.

b. San. 67a--*Aqiva says* + same as above.

y. Soṭ. 5:6--*Aqiva expounded* + verse + exegesis + *Said to him Eleazar* + objection + exegesis.

Sifré Deut. 50--Two verses + *words of Jacob* + *Said to him Eleazar* + question + verse + lemma + verse.

Pesikta de Rav Kahana, p. 211--Eleazar b. Azariah and Eleazar HaModai + one says + lemma + one says + lemma + verse + question + verse.

Pesikta, p. 316--*dylmh* + Leazar b. Azariah and Leazar HaModai sitting + verse + said b. Azariah to HaModai + question + he said to him + lemma + verse.

C

Glosses: None.

D

Combinations or juxtapositions of independent lemmas:

There are four items combining independent lemmas and three clearly artificial pericopae.

b. Yeb. 63b--Eliezer/Eleazar/b. Azzai *says* + lemma + verse.

b. San. 99a--*Eliezer says* + lemma + verse + *Eleazar says* + lemma + verse + gloss + Rabbi says, etc. (*re*: messiah).

Sifré Deut. 1--Verse + lemma + said Tarfon/Eleazar/ Aqiva + exclamation + lemma (*re*: reproof).

Sifra *Aḥare*, *par*. 1:2--Verse + *Yosé the Galilean says* + lemma + *Aqiva says* + three verses + lemma + *Eleazar says* + lemma (*re*: death of Aaron's sons).

b. Pes. 117a--Hallel: Who said it? + seven answers with same verses.

b. M.Q. 28b--Protasis + glosses + Ishmael opened + saying + Answered Tarfon/Yosé/Eleazar/Aqiva + verse + Is not the matter a *qal veḥomer*? + lemma (an artificial construction).

Sifré Deut. 32--Protasis + *answered* Tarfon/Joshua/
Eleazar/Aqiva (*re*: Eliezer).

E

Stories: Seven are preceded by *m'śh b* and six are not.

T. Soṭ. 7:9-10--*m'śh b* + story + exegeses.

y. Ber. 4:1--*m'śh b*: + deposition narrative.

b. Ber. 27b-28a--*m'śh b* + deposition narrative.

y. Suk. 2:4--*m'śh b* + Eleazar and Aqiva on ship.

Sifré Deut. 43--Story of rabbis entering Rome (*wkbr*).

Kal. Rab. 1:5--*m'śh b* + story + Eleazar made a proclamation.

Kal. Rab. 7:1--*m'śh b* (four elders, philosopher).

Ex. R. 30:6--*m'śh b*: four rabbis.

b. Shab. 54b--Said Rav: Eleazar used to tithe...; biographical tradition.

y. Pes. 6:1--Protasis + list of three + said Rabbi, No, etc. (*re*: deposition).

y. Yeb. 1:6--Dosa recites verses on three rabbis (Joshua, Aqiva, Eleazar).

b. Yeb. 16a--as above.

b. Men. 53a--Amoraic tradition that Eleazar was tenth to Ezra.

y. Ket. 11:3--Story (*re*: Yosé's wife).

(y. Qid. 4:1--Huna said in the days of Eleazar, etc.)

Three other items are traditions about Eleazar.

M. Soṭ. 9:15--When Eleazar died, etc.

b. Ber. 57b--If one sees Eleazar in a dream (in list of rabbis).

ARN A 18--Judah the prince used to list the praise of the sages, etc. = b. Giṭ. 67a.

The following chart summarizes the forms:

Form	*% of Total Traditions*	*% of Legal Traditions*
A	28	15
B	16	16
C	10	18
D	22	31
E	21	19
none	5	4

The discussion below will deal exclusively with the legal traditions, except where noted.

Our analysis of the above catalogue of forms proceeds as follows. First we make some general comments concerning the distribution of the traditions amongst the various types of forms; the materials preserved in each form are listed according to the attestations; we examine the legal agendum of the traditions and ask whether a particular form has a predilection for a certain subject matter. Then we list the masters associated with Eleazar in the items in forms B and D and compare the use of forms in Eleazar's tradition with the legal corpuses of Eliezer, Joshua, Ishmael, and Gamaliel. Based on this comparison, we may be able to make some historical observations. Finally, we turn to the relationship between form and redactional setting.

For, as we see from the list above, about 65% of the material has been preserved in some variation of the dispute form (B+C+D). However, upon closer examination we note that almost half of that sample is given in list D which represents the loosest variations of the dispute. Few of the traditions even in form B exhibit the traits of the dispute which we have come to expect based on a study of the Houses' disputes. That is to say, few contain evenly balanced apodoses or show signs of a conscious attempt to establish a mnemonic pattern. Some lack a protasis. Others contain one or more glosses interior to the pericope. We return to these observations at the end of this chapter.

ii. *Forms and Attestations: The Strata*

We turn now to an examination of the forms based on their attestations. The following chart summarizes each group of forms according to the attestations using the numbers assigned to the traditions in the preceding chapters:

	A	*B*	*C*	*D*	*E*
Attested to Usha	58	2, 60	9	8, 22, 24 30	- - -
Chains	- - -	- - -	6, 13, 54, 59, 31, 5	- - -	3, 15, 38, 39
M.-T.	1, 26, 48, 49	14, 23, 57, 67	16, 27, 28, 45, 61, 68	7, 29, 36, 40, 47, 52, 56, 62, 64	4, 11, 17, 44
Tannaitic Midrashim	32, 34	37, 51	- - -	18, 46	12, 21
b. and y.	41, 42, 63	12, 20	43	25, 33	- - -
Other	35	- - -	- - -	- - -	55

While the sample is small, we may still note the following: 45% of forms A are attested to M.-T. or earlier; 55% of form B; 92% of form C; 71% of form D; 62% of form E. Taking B, C, and D together, all the variations of the dispute, 73% is attested to M.-T. or earlier. Now these figures are suggestive and may indicate that materials preserved in variations of the dispute-form are more reliable since they may be better attested. It should be noted that our definition of attestations (see above p. 223), however, allows us to better attest traditions in which another party is present, e.g., the disputes. Therefore, the results are inclusive.

iii. *Forms and the Legal Agendum*

The legal agendum encompassed in the materials preserved in each form is illustrated in the following chart which should allow us to see if one form tends to preserve legal material within a proscribed range. A fuller discussion of the legal agendum will be given in Chapter VII. (The total number of discrete traditions is listed for each instance.)

	A	B	C	D	B+C+D	E
Liturgy	1	1	--	1	2	2
Agricultural laws	--	3	3	4	10	2
Sabbath, festival	1	1	1	2	4	4
Divorce, etc.	3	--	1	3	4	--
Civil and commercial	3	1	--	2	3	2
Sacrifice	--	1	1	1	3	--
Purity laws	1	2	4	4	10	1
Other	2	1	2	4	7	1

No significant pattern can be seen within any *one* of the forms. However, taken together the disputes tend heavily towards agricultural and purity laws with Sabbath and divorce laws next. No form though can be said with certainty to favor a specific legal area.

iv. *Forms and the Named Masters*

We next ask whether within the items in which Eleazar appears with another named sage (B and D) there is a tendency to favor a specific name or group of names. We also wish to know whether the clear disputes (B) show any preference not reflected in the artificial composites (D). The following chart summarizes the frequency of the masters in both forms B and D. (Note that we have distinguished between Di and Dii, iii, and iv. Di alone attempts to represent itself as a dispute by combining independent opposing rules. Dii, iii, and iv clearly preserve the autonomy of Eleazar's saying, merely juxtaposing it with another rule. Different redactional processes are indicated here.)

	B	*Di*	*Dii, ii, iv*	*Total*
Aqiva	3	9	3	15
Joshua	1	2		3
Ishmael	1	2	1	4
Eliezer		2		2
Ṭarfon	1	2		3
Sages	5	2	3	10
Ben Azzai, Judah b. Batyra, Ḥanan b. Menaḥem, Eleazar Ḥismȧ, Simeon b. Ġamaliel, Yosé (the Galilean)		1 (each)		6
Simeon b. Eleazar			1	1
Meir		1	2	3
Simeon		2		2
Yosé		1		1

Appearing with Eleazar in the items in dispute-form (B) are only Yavneans and sages. Aqiva predominates among the named masters although sages appear as the disputants in almost half the cases. This pattern breaks down completely in the items in group D as several minor figures and even Ushans appear in the same pericope with Eleazar. We can correlate the loosening up of formal characteristics with a diversification of names within items in D. Aqiva dominates the list, appearing in 12 of 21 traditions in D, which indicates the hand of Aqivan redactors at work. The appearance of Ushans, the loosening of the form and the diversity of names all seem to argue either for a later date of redaction for materials classified under D, or for an unusual redactional process transmitting Eleazar's traditions at an earlier date. In the concluding section of this chapter we return to this issue.

v. *Forms of Eleazar's Tradition and Those of Other Yavneans*

Our next area of investigation with regard to the forms is how the forms described above for Eleazar compared with the forms of the traditions of other masters. First we compare the proportion of forms used within various traditions. How much of a tradition has been transmitted in the dispute-form and variations of it? How much as stories? How much in the standard attributive form, autonomous of the tradition of another master? The following chart summarizes the proportions in the traditions of five major Yavnean figures. (Note that the first column gives the percentage for the entire Eleazar corpus, legal and non-legal so that it may be compared with Eliezer's traditions for which the percentage of the whole is also given. The third column gives the percentage of the legal traditions appearing in the various forms so that a comparison may be made with the three other masters' traditions for which we only have similar figures.)

	Eleazar: total	Eliezer[4]	Eleazar: legal	Joshua[5]	Ishmael[6]	Gamaliel[7]
Standard attributive form	28	7	15	20	9	9
Variations of dispute	48	86	65	60	56	45
Stories	21	6	19	5	8	49

The chart shows two facts clearly. First, a significantly large percentage of Eleazar's traditions are preserved independent of any conjunction with another named master. The bulk of the traditions thus preserved are non-legal and found first in later documents, not in M.-T. There is nothing unusual about the proportion of legal traditions of Eleazar preserved by themselves. Second, the proportion of stories in Eleazar's traditions is significantly greater than that of any other master, save Gamaliel. Kanter has suggested that the story or *m'śh* may derive from the courthouse setting rather than the schoolhouse. Thus it is not surprising that Gamaliel, a patriarch, is associated with a large number of such traditions.[8] Eleazar was alleged to have served as patriarch and the proportion of *m'śh*-stories may in some way reflect that tradition for it is significantly different from that expected for a Yavnean master.

The chart seems to show, however, a remarkably consistent proportion of the materials of all of the masters (except Gamaliel) preserved in variations of the dispute-form. It does not give, though, an accurate picture of the situation. Eliezer's and Joshua's traditions contain a significant proportion of standard disputes with attention to balance and little variation of form (approximately 35% for each). Ishmael's corpus also holds a good percentage of pericopae in the dispute-form. Porton has shown a sizable number of these to be "artificial" disputes.[9] The fact remains, however, that somewhere in the process of redaction, the traditions of Eliezer, Joshua, and Ishmael became attached to traditions of other masters within the tight limits of the dispute-form.

Eleazar's traditions show a much lower incidence of disputes cast within well-defined limits. The variation of the form is much greater. It takes on a looser character. Neusner has argued that the looser form comes later than the tighter one. With less attention paid to balance and construction, more variation of form enters the pattern of expression.[10]

vi. *Forms and their Redactional Contexts*

a. *The Compilations*

We may further refine our results by asking about the distribution of the forms within the various *documents* before us. The following charts give the percentages of the forms within the documents:

Percentage of the total number of each form (read across):

	M.-T. (42%)	Midrashim (18%)	b. (20%)	y. (8%)	Later Compilations (13%)	Total no.
A	25% (9)	33% (12)	14% (5)	3% (1)	25% (9)	36
B	35% (6)	17% (3)	24% (4)	12% (2)	12% (2)	17
C	92% (11)	- - -	8% (1)	- - -	- - -	12
D	54% (15)	18% (5)	29% (8)	- - -	- - -	28
E	33% (9)	7% (2)	22% (6)	22% (6)	15% (4)	27

Percentage of the forms within each document (read down):

	M.-T.	Midrashim	b.	y.	Later Compilations	Total %
A	18%	55%	21%	11%	60%	30%
B	12%	14%	17%	22%	13%	14%
C	22%	--	4%	--	--	10%
D	30%	22%	33%	--	--	23%
E	18%	9%	25%	66%	16%	23%
Totals	50%	22%	24%	9%	15%	

With these charts before us we may ask whether the formulaic traits of our corpus derive mainly from the tradental process of formulation, or do the documents impose their own forms on the materials? Several observations may immediately be made. First, it is clear that the Midrashim favor form A, the standard attributive form. M.-T. accounts for almost all of the traditions in form C, the gloss form. Together with b., M.-T. contains a great majority of the disputes (form B) and items in form D. It is clear, therefore, that any study of the forms must pay careful attention to the preferences of each document.

b. *Mishnah: A Detailed Study--Redactor* versus *Tradent*

Turning to M.-T., specifically, we may further ask whether the formulaic traits of redaction within the various chapters under analysis dictate the form in which Eleazar's tradition appears. It is clear that Eleazar's corpus seems to bear evidence of loose redaction, unlike the traditions attributed to other Yavnean masters. May we say that Eleazar's corpus went through a different tradental process and thus account for the deviation from the expected norm? Or do the contexts in which the traditions appear impose their formal traits on Eleazar's material?

Let us look at the chapters in M. in which Eleazar's traditions appear and get an idea of the general state of the use to which his traditions were put within the framework of the redactional preferences and traits of the tractates.[11] Can we show the formulary patterns of the tractates to be the determining factor in the present formulation of a significant number of Eleazar's traditions? If so, we may then argue that it is not the tradental process which accounts for the variation in the forms of Eleazar's corpus, but the redactional process. Accordingly, we may suggest that some of Eleazar's materials entered the redactional stream at a point that allowed the hand of the redactor to reshape them freely.

Of the forms enumerated above, the one which we have called the "loosest" is form D (combinations or juxtapositions of independent lemmas). Traditions in forms A, B, C, and E are common among the Yavneans. Thus, we turn first to those listed under D to inquire as to whether their traits derive from tradental hand, or from editorial hands. Of the fifteen items listed under D in M.-T., eleven may be found in M. They are listed below along with a brief description of their redactional context:

1. *M. Sheb. 1:8*: This pericopae appears at the conclusion of the chapter. The protasis takes the form of a question, "Until when may they be called saplings," followed by the responses of Eleazar, Aqiva, and Joshua. Chapter Two begins with a question relating to a different matter but phrased in exactly the same fashion as the preceding tradition, "Until when..." Thus redactional considerations have clearly entered into the formulation of the pericope.
2. *M. Sheb. 3:3*: Chapter Three is an Ushan chapter replete with several attributions to Meir, Judah, and Yosé

(3:1); Simeon (3:2); Simeon, Meir, and Eleazar b. Azariah (!) (3:3); Simeon b. Gamaliel (3:4); Meir and Yosé (3:9). The redactional language of the pericope ("One may make...") is used throughout to express the rulings of Simeon, Meir, and finally Eleazar. Clearly Eleazar has been inserted into an Ushan unit.

3. *M. Beṣ. 2:8*: M. 2:6 has a list of three things in which Gamaliel rules stringently followed by his three lenient rulings in 2:7. 2:8 then gives us three lenient rulings of Eleazar. The work of a redactor is evident.
4. *M. B.Q. 6:4*: The chapter is characterized by the use of the phrase, "He who..." to introduce a case. Our pericope has "He who ignites a fire on his property... how far may the fire spread"? The protasis is shaped by the needs of redaction.
5. *M. Mak. 1:10*: The pericope is clearly a miscellany at the end of a chapter. The rules in the chapter deal with witnesses. Then a ruling is given that the Sanhedrin applies in the Land and outside, followed by our pericope, "A Sanhedrin which executes..."
6. *M. Arak. 8:4*: Our pericope gives two related rulings on the limits for dedicating one's property. 8:5 begins, "He who dedicates..." 8:7 has "One may dedicate..." as in our pericope. The tradition serves as an introduction to a new unit within the chapter.
7. *M. Ker. 2:5*: Eleazar says, "All the forbidden relations were explicitly mentioned and what was left out?..." 2:4 uses the phrase "all the forbidden relations (*kl h'rywt*)" three times and 2:6 has it once. The language used by Eleazar may be shaped by the linguistic preference of the chapter.
8. *M. Kel. 3:8*: The chapter is characterized by apocopation--case + clean/unclean. Eleazar's rule is given as follows: "A funnel which was stopped up...Eleazar declare unclean (*mṭm'*)." The pericope makes use of the chapter's trait of apocopation.
9. *M. Neg. 7:2*: The pericope has, "If their appearance changed + glosses + clean/unclean." 7:1 has "If they...

clean/unclean." Likewise 7:3 has the apocopated construction, "Case + must be shut up/subject to decision." The apocopation of the chapter is evident.

10. *M. Miq. 8:3*: The pericope has the formulary pattern "He who...clean/unclean" three times in succession. 8:4 also gives a case + clean/unclean. The apocopation of the redactor shows up in this pericope as well.
11. *M. Maksh. 6:6*: This classic example gives a list of things which render unclean and susceptible to uncleanness. The list is then glossed separately by Eliezer, Eleazar, and Simeon. The next pericope gives us the contrary list of things which render neither unclean nor susceptible. It too is heavily glossed (by Yosé, the Ushan Eleazar and Simeon b. Eleazar).

Thus of the eleven pericopae in form D (combinations and juxtapositions of independent rulings), nine show traces of reworking by the hands of the redactor; only two (5 and 6) do not. As we expected, those traditions which most markedly deviate in form from the parameters established among Yavneans through the analysis of the traditions of the major figures of that period, follow most closely the formulary patterns of the chapters and tractates in which they appear.

Let us turn now to the other forms. Do we find that the bulk of the traditions, regardless of form, reveals traces of the hand of the redactor at work? Or are most of the traditions preserved in M. formally and linguistically distinct from their present context? Can we make a case for the claim that the majority of the forms are the work of redactional processes, or have tradentally shaped materials been inserted virtually unaltered into appropriate contexts? The evidence clearly shows that the latter is the case in a statistically significant number of instances as the list which follows illustrates:

The standard attributive form (A)

1. *M. Ber. 1:5*: The pericope does not follow the formulary pattern of the chapter, which uses the present participle.
2. *M. Yoma 8:9*: The item is appended to the tractate and shares no distinctive formulary traits with it.
3. *M. Ket. 4:6*: Formally distinct.
4. *M. Ned. 3:11*: Redacted in a long pericope but preserves its own formal traits.
5. *M. Abot 3:17*: Shows exceptional balance but no direct link to the rest of the chapter.
6. *M. Neg. 13:6*: *Follows* the pattern of the chapter ("he who enters etc.").

Disputes (B)

1. *M. Ber. 4:7*: Unrelated to the preceding or following pericopae in form, language, or content. Comes at the end of a chapter on prayer and introduces a new issue, the additional service.
2. *M. Shab. 4:2*: The dispute follows a list enumerating the articles with which one may insulate pots. Formally and linguistically, the dispute stands outside its context.
3. *M. M.Q. 1:2*: The chapter is loosely redacted, mentioning various acts permitted or prohibited on the intermediate days of the festival. The redactor has reshaped the sages' position to enable him to add further rulings.
4. *M. Neg. 8:9*: The protasis seems to resemble the style of the chapter: "One who comes all white..." (cf. 8:7, 8:8). However, the mention of large and small bright spots is new, not known elsewhere, indicating preservation of tradental formulation.
5. *M. Ṭoh. 7:7*: Apocopated, a trait of the chapter.
6. *M. Yad. 4:3*: Linked to the chapter by redactional language ("On that day they said"). Otherwise independent.

Glosses (C)

1. *M. Maas. 5:1*: Eleazar's gloss is formally different from the rest of the chapter. The chapter makes the "one who" grows or prepares food the subject of its rules. Eleazar makes the produce the subject of his ruling--"lo, they are liable."
2. *M. Shab. 19:3*: The ruling shares the phraseology of the preceding law and thus of the chapter, even though the ruling seems to be out of place.
3. *M. Ket. 5:1*: The gloss preceding Eleazar's rule links it to the preceding anonymous law. Otherwise, Eleazar's lemma stands independent of the chapter.
4. *M. Naz. 6:2*: The pericope shows signs of thorough editing. Eleazar's ruling *follows* the formal literary traits of the unit ("he is not liable until").
5. *M. Men. 13:6*: Clearly a formally independent gloss.
6. *M. Miq. 3:2*: A formally independent gloss.
7. *M. Uqṣ. 1:5*: The gloss *follows* the form of the chapter.

Stories (E)

1. *M. M.S. 5:9*: Stands as an illustration of the law preceding it ("one who..." following the form of 5:7) but not reworked in any way to accommodate the formal traits of the chapter.
2. *M. Erub. 4:1*: The statement of law based on the *m'śh* precedes it. The story does not exemplify any of the literary characteristics of the chapter. Another story, however, follows ours before the chapter continues its standard form ("one who..." M.s 4:3,4,5,7, 10,11).
3. *M. Shab. 5:4*: The lemma is not in *m'śh b* form but reports a precedent. It clearly glosses a ruling in a list and uses the language of the list.

Thus sixteen items clearly stand independent of the formal traits of their respective contexts. Only four can be shown to follow the strict literary traits of the chapters in which they stand. This is sharply in contrast with the results obtained in the analysis of the traditions we have listed under form D. There we found nine of eleven items related in form to their contexts.

It is clear that approximately one third of the traditions we have examined in M. have been reshaped by the redactor in some way. Though we may draw no probative conclusions from this observation, we have suggestive evidence to support the supposition that a significant portion of Eleazar's materials underwent editing by a redactor at a later date. We may therefore reject the hypothesis that the loose nature of the forms of Eleazar's traditions stems from a separate and different tradental process. Time and again we have shown that redactional considerations were the determining factor.

Redactional traits and preferences have been systematically studied for a substantial portion of Mishnah. At this point our work in the examination of the role of the redactional process in the formation of Eleazar's traditions may proceed with some confidence for those pericopae in Mishnah. Work on the stylistic and formal traits of other compilations must be undertaken before any analysis of the redactional contribution to the formulation of traditions in those documents can be attempted.

To sum up, we have suggested that the loose formal characteristics of a substantial number of Eleazar's traditions in M. may be attributed for the most part to the activity of redactors, rather than tradents.

NOTES

CHAPTER V

[1]*HMLP*, *Kelim*, III, pp. 192ff. Also see *Eliezer*, II, Chapter 6 and *Pharisees*, III, *passim*.

[2]There are not enough examples of each to make differentiating among them worthwhile.

[3]See *Eliezer*, II, p. 39. Neusner tentatively dates the emergence of this form to the end of the Jerusalem period or the beginning of the Yavnean era.

[4]*Eliezer*, II, Chapter 6.

[5]Green, *op. cit.*, Chapter 7.

[6]Porten, *op. cit.*, Chapter 8.

[7]Shammai Kanter, *Legal traditions of Gamaliel II*, Ph.D. dissertation, Brown, 1974, conclusions.

[8]Kanter, *ibid.*

[9]Porten, *ibid.*, and *The Artificial Dispute: Ishmael and Aqiva*, in J. Neusner, ed., *Christianity, Judaism and other Greco-Roman Cults: Studies for Morton Smith at Sixty*, Vol. IV, p. 23.

[10]*Eliezer*, II, p. 37.

[11]See Neusner, *HMLP*, Vols. 1-22. He has shown that chapters of M. follow careful formulary patterns.

CHAPTER VI

THE CIRCLES: A TRADENTAL-REDACTIONAL STUDY

In this chapter we examine all of the traditions in our corpus in which Eleazar appears with another master. Our main purpose in this study is to attempt to discern any tendency within the materials to favor a named master or specific circle. The redactional traits of the traditions come into sharper focus when the items are examined by attention to the individual pericopae in each document divided according to the named masters associated with the traditions. For the pericopae in M.-T. we see whether careful attention to the names associated with the traditions and the forms attendant to them reveal any pattern of conjunction between redactional circles. Thus we ask whether there is any evidence that Aqivans, for example, are responsible for the preservation, transmission, or formulation of Eleazar's traditions.

Our second line of inquiry is to ask whether the traditions in the midrashim, b. and y., or later compilations follow the lines defined by the traditions in Mishnah-Tosefta or diverge from them in a significant way. Each master and document is considered separately.

i. *Mishnah-Tosefta*

A. *Aqiva*: Aqiva appears together with Eleazar in fourteen of the thirty traditions in M.-T. containing names. As we see, there is no indication that Aqivan redactors took Eleazar's rulings and molded them into balanced disputes with Aqiva. In the instances listed below, Eleazar stands formally outside of the Aqivan disputes with other masters. Furthermore, in the two instances in which only Eleazar and Aqiva appear together presenting legal rulings, no balanced dispute is given. Note also that the two stories of the four masters on a ship serve as the point of origin for the five pericopae in other documents containing those same named masters together.

1. *Eleazar and Aqiva alone*: Nos. 3, T. Ber. 1:2; 17, T. Shab. 3:3; and 28, M. Naz. 6:2. Two of the three traditions are stories which serve as precedents for a legal ruling (3, 17). Both have Judah as the tradent. In one instance Eleazar and Aqiva recite the *shema'* (3). In the second they enter a bathhouse on the festival day (17). The third tradition is a complex pericope in which Aqiva appears to dispute Eleazar's ruling on the liability of a Nazirite for eating grapes (28).

2. *Eleazar + an Aqivan dispute*: In five instances Eleazar's opinion is redacted together with a dispute between Aqiva and another rabbi. As our literary analysis has shown in each case, the dispute between Aqiva and the second sage is balanced and clearly separate from Eleazar's lemma.

   Eleazar, Joshua, and Aqiva: No. 7, M. Sheb. 1:8. The protasis of the pericope clearly serves Eleazar's lemma best as he answers the question directly ("Until when may they be called saplings"?). The dispute between Aqiva and Joshua is appended.

   Eleazar, Eliezer, Aqiva, Simeon: No. 36, M. B.Q. 6:4. Here the protasis serves the opinions of the dispute between Eliezer and Aqiva. Eleazar's view is added. Simeon introduces another issue.

   Eleazar, Ishmael, Aqiva: Nos. 50, M. Ker. 2:5, and 62, M. Miq. 8:3. In the first item Eleazar repeats Aqiva's opinion. Ishmael and Aqiva form an autonomous dispute. In the second pericope as well, Ishmael and Aqiva give their views as a balanced dispute with Eleazar's lemma clearly standing outside that subunit.

   Eleazar, Eleazar Ḥisma, Aqiva: No. 56, M. Neg. 7:2. Eleazar's ruling can stand alone. Aqiva's and Eleazar Ḥisma's lemmas balance each other as a dispute.

3. *Eleazar + a related ruling of Aqiva*: Nos. 40, M. Mak. 1:10, and 52, M. Kel. 3:8. In the former (40) Aqiva together with Tarfon rules on the Sanhedrin. Eleazar's lemma responds to the preceding anonymous ruling. Aqiva's does not but comments on his view of capital punishment. In the latter (52) Aqiva's lemma is glossed by Yosé. Eleazar's stands separately.
4. *Eleazar and Aqiva in a list of opinions*: In these two instances the names of Aqiva and Eleazar are attached to two of a list of several lemmas.
   No. 29, T. Soṭ. 1:2: Eliezer, Joshua, Ben Azzai, Aqiva, Judah b. Batyra, Eleazar b. Azariah and Ḥanan b. Menaḥem give different definitions for the time required for intercourse.
   No. 30, T. Giṭ. 9:1-5: Eleazar, Tarfon, Yosé the Galilean, Simeon b. Eleazar, and Aqiva present arguments against Eliezer's ruling regarding conditional divorce in a clearly artificial pericope.
5. *Eleazar, Joshua, Gamaliel, Aqiva*: As we shall see, these four names reappear together in subsequent documents.
   No. 11, M. M.S. 5:9. The four are travelling on a ship and separate tithes. The four travelling together is a common motif.
   No. 19, M. Erub. 4:1: Eleazar and Gamaliel dispute Aqiva and Joshua over the Sabbath limit on a ship. The dispute is followed by a story.

Conclusions: After examining the remainder of the traditions in which Eleazar appears with other named masters, it will be more evident that the bulk of the material seems to have been passed on by Aqivan redactors. We have seen five types of materials above. First, there are those traditions in which only Aqiva and Eleazar appear. Two stories and two other traditions in M.-T. resemble disputes. Second, several traditions combine an Aqivan dispute with a separate ruling attributed to Eleazar. Although the sample is small, it is conclusive. No material before us gives a lemma attributed to Eleazar tightly redacted together with an Aqivan tradition in a balanced dispute. The Eleazar-corpus seems to have undergone a redactional process different from and later than the traditions attributed to Ishmael, Joshua, or Eliezer, which in many instances are closely linked to Aqivan lemmas with care and balance.

The remaining three types of traditions listed above include related rulings redacted together, clearly artificial pericopae and traditions about the four masters travelling on a ship.

B. *Joshua*: In the section on Aqiva we have dealt with half of the traditions in M.-T. associating Eleazar and Joshua. Those dealt with above are nos. 7, 11, 19, and 29. The remaining traditions are as follows:

1. *Eleazar, Eliezer, and Joshua*: Nos. 6, T. Peah 3:2 and 13, T. Ḥal. 1:6. In these two pericopae Ilai gives a dispute between Eliezer and Joshua. Eleazar merely comments on the opinion of Eliezer.
2. *Eleazar and Joshua*: No. 74, T. Soṭ. 7:9-10: Joshua is portrayed as an outcast rabbi inquiring after the proceedings of the study hall. He is told of Eleazar's exegeses and praises them.

Conclusion: No significant sample of traditions associates Eleazar with Joshua. Thus we cannot say that Joshua's tradents are responsible for preserving any major portion of our corpus.

C. *Eliezer*: Eight traditions in M.-T. associate Eliezer's name with Eleazar. Two of those have been discussed above in connection with Joshua (6, 13). Three have been mentioned in our analysis of traditions associating Eleazar and Aqiva (29, 30, 36). The remaining three are as follows:

1. *Eleazar and Eliezer*: No. 47, T. Arak. 4:23. Related rulings on dedicating one's property are juxtaposed.

2. *Eleazar, Eliezer, and Simeon*: No. 64, M. Maksh. 6:6. The three gloss and dispute different anonymous rulings within a pericope. Their lemmas are unrelated to one another.
3. *Eleazar, Ṭarfon, Ishmael, and Eliezer*: No. 67, M. Yad. 4:3. Eleazar and Tarfon dispute and then debate an issue. Ishmael debates Eleazar on the same issue. Eliezer approves of Tarfon's opinion indirectly never mentioning his name. The reference to Eliezer is tacked on to the pericope and bears no integral relationship to it.

Conclusions: There is no indication that Eleazar's traditions circulated together with Eliezer's alone. Material from the two masters circulated independently until some stage of redaction at which the traditions were joined. Aqivan redactors seem to have drawn upon the materials of both masters. In sum, there is little evidence of any direct relationship between the redactional circles of Eliezer and Eleazar.

D. *Ishmael*: Of the five traditions in M.-T. linking the two men, three have already been discussed above. In two, Ishmael disputes Aqiva (50, 62). In one Ishmael interrupts a debate between Tarfon and Eleazar (67, see above under Eliezer). The two remaining pericopae are as follows:

Ishmael and Eleazar alone:
No. 4, T. Ber. 1:4. They debate the correct posture for the recitation of the *shema'*.
No. 57, M. Neg. 8:9. They appear in a nicely balanced pericope which takes up the issue of one who turned all white before the tips of his limbs reappeared.

Conclusions: The sample is too small for any decisive conclusion to be drawn from it. We do have an indication of the conjunction of the two outside of the Aqiva redactional circle in one debate and one dispute. There is an echo of a relationship between the two redactional circles. Nothing conclusive can be said though.

E. *Gamaliel*: In the items in which Eleazar and Gamaliel appear together they appear with Joshua and Aqiva. (See 11, 19, above, section A.) This strongly suggests that their names are associated as a convention and nothing more. Aqivan tradents may be responsible for the creation of the traditions mentioning the four names.

F. *Ṭarfon*: The two appear together in three pericopae in M.-T., all of which have been mentioned above (30, 40, section A; 67, section D). One tradition has a balanced dispute between the two. It is likely that Aqivan redactors are responsible for the conjunction of the two names.

G. *Yosé the Galilean*: One tradition associates the two (30, section A, above).

H. *Ben Azzai*: The tradition associating the two has been discussed above (29, section A).

I. *The sages*: The traditions associating Eleazar and the sages form a significant segment of the corpus in M.-T., eight items in all. Six of the items are disputes showing careful redaction. Two mention that Eleazar acted against the will of the sages, but do not appear in the dispute form.

1. *Eleazar and the sages alone.*
   No. 10, T. Maas. 3:8: Judah cites Eleazar *vs.* sages--dispute.
   No. 14, M. Shab. 4:2: Eleazar *vs.* sages--dispute.
   No. 23, M. M.Q. 1:2: Eleazar *vs.* sages--dispute.
   No. 60, M. Ṭoh. 7:7: Eleazar *vs.* sages--dispute.
2. *Eleazar, sages, third party.*
   No. 2, M. Ber. 4:7: Judah glosses the dispute with a compromise.

No. 24, T. Moed 1:1: Meir gives a third opinion.

3. Nos. 15, M. Shab. 5:4 and 22, M. Bes. 2:8: *Eleazar acted against the will of the sages.*

Conclusions: This segment shows careful redaction but tells us little about the circles responsible for the transmission of Eleazar's traditions. We have no evidence to indicate that the traditions associating Eleazar with the sages reached their present form before the Ushan period.

J. *Other masters*: The following appear with Eleazar once in traditions already listed above (section A): Eleazar Hiṣma (56), Simeon b. Eleazar (30), Judah b. Batyra and Ḥanan b. Menaḥem (29), Yosé (52), Simeon b. Gamaliel (40). Judah appears twice (2, 22) (section I). Meir appears twice (8, 24). Ilai is the tradent of two pericopae (6, 13). The following have not been alluded to above: Boethus b. Zunin (in 38, T. B.M. 4:2); Ḥuspit, Yoḥanan b. Nuri, Yeshabav, and Ḥalafta (53, T. Kel. B.B. 2:2); Eleazar (58, M. Neg. 13:6).

Summary: We see that first, the major portion of the named traditions are associated with Aqiva. Second, the mode of association is clear--the traditions are combined with Aqivan items but not completely reshaped by the tradents. Third, a significant proportion of the traditions are associated with the sages. The first two conclusions lead us to surmise that Eleazar's lemmas were attached to Aqivan material *after* that material had undergone a primary level of redaction into balanced disputes. Eleazar's corpus was transmitted through a different tradental process at some of the early stages until finally being incorporated with Aqivan teachings and passed on by post-Aqivan tradents in the later stages.

ii. *The Tannaitic Midrashim*

We turn next to the midrashim for the picture they portray of the circles of masters. Not surprisingly, the picture is even clearer in this strata of the material. All of the traditions mention Aqiva, except two, which give disputes between Eleazar and the sages. The list of the traditions follows.

(Nine of the eleven traditions in the Tannaitic Midrashim containing names of other masters have Aqiva as one of the rabbis mentioned. The other two traditions mention the sages (nos. 31 and 50). The list includes all of the instances in which Joshua, Ishmael, Tarfon, Yosé, and Gamaliel appear with Eleazar. Eliezer does not appear with him in the midrashim.)

1. *Eleazar* vs. *Aqiva: Exegeses: Four traditions.*
   No. 20, Mekh. Simeon, p. 13. Conflicting legal exegeses on how long the Passover sacrifice may be eaten.
   No. 46, Sifra *Ṣav* 11:4-6. Eleazar's view based on tradition is appended to Aqiva's lengthy exegesis concerning the amount of oil offered with the Thanksgiving-offering.
   No. 37, Mekh. Simeon, p. 179. Aqiva responds to Eleazar's exegesis on the culpability of the owner of an ox and then gives his own exegesis.
   No. 106, Sifré Deut. 50. Eleazar and Jacob (probably Aqiva) give differing exegeses of Ex. 23:29.
2. *Eleazar, Aqiva + another master.*
   Eleazar, Aqiva, Yosé the Galilean: No. 99, Sifra *Aḥare, par.* 1:2. Aqiva repeats Yosé's view and disputes Eleazar's.
   Eleazar, Aqiva, Tarfon: No. 95, Sifré Deut. 1. The opinions of the three are exchanged in the differing versions of the pericope.
3. *Eleazar, Joshua, Gamaliel, Aqiva.* Nos. 21, Sifra *'Emor, pereq* 16:2 and 94, Sifré Deut. 43. In both cases the four are on a ship.

4. *Eleazar, Joshua, Tarfon, Aqiva*: No. 93, Sifré Deut. 32. The four visit Eliezer.

Summary: Aqiva and Eleazar are presented in several cases in dispute form, all of course exegetical. M.-T. has only one exegetical item, no. 50. That has Eleazar together with a dispute between Aqiva and Ishmael. The portrayal of the two as disputants in exegesis appears in b. and y. as well. Two more items mentioning the four rabbis on a ship appear in the midrashim.

iii. *Babli*

The pattern of M.-T. is continued. Aqiva seems to be the central figure. Joshua, Gamaliel and Ben Azzai do not appear with Eleazar in b. Where Tarfon, Yosé the Galilean, and the sages appear, they do so along with Aqiva (82, 85, 91). One pericope juxtaposes the opinions of Eleazar, Eliezer, Rabbi, and R. Hillel (92). Otherwise Eliezer appears with Aqiva (93, cf. 30). Ishmael appears together with Eleazar in one standard list (91) and one questionably authentic pericope (69a). Otherwise, he too appears with Aqiva (85). Several new names are associated with Eleazar in b. though: Ḥaninah the son of Joshua's brother (43); Isi b. Judah (51); Eleazar HaModai (43, 82); Eliezer b. Jacob (91).

Eleazar and Aqiva appear together in seven traditions in b.:

1. *Eleazar and Aqiva alone*: They appear together in three traditions: Nos. 12, b. Yeb. 86a-b, 86, b. Ḥag. 14a, and 87, b. San. 67b. No. 12 is a legal dispute followed by an Amoraic discussion and a story. As we have shown above, it is related to the story in item no. 11. The other two instances portray Eleazar as ridiculing Aqiva's exegesis and presenting his own. These are isolated pericopae, for the other exegetical disputes have no trace of sarcasm in them.

2. *Eleazar, Aqiva + another master*: Two examples: No. 18, b. Yoma 85a-b. Ishmael. This pericope is clearly an artificial construction. The attribution to Eleazar is questionable.
   No. 25, b. M.Q. 24b. Simeon b. Eleazar. The three rule on related issues.
3. *Eleazar and Aqiva in a list*: No. 82, b. Pes. 117a. Seven masters give varying views on the authorship of the Hallel.
   No. 85, b. M.Q. 28b. Ṭarfon, Yosé the Galilean, Eleazar, and Aqiva console Ishmael. These four also appear in T. (no. 30) as the rabbis who respond to Eliezer's opinion.

Summary: b. follows M.'s pattern. The only significant trend to be noted is the portrayal of the overt tension between the two masters in two exegeses. This is new and could not have been generated by any traditions in M.-T.

iv. *Yerushalmi*

Except for two traditions (12, a dispute between Eleazar and Joshua, and 89, a story linking him with Yosé the Galilean), the conjunction of names in the traditions in y. again shows Aqivan domination of the list. He appears in five items.

1. *Eleazar and Aqiva alone*: Three traditions contain only the names of the two. No. 12, y. M.S. 5:5, has the story of Eleazar giving back his tithes because of Aqiva's argument. No. 84, y. Suk. 2:4, another story shows Eleazar ridiculing Aqiva's ruling that a *sukkah* may be built on a ship. No. 90, y. Soṭ. 5:6, is a simple exegetical dispute.
   No. 77, y. Ber. 4:1. The deposition story. Aqiva's place in this tradition is difficult to interpret. He reproves Eleazar at the outset, telling him that he is not worthy of the position of patriarch since he is

not entitled to inherit it. Later in the narrative, Aqiva is sent to appease Eleazar. b.'s version of the story makes Aqiva's objection to the appointment of Eleazar explicit. The reasons for appointing Eleazar and not Aqiva are given in detail. Moreover, at the conclusion of the story Aqiva is the rabbi appeased by the messenger. The primary interest of the narrative is, of course, the dispute between Gamaliel and Joshua. Eleazar and Aqiva play secondary roles. It is interesting to note that the four names in the story are those usually associated with each other travelling on a ship (to Rome).

No. 79, y. Yeb. 1:6. Dosa recites the praise of Eleazar, Joshua, and Aqiva.

Summary: Stories characterize the y. traditions attributed to Eleazar. We can tell little about the status of the transmission and formulation of Eleazar's traditions from these items other than the fact that no new names are associated with the two masters and no radically new motifs appear.

v. *Later Compilations*

Five of the six traditions in later compilations which give opinions of other named masters along with Eleazar's have Aqiva. One (116) has Eleazar with Eleazar HaModai.

No. 118, Tanḥ. *Teṣaveh* 1. Eleazar comments on Aqiva's statement concerning the Song of Songs.

No. 88, B.R. 34. Eleazar, Ben Azzai, and Aqiva give opinions on the merits of procreation. The pericope is exegetical.

No. 91, ARN A 18. Tarfon, Aqiva, and Eleazar are listed as three rabbis and their praise is given.

Nos. 115, Kal. Rab. 7:1 and 119, Ex. Rab. 30:6. Eleazar, Joshua, Gamaliel, and Aqiva travel together.

Summary: Only one tradition deviates significantly from the pattern established in earlier documents. That has Eleazar comment on Aqiva's lemma, a phenomenon not seen before in the tradition. Otherwise there is nothing of note.

vi. *Conclusions*

The picture which emerges from a consideration of the entire tradition is striking. The centrality of Aqiva's name in the traditions which associate Eleazar with another master first emerges in M.-T. The evidence there indicates that post-Aqivan tradents combined Eleazar's traditions with completed units of tradition for transmission. Aqiva remains the central figure in all of the groups of later traditions--in the midrashim, b., y., and other compilations. The following chart summarizes the frequency of the appearance of the various masters with Eleazar in the pericopae:

	M.-T.	Midrashim	b.	y.	Later Compilations	Totals
Aqiva	14	9	7	5	6	39
Joshua	7	3	0	3	2	15
Eliezer	8	0	2	0	1	11
Ishmael	5	1	3	0	0	9
Gamaliel	2	2	0	1	2	7
Tarfon	3	2	1	0	1	7
Yosé the Galilean	1	1	2	1	0	5
Ben Azzai	1	1	0	0	1	3
Sages	8	2	1	0	0	11
Judah and Meir	4	0	4	0	0	8
Others	11	2	10	1	1	25

Even though other names appear to be sure, Aqiva predominates. The tradition thus shows a remarkable consistency.

It would seem then that we may conclude with some certainty that post-Aqivan tradents and redactors played a large role in the preservation and formulation of Eleazar's traditions whether in M.-T., the midrashim, b. and y., or elsewhere. But this is one of the only cogent and consistent tendencies of the corpus as a whole. Above (pp. 255-56) we show that the forms of the traditions vary from compilation to compilation. Below (pp. 297ff.) we demonstrate that the central themes and concerns expressed in traditions in one compilation are not developed in another. The consistent result in the present instance then is all the more striking. Though the form and content of traditions attributed to Eleazar differs in each compilation, the data suggests that many pericopae in the several compilations have passed through Aqivan or post-Aqivan hands at some stage of their tradental history. But this is no surprise, for the rabbinic tradition itself claims, "all follows R. Aqiva" (b. San. 86a).

CHAPTER VII

THE LAW

The laws in M.-T. interrelate like the strands of a finely woven cloth. The rulings of individual masters or generations of rabbis form the warp of the fabric. The strands of its woof are the laws, passed on from one generation to the next and in the process refined and developed. So closely are the threads of the cloth intermeshed that it is often difficult to separate one from another.[1] In this chapter we penetrate into a portion of the law's fabric. First we list those elements of the 'warp,' the horizontal part of our cloth, attributed to Eleazar b. Azariah. We examine the content of those rulings bearing several issues in mind. The content of Eleazar's traditions is compared with that of other Yavnean masters. Then we inquire whether the rulings, the "threads" of the tradition, form a significant part of any one tractate of M.-T. Is a tractate or chapter spun out of the conceptions presented in Eleazar's rulings?

Another closely related line of inquiry is the question of the relationship of Eleazar's traditions to the "woof" of the fabric in general. Do subsequent laws contradict, ignore, or develop Eleazar's rulings? That is, are the rulings central in any way to the fabric of the law, or are they better characterized as stray threads at the periphery of the cloth?

Finally, we return to the individual rulings and summarize the principles which we discern underlying them. Presumably, the rulings are based on a legal philosophy, on the application of a set of principles to specific cases. Thus we search for those principles and try to reconstruct the general outlines of Eleazar's legal thought processes.

To illustrate the traditions and facilitate our undertaking, we present the legal rulings in a chart. The first column briefly summarizes each ruling. The second traces Eleazar's role in the development of the law in M.-T., taking into consideration the questions mentioned above. The final column restates the principle which serves as the basis of the law. The entries of the chart are divided as follows: pericopae attested at Usha are listed first, then the remainder of the items in M.-T. The laws are divided into seven general categories: agriculture, purity, liturgy, Sabbath and festival, civil, family, Temple laws and vows.

Agricultural Laws

Column One--Rulings	*Column Two--Eleazar's Role in the Law*	*Column Three--Principles*
6. T. Peah 3:2. *Sheaves*. Eleazar comments on the Houses'/Joshua, Eliezer dispute, affirming Eliezer's opinion on the definition of sheaves.	6. Commentator on a common Yavnean issue (M. Peah 6:2-3).	6. Bases decision on tradition.
9,10. M. Maas 5:1, T. Maas. 3:8. *Tithes of Seedlings*. Produce gathered to be sent to another party is liable to tithes if its kind is sold in the market. T. illustrates and attests M.'s ruling. [See Nos. 11,12 on tithes.]	9,10. The law presumes the existence of basic tithing requirements. Eleazar's ruling makes produce which changes hands subject to tithes. Contrary views require only that which is consumed by the producer to be tithed by him. Eleazar thus is responsible for a stringent secondary ruling. Sages contradict, *ad loc*. T. 3:8 illustrates the principle which Eleazar set down.	9,10. Liability to tithes is determined by an objective formal criterion--if the produce is sold in the market (intention plays no role).
8. M. Sheb. 3:3. *Storing dung*. On the Seventh year dung may be set out little by little on rocks or raised/lowered from the ground.	8. The law refines the presumed ruling that one may not fertilize a field on the Seventh year. Nothing more is made of Eleazar's rule in M. A secondary ruling.	8. An action's objective appearance is important, regardless of intention. Cf. No. 23, the bathhouse.
24. T. Mo'ed 1:1. *New spring*. One does not water from a newly flowing spring on the intermediate days of the festival. Cf. No. 23.	24. Law presumes agricultural restrictions on festival days. Meir and sages disregard the ruling and dispute whether a householder's or	24. No perceptible principle. Restrictive.

Column One	*Column Two*	*Column Three*
	irrigated field may be watered. Secondary ruling.	
Purity Laws		
54. T. Kel. B.B. 2:6. *Immerse torn objects*. Eleazar rules that one may immerse torn objects as they are.	54. Presumes and glosses the law that objects are unclean even if torn, as long as they serve as containers (cf. M. Kel. 23:1).	54. Stuffing is connected to the container and therefore does not interpose (contra MA). The owner intends that it hold what is in them. On connection, see also 52.
58. M. Neg. 13:6. *House which shades a house which bears the plague*. One may enter the outer house. Cf. 59.	58. Based on the assumption that the house interposes for itself (M. Ohal.). Sens: cf. M. Neg. 13:3. MA: cf. M. Neg. 13:11. The ruling is congenial to the Ushan view comparing uncleanness of plagues and corpse-uncleanness. The house/tent interposes. Cf. Neusner, *HMLP*, VIII, p. 196. A secondary ruling. Theoretical case.	58. Stone is not an integral part of the house, therefore the house may interpose. Ushan Eleazar gives contrasting view in the same pericope.
59. T. Neg. 7:3. *One who touches inside of a house which bears the plague*. Clean.	59. Eleazar's ruling is cited as support for an authority in later dispute. Rabbi's circle seems to be reworking this law, already addressed by Yavneans. Eleazar rules that touching does not convey uncleanness in this case. Secondary ruling. Theoretical.	59. The hand does not convey uncleanness. May be based on a literal understanding of Scripture.

Column One	*Column Two*	*Column Three*
60. M. Toh. 7:7, T. Toh. 8:7. *Clothes left in a wall niche.* Clean.	60. Presumes that doubts are an issue. Unguarded clothing may have been touched by an *'am ha'areṣ*. Sages contradict the ruling, *ad loc*. Judah refines Eleazar's ruling in T. 8:7. Secondary ruling. Theoretical.	60. A matter of doubt in entry is clean. Lenient.
Liturgy		
2. M. Ber. 4:7. *Additional Service.* Only said with the congregation of the city (cf. 1,3,4).	2. Assumes the additional service is part of the liturgy, a fact not explicit in M. A basic ruling. Sages expand on the law: It is said with and not with the congregation. Judah compromises between the two rulings.	[2. Regulation of liturgy.]
3. T. Ber. 1:2. *Time for the shema'.* Story. Eleazar recited too late.	3. No ruling/report of a story. T. Ber. 1:2 says it may be said until sun-up. M. Ber. 1:2 says until the third hour.	[3. Regulation of liturgy.]
[5. b. Ber. 15a. *Audibility of the shema'.*] (Appears in b.)	[5. M. Ber. gives this ruling in Yosé's name.]	[5. Scripture.]
Sabbath and festival law		
22. M. Beṣ. 2:8. *Curry cattle.* Eleazar permits on the festival.	22. T. Shab. 2:17 asks, What is currying? commenting on the dispute between Eleazar and Judah. Eleazar's ruling presumes that scratching an animal may be	22. One does not intend to scratch the animal, only to curry it. Therefore one may do so in spite of the resulting wounds. Intention is taken into account in this case.

Column One	*Column Two*	*Column Three*
	prohibited. Since currying causes scratches, it is a problem. Eleazar permits.	
Civil Laws		
38. T. B.M. 4:2. *Sale of a field*. Judah reports that Boethus followed Eleazar's ruling.	38. Third hand report of Eleazar's ruling. No other law on the mortgage of a field is given in Eleazar's name.	38. No clear principle.
Family Law		
30. T. Giṭ. 9:1-5. *Conditional divorce*. Eleazar does not allow. On divorce, see 27, 31.	30. Comments on a ruling of Eliezer. (M. Giṭ. 9:1) Yosé and Rava affirm Eleazar's comment in b.'s version. Other views, *ad loc* ignore Eleazar's lemma.	30. Simple exegesis of Scripture.
Temple Law		
13. T. Ḥal. 1:6. *Dough-offering of cakes of Thanksgiving and wafers of a Nazirite* [also an agricultural law]. Eliezer/Joshua dispute. Cf. 46 on Thanksgiving and Nazirite's offerings.	13. Commentator on a Yavnean dispute, as in No. 6.	
M.-T. Stratum		
Agricultural Laws		
7. M. Sheb. 1:8. *Saplings in Seventh year*. Sapling becomes a	7. Eleazar provides one definition of a sapling, Aqiva and Joshua	7. Eleazar makes use of a ruling regarding agricultural taboos to

Column One	*Column Two*	*Column Three*
tree in the fourth year. Cf. 8, 23 on Seventh year.	provide others. Several circles at Yavneh rule on the same issue. The ruling presupposes the Seventh year rulings of a sapling (i.e., Ch. One of *Shebi'it*). Nothing is built on this specific ruling in its context, though. Eleazar's lemma is omitted from T.	define the process of maturation of a tree *vis a vis* the Seventh year.
9,10. As above in section on Ushan rulings.	- - - -	- - - -
11. M. M.S. 5:9. *Tithes*. Story. Cf. 9,10,67.	11. No ruling.	11. No clear principle.
23. M. M.Q. 1:2. *Digging a water channel*. One may not dig a new channel on either the festival or the Seventh year.	23. Repairs presumably may be made. Sages modify the rulings in the pericope. A secondary issue.	23. For the Seventh year: the appearance of an action matters regardless of intent--consistent with 8 and 17. For the festival: initiatory activity on the festival prohibited as it requires great exertion--consistent with 24.
67. M. Yad. 4:3. *Tithes in Ammon and Moab*. Eleazar decreed that in the Seventh year Second tithe should be given. Cf. 9,10, 11.	67. Common Yavnean issue. None of the others in the discussion accept Eleazar's decision.	67. Stringent ruling. Follows the order of the years. Reasons by analogy to other cases. [Tithes go to Temple not to the poor.]

Column One	Column Two	Column Three
Purity Laws		
52. M. Kel. 3:8. *The funnel stopped up with pitch.* Unclean.	52. Aqiva and Yosé dispute a refinement of Eleazar's ruling--whether the funnel was wooden or earthenware.	52. Definition of vessel or, alternatively, connection. Intention of the owner may be crucial (cf. 54).
56. M. Neg. 7:2. *Color change in a bright spot.* Change does not affect the spot which was clean at the outset.	56. Eleazar's theory, the priestly theory of spots, is left undeveloped in the tractate. Aqiva's conception takes the history of the spot into account (cf. *ad loc*). Theoretical and primary.	56. Once a spot is clean it remains so.
57. M. Neg. 8:9. *Quickflesh spread and receded.* Eleazar says it is like the 'small bright spot.	57. Ishmael compares the case to the large bright spot. One hears of neither the small nor the large bright spot elsewhere in M.-T. The ruling is a peripheral one yielding no further rulings. An 'abstract' ruling.	57. No clear principle.
61. M. Miq. 3:2. *The cistern*: May be purified only by being replenished (or by contact with another pool--GRA).	61. The ruling presumes that drawn water invalidates a pool. Purification of the pool is a basic issue though.	61. No clear principle.
62. M. Miq. 8:3. *Discharge of semen.* After two days, semen discharged does not cause uncleanness in a woman.	62. Lemma presumes a knowledge of the law of M. Kel. 1:1: semen is a father of uncleanness. Aqiva and Ishmael refine the ruling, or a similar one, in new terms. Ruling given anonymously in M. Shab. 9:3.	62. Exegesis of Scripture (not given).

Column One	*Column Two*	*Column Three*
64. M. Maksh. 6:6. *The blood of a menstruant*. It is not a liquid to render objects susceptible to uncleanness.	64. Disputes the anonymous rule. Presumes system of uncleanness rules. Anonymous law in M. Nid. 7:1 contradicts Eleazar.	64. No clear principle.
68. M. Uqṣ. 1:5. *Fruitstalks of beans*--clean. Of other legumes--unclean.	68. Presumes separate status of handle (M. Uqṣ. 1:1).	68. Connection to receive and convey uncleanness where intention is clear to use stalks as handle.
Liturgy		
1. M. Ber. 1:5. *Mention Exodus at night*. Eleazar cites b. Zoma's lemma. On *shema*ʿ liturgy see: 3, 4,5.	1. No ruling.	
4. T. Ber. 1:4. *Reclining/sitting for shema*ʿ.	4. No ruling. Story.	
Sabbath and festival laws		
14. M. Shab. 4:2. *Insulation of foods*. One should take foods from the basket by tilting, not by taking pot out of insulation.	14. Presupposes insulation laws for Sabbath. Nothing built on this ruling. Sages contradict it, *ad loc*.	14. Replacing pot equals reinsulation, therefore prohibited. (Intention not taken into consideration).
15. M. Shab. 5:4. *Eleazar's cow*. Story.	15. No ruling. Sages allegedly condemn his behavior, *ad loc*.	
22. M. Beṣ. 2:8. *Three rules contra sages*. May grind pepper on festival. (Also see Usha, 22 and 15 above.)	22. T. Beṣ. 2:16 gives same ruling in Gamaliel's name. Sages forbid, *ad loc*.	22. No clear principle.

Column One	*Column Two*	*Column Three*
16. M. Shab. 19:3. *Washing child.* May wash on third following circumcision (cf. No. 18 for possible correlation).	16. Ruling not related to the common issue regarding preparations for the circumcision on the Sabbath. Thematically distinct. Not developed further in M.-T. Given anonymously in M. Shab. 9:3.	16. Exegetical; proof text supplied.
17. T. Shab. 3:3. *Bathhouse whose openings were stopped up.* Story.	17. No ruling.	17. No clear principle.
19. M. Erub. 4:1. *Sabbath limit.* Story and ruling that one may traverse the limit of an enclosed area outside the Sabbath limit.	19. Gamaliel and Eleazar *vs.* Aqiva and Joshua regarding a middle case defining the Sabbath limit. Abstract, central to the law.	19. Sabbath limit depends on defined domains, not distance alone.
23/24. *Water channel on festival,* see Usha.	- - - -	- - - -
Family Laws		
26. M. Ket. 4:6. *Maintenance of daughters.* Not an obligation for the father.	26. A basic issue. Context of the ruling discusses rights and obligations of father/husband. T. Ket. 4:8 contradicts the ruling.	26. Ruling based on exegesis of the *ketubah.*
27. M. Ket. 5:1. *The marriage settlement.* Only a married woman collects extra, a betrothed woman does not. Cf. 30,31 on divorce.	27. One of a number of miscellaneous rules not developed further. A secondary refinement of the law.	27. Original intent of the contract is binding *re* the sum of the added amount of the *ketubah.*
29. T. Soṭ. 1:2. *Time for intercourse.*	29. One of seven opinions. All parallels omit Eleazar's name.	29. Definition of time.

Column One	*Column Two*	*Column Three*
50. M. Ker. 2:5. *The halfbond-woman*. Explains Lev. 19's case.	50. Eleazar repeats Aqiva's view.	50. Exegetical; a difficult verse is expounded.
Civil Laws		
36. M. B.Q. 6:4. *Liability for a fire*: which spreads from one's own domain is limited to a *beit kor*'s area. (Curiously correlated to No. 7.)	36. Aqiva and Joshua dispute. T. omits Eleazar. Law ignores his view. A primary ruling.	36. Uses Sabbath definition of garden for defining liability (cf. M. Erub. 2:6).
Vows, Temple Law and Nazirites		
28. M. Naz. 6:2, T. Naz. 4:1. *The liability of a Nazirite*. Eleazar rules that he is liable for consuming either a quarter-*log* of wine or two grapes and their skins.	28. The liquid minimum appears in Eleazar's name in T. M. attributes it to *mišnah rišonah*. Aqiva disputes. The issue of solid measure is developed in M. by Yosé and Judah who discuss the terms used in Eleazar's lemma. The issue is basic to the development of the law of Nazirite, central to the tractate.	28. Definition--minimum for liability.
45. M. Men. 13:6. *Pledge of a Burnt-offering*. Must bring dove or pigeon.	45. Defines an unspecified pledge. Further refinements given *ad loc*.	45. Definition.

Our summary of the chart considers the data of each column separately.

i. *The Agendum of Legal Issues* (Column One)

It is clear that for both the Ushan substratum of M.-T. and in the entire corpus of rulings in M.-T., agricultural and purity laws make up the largest segment of the tradition. Over 60% of the materials attested to Usha (8 items of 14) relate to those two general categories of legal concern. For M.-T. as a whole, the figure stands at nearly 50% (20 items of 42). We give the figures for the distribution of the remaining rulings in the following chart listing the percentage of pericopae in M.-T. dealing with each of the subtopics. Alongside the figures for Eleazar, we list the correlative figures currently available for other Yavnean masters and the Houses. These figures too are based on all the traditions in M.-T.

We list the figures for the other masters and the Houses to illustrate that Eleazar's agendum of issues falls squarely within the parameters of concerns expected of a Pharisee at Yavneh.[2]

	Eleazar	Gamaliel[3]	Eliezer[4]	Ishmael[5]	Houses[6]	Deviation[7] from mean,%
Agricultural	21	17	18	20	22	+2
Purity	26	14	29	25	28	+2
Liturgy	10	10	2	9	6	+3
Sabbath and Festival	19	33	15	18	23	-3
Civil	5	8	3	7	2	0
Family	12	14	10	4	13	+2
Temple, vows	7	5	16	10	6	-2
Others	--	--	6	7	--	-3

Eleazar provides us with neither the highest nor the lowest figure in each subcategory and deviates an average of only 2% from the mean. This data confirms that Eleazar was a Pharisee, and shared the general concerns of many of the Yavneans.

ii. *The Topics of the Rulings. Eleazar and the Formation of Mishnah*

The data in column one also enable us to summarize and correlate the more specific areas of concern within each of the seven categories. As the accompanying list shows, it is clear that few legal themes recur more than once or twice:

Sabbath and festival laws: Preparation of food (2 rulings); handling of cattle (2); Sabbath limit (1); use of baths (1); therapeutic bathing (1); preparation of fields (2).

Purity laws: Cleanness of utensils (2); *nega'im* (2); plague of houses (2); doubts in impurity; semen; menstrual blood; handles of produce (one each).

Liturgy: *shema'* (3); additional service (1).

Civil law: mortgage; liability for damage (1).

Agricultural laws: Tithes (4); preparation of field (4); sheaves (1).

Family laws: Divorce (2); paternal obligations; miscellaneous (2).

Temple, Vows: Sacrifices (2); Nazirite (1).

Tithes and the *shema'* are the only topics recurring three or more times (preparation of a field is a general subcategory). Clearly we see that the specific legal rulings form a remarkably heterogeneous group.

We may still ask whether the traditions, diverse as they are, form conceptual basis for a chapter or tractate of M. Let us first consider how the pericopae are distributed throughout M. As the accompanying chart illustrates, they are scattered about, throughout the tractates.

The distribution of Eleazar's traditions in M.-T. is as follows: (number of rulings per tractate).

Zera'im	*Mo'ed*	*Nashim*
Berakhot-5	Shabbat-4	Yebamot
Pe'ah-1	'Erubin-1	Ketubot-2

Zeraʿim
Demai'
Kila'im
Shebiʿit-2
Terumot
Maʿaserot-2
Maʿaser Sheni-1
Ḥallah-1
ʿOrlah
Bikkurim
Total: 12, 26%

Moʿed
Pesaḥim
Shekalim
Yoma'
Sukkah
Beṣah-1
Rosh Hashanah
Taʿanit
Megillah
Moʿed Qatan
Ḥagigah
Total: 8, 17%

Nashim
Nedarim
Nazir-1
Soṭah-1
Giṭṭin-1
Qiddushin
Total: 5, 11%

Neziqin
Baba' Qamma'-1
Baba' Meṣiʿa'-1
Baba' Batra'
Sanhedrin
Makkot-1
Shabuʿot
ʿEduyyot
ʿAbodah Zarah-1
'Abot
Horayot
Total: 4, 9%

Qodashim
Zebaḥim
Menaḥot-1
Ḥullin
Bekhorot
ʿArakhin-3
Temurah
Middot
Qinnin
Keritot-1
Meʿilah
Tamid
Total: 4, 9%

Ṭoharot
Kelim-3
Ohalot
Negaʿim-4
Parah
Ṭoharot-1
Miqva'ot-1
Niddah
Makhshirin-1
Zabim
Ṭebul Yom
Yadayim-3
Uqṣin-1
Total: 14, 30%

It is clear from the chart that Eleazar does not contribute a significant number of rulings to any one tractate. The one notable exception to the random distribution is Mishnah-Tosefta Ber. which contains four rulings attributed to Eleazar. Three of them deal with the *shema'* as we have noted. May we say that these rulings form the basis of a chapter of law? That is, are later conceptions which are integral to the chapter or tractate generated from his rulings? To answer these questions, we consider more closely the structure of the first four chapters of M. Ber. Briefly sketched, they are:

Chapter I

Times for reciting the *shema*' evening and morning
Posture for reciting
Blessings before and after
Exodus at night (see T. 2:1)

Chapter II--procedure (continued)

Intention
Interruption of recitation
Audibility
Mistakes in recitation
Place of recitation
Those exempt from recitation

Chapter III

Those exempt, person with an emission

Chapter IV

Times for morning and evening prayers
The short prayer
The eighteen-standardized prayer
Posture for prayer
The additional prayer, etc.

Two rulings in Eleazar's name appear in M., one in Chapter One, one in Chapter Four (1:5, 4:7). The other traditions attributed to Eleazar related to M. Ber. appear in b. and T., but turn up in different forms in M. (cf. T. 1:2, M. 1:2, M. 1:3, M. 2:3). Although Eleazar rules on important issues in all four items, they are not developed or refined in other pericopae in M. They generate no further legal rulings in the tractate.

Accordingly, we conclude that Eleazar's traditions, though freely integrated into M., as far as we can see, do not form the generative, conceptual basis for either a tractate or even a chapter of M. May we say that the pericopae generate no further logical developments? To examine this question, we return to the data of column two of our chart above (pp. 281-89).

iii. *Eleazar's Contribution to the Law* (Column Two)

What role do Eleazar's rulings play in the development of the law? That is to say, do they spell out primary elements in a given legal structure or answer to secondary concerns, providing generalizations or refinements of law? Moreover, we wish to know whether the rulings are central to the concerns of their immediate settings in M.-T., if not to their chapters or tractates, or do they introduce peripheral issues which lead away from the development of major themes. Accordingly, we seek to determine whether the rulings are basic in their nature. If so, we ask whether they generate logical developments, within a given chapter or tractate, and yield subtle distinctions, or are left by the wayside as interesting, but not integral lemmas.

To decide which rulings are central and which peripheral, we establish the following criterion. We consider a ruling peripheral if neither it nor the contrary ruling, if it is contradicted *ad loc* or elsewhere, serves as the generative basis for further laws in M.-T. A ruling is not central if its content is ignored in virtually all other pericopae which serve as part of the structures of legal thought in M.-T.[8]

Our evidence then yields the following. Several rulings directly generate further laws. These include Nos. 2, 22, 23, 28, 61, 62, and 68. To this group we may add Nos. 52, 54, 58, 59, and 60. These items are in some way refined and developed in M.-T., and thus become a more integral part of the larger fabric of the law. We reiterate that in no case is a tractate or even a chapter built upon the legal conception of one or more of Eleazar's rulings. They are limited in the scope of the further logical developments which they generate.

Several items provide opinions alternative to central generative rulings. These include Nos. 7, 9, 10, 14, 22, 24, 60, 64, 67, and perhaps 30, 36, 38, and 45. Stories are directly illustrative of central concerns (Nos. 1, 3, 4, and 11), or of an alternative view (No. 15), or neither (Nos. 17 and 19). In several pericopae Eleazar comments on or repeats a ruling attributed to another master (Nos. 6, 13, and 50). Only six rulings remain wholly peripheral to the law, Nos. 8, 16, 26, 27, 56, and 57. The latter two are entirely out of phase with the conception of the law expressed in all other pericopae in their tractate. The other four are appropriate to their respective contexts but neither generate further rulings nor provide alternatives to other existing laws.

Turning to the question of the inherent character of Eleazar's individual rulings, we observe that very few are basic rulings, laying groundwork at the most primitive stage of the law (cf. 2, 26, 36, 28, and 56). Most rulings stand at a secondary or tertiary level presuming the knowledge of a fair amount of law.

These then are the major traits of Eleazar's legal rulings. To review, we may say that we have reached a number of negative conclusions. We found the role Eleazar's rulings play in the development of the law of M.-T. is complex. In some instances Eleazar's lemmas serve as threads for the weaving of larger legal units. But in many they do not directly generate any further logical developments. Few of the rulings address the basic, primary concerns of a tractate. In the main, Eleazar's rulings do not loom central in the growth and development of rabbinic law in M.-T.

iv. *The Legal Principles* (Column Three)

The rulings attributed to Eleazar in M.-T. seem to be based on a variety of legal principles. From these, however, we cannot reconstruct any single pattern of thought or philosophy of the law. Even in those instances where clear principles may be discerned, our evidence gives us a contradictory picture of Eleazar's basic legal conceptions. For example, several rulings deal with middle cases, gray areas of law. In those, the actor's intention is contrary to the objective appearance of his behavior. How does Eleazar rule in such instances? Our evidence is split. In five cases he rules that objective criteria, such as 'appearance', determine the decision. They are nos. 8, 9, 10, 14, 23. In four others it appears that intention is the key factor in establishing the ruling, i.e., 22, 27, 52, 68. It is clear that Eleazar makes use of a number of other principles as well. But these do not appear to cohere to form a definite pattern of thought. Thus, in three purity rulings, connection seems to be the deciding issue, i.e., nos. 54, 52, 68. Four other pericopae involve the issue of defining the minimum or limits for liability. But no one, uniform principle or approach to this problem emerges from these rulings, nos. 28, 29, 45, 52. Correspondingly, five items are exegetical. However, no single principle of exegesis is employed in these pericopae.

The nine remaining pericopae break down as follows: Two utilize a ruling in one area of law to determine the law in a second instance, nos. 7, 36, curiously similar in many respects. One purity law declares clean a case involving doubts (no. 60). The remaining rules are diverse, unrelated to each other and to the pericopae for which we have been able to discern clear principles. These are nos. 58, 23, 67, 19, 56. Accordingly, it is clear that Eleazar's rulings are not based on a single legal principle, but rather on a set of several varied legal considerations.

Our consistent result in this study of the law is the discovery of the basic lack of consistency and cogency in Eleazar's tradition. As we have said, regarding the specific subjects dealt with by the rulings, they seem to be diverse. Moreover, the role of Eleazar's rulings in the development of the law is complex and varied, evincing no clear pattern. The legal principles behind the rulings also do not gravitate to a single pole. Our one positive result, though, is highly suggestive. Eleazar is surely a Pharisee, as his agendum strikingly indicates.[9]

If we are to characterize the legal thought of Eleazar in one phrase, we may resort to the tradition itself. It supplies an apt description. "Eleazar b. Azariah: a spice peddler's basket, a salesman's sample case."

v. *The Later Legal Rulings*

Our final problem in this chapter is the consideration of the relationship between the legal rulings attributed to Eleazar in the Tannaitic Midrashim, b. and y., and later compilations, and the laws assigned to him in M.-T. We wish to determine which issues are introduced for the first time by the later sources and of those, which may be developments of, or bear some relationship to, pericopae appearing first in M.-T.

a. *The Tannaitic Midrashim*

The midrashim contain twenty pericopae dealing with legal issues. Nine of them parallel traditions appearing in M.-T. Eleven are new issues which relate in at most a marginal way to the material preserved in M.-T. The following chart considers each of the Tannaitic Midrashim separately, listing the legal pericopae. First we offer a brief summary of the issue of each tradition. Second, we note any relationship between the pericope and any other item in the corpus of traditions. Next, we review data which might cast doubt on the accuracy of the attribution. The prominent exegetical traits of the pericopae are also listed. Our main concern throughout, however, is the relationship between these sources and the traditions in M.-T. Finally, if the item bears a questionable attribution or is unrelated to issues raised in the pericopae in M.-T., or both, we classify it as a "poor" tradition. As we shall see almost all of the items listed below are poor traditions. Accordingly they are of little value in reconstructing the thought of Eleazar or his circle.

Mekhilta de R. Ishmael

18. *Mekh. Shab. I. Mortal danger on the Sabbath.* Eleazar says that since circumcision overrides the prohibitions of the Sabbath, then *a fortiori*, mortal danger overrides the Sabbath. T.'s version of the pericope attributes the lemma to Eliezer. He is a much more likely candidate for author of the lemma since we have explicit references to his concern with the procedures for circumcision on the Sabbath. However, since we do have one tradition attributing concern for the circumcised child on the third day if it is the Sabbath (16), we may have an accurate attribution in Mekh. At most though we may marginally accept the association of this pericope with Eleazar. No exegesis is employed by Eleazar in this pericope. It is a poor tradition.
32. *Mekh. Neziqin 1. Gentiles judge.* Mekh. supplies an exegetical basis for Eleazar's lemma. Gentiles may not employ Jewish law. The example given is that of a *geṭ* made by gentiles. We have no rules attributed to Eleazar elsewhere relating to either the gentiles or to actual procedure for divorce. One pericope we have regarding divorce deals with the monetary settlement (27). Our pericope does not conform to the previous agendum of specific issues which we have for Eleazar in M.-T. We have no particular warrant, aside from the attribution, for assigning to Eleazar such a ruling. The exegesis is straightforward. A poor tradition.
36. *The spread of fire re: liability.* (See M.)
62. *Woman discharges semen on the third day.* (See M.)

Mekhilta de R. Simeon b. Yoḥai

Except for the parallel to 62 (the woman's discharge

of semen on the third day), this compilation gives us entirely new material, unrelated to any previous pericopae in Eleazar's corpus. All poor traditions.

20. *Passover eaten until midnight.* Eleazar disputes Aqiva. His ruling is based on a *gezerah shava*, the use of a common word in two verses, a principle not found elsewhere in the corpus of traditions associated with Eleazar. Aqiva assigns a different exegesis to the word. The ruling appears anonymously in M. Zeb. 5:8b. Eleazar's only previous connection to the Passover sacrifice is in M. Zeb. 1:2. There, however, he is mentioned only to set the stage for a ruling cited by b. Azzai. The tradition appears several times in b.
34. *The slave or master who took sick.* Eleazar's simple exegesis deduces that if either slave or master take sick during the period of servitude, the slave may not elect to have his ear pierced and remain with the master until the Jubilee year. Sifré cites the tradition without the attribution to Eleazar.
37. *Liability of the owner of an ox.* Mekh.'s version of the exegetical pericope omits the attribution to Eleazar.
62. *Woman discharges semen on the third day.* See above.

As we said, the agendum of Mekh. de R. Simeon is unrelated to and inconsistent with the previous agendum of issues associated with Eleazar.

Sifré Deuteronomy

31. *Sifré Deut. 270. Remarriage.* Eleazar rules that after betrothal, the wife may remarry the husband, but after marriage to another, she may not. The appropriate verse is given as simple proof. Sages dispute the ruling and apply the verse to another question. Eleazar rules on conditional divorce in T. (30). Accordingly, the issue at hand may be marginally within the bounds of the earlier legal agendum.

Other legal rulings found in the earlier strata of the tradition include:

1. *Mention Exodus at night.* (See M.)
4. *Reclining/sitting for* shema'. (See M.)
30. *Conditional divorce.* (See M.)

Sifré Numbers

51. *Sifré Num. 112. Reviling the Lord.* Eleazar and Isi b. Akabiah give two Aramaic proverbs to explain the biblical phrase. b. provides us with an interpretation of the meaning of those epigrams. Eleazar thinks reviling the Lord means worshipping idols. We have no other tradition linking Eleazar with the issue of idolatry.

Also in Sifré Numbers:

28. *The liability of a Nazirite.* (See M.)

Sifra

21. *'Emor, pereq 16:2. The* lulav *on a boat.* The four "standard" rabbis were travelling on a boat and used one *lulav* to fulfill the obligation. No other tradition deals with the *lulav*. The same list of names appears in M. M.S. 5:9 (11).
46. *Ṣav, pereq 11:4-6. Oil for offerings; the menstrual period.* Eleazar rejects the exegetical basis for Aqiva's ruling regarding the oil of the Thanksgiving offering, but accepts the ruling based on tradition. Two other rules are cited: The oil of the Nazirite's offering is a quarter-*log* and there are eleven days between menstrual periods. The three rules were handed down directly from Sinai and need no exegetical basis, Eleazar says. T. Ḥal. 1:6 has Eleazar declare the ruling that cakes of a Thanksgiving offering and wafers of the Nazirites offering are free from the obligation to Dough offering was handed down from Sinai (13). That provides a link between Eleazar and the issues of the two offerings, although in

T. he does not refer to the requirements for the oil to be brought with it. Eleazar refers to the discharge of semen and the status of menstrual blood (62, 64) but he does not rule in M.-T. on the duration of the menstrual period. Thus we have only a tenuous link between this pericope and preceding materials.

Also in Sifra:
47. *Dedicate only part of one's property.* (See M.)
50. *Half-bondwoman.* (See M.)
56. *Appearance of a bright spot changed.* (See M.)

At best, we find three traditions marginally related to issues taken up in Eleazar's traditions in M.-T., Nos. 20, 31, 46.[10] For all practical purposes, the relationship between the legal traditions in M.-T. and those in the midrashim is limited to the direct parallels of items appearing in both (9 items). For the remaining, only the attribution to Eleazar links the pericope to our master. Accordingly, we conclude that the authenticity of the attribution to Eleazar of all the new, legal pericopae in the Tannaitic Midrashim is dubious at best. These later traditions provide us with little information to add to the picture we have of Eleazar based on the traditions in M.-T.

b. *Babli and Yerushalmi*

Five legal rulings new to Eleazar's agendum are designated as Tannaitic in b. and y. One of these seems to comment on a completed M. pericope, reading into Eleazar's ruling a distinction which it does not make (63). Our list reviews the major issue of each ruling and discusses the relationship of the pericope to items in M.-T. Two items relate directly to issues attributed to Eleazar in M.-T. (5, 12). These then are the only traditions not classified as "poor."

Tannaitic pericopae in b. and y.

12. *b. Yeb. 86a-b. Tithe to Priest.* b. designates the dispute over whether tithes go to the priest or Levite between Eleazar and Aqiva as Tannaitic. y. attributes a similar dispute between Eleazar and Joshua to Abbahu. In both versions a debate follows the dispute. To conclude, a story is given which has Eleazar retract his opinion and return all the tithes he had taken. b. has a neater and fuller version of the story but omits one of y.'s crucial details--the return of tithes by Eleazar. Eleazar's ruling, and the dispute in toto, are not to be found in M.-T. But as we have shown, a distant echo of the issue is present in M. (See comment to 11.) Furthermore, Eleazar's concern for tithing is a major component of his early agendum.

33. *b. Qid. 17b. Furnishing a slave.* How much must be given a Hebrew slave upon his release? If the slave was productive, he is rewarded accordingly. Eleazar dismisses the phrase in Scripture, "You shall furnish him liberally" as a colloquialism in which Scripture had indulged. The legal issue and the exegetical principle appear nowhere else in the range of Eleazar's agendum.

39. *b. B.B. 13b. Attaching scrolls together.* Eleazar reportedly allowed scrolls of the prophets to be attached together. We have noted that Eleazar plays no active role in the pericope. He is used as an authority figure lending support to a ruling. The issue of the tradition is unrelated to other pericopae.

63. *y. Shab. 9:3. Definition of a period.* Eleazar is credited with the definition of a day or night as a period in determining the time that elapsed after intercourse. This seems hardly appropriate since the ruling attributed to Eleazar in M. to which this relates does not mention periods. It deals with days. The second half of this pericope spells out the

consequences of Eleazar's ruling in M. It can apply to a discharge which takes place anywhere from just over one day to just under two (see comment to 62).

5. *b. Ber. 15a. Audibility for the shema'.* (We have listed this pericope above with the Ushan sub-stratum of M.-T. since it is attested to Usha. Of course, it appears first in b. and thus must be considered here as well.) Eleazar rules that the recitation of the *shema'* must be audible, citing an appropriate proof text. The issue of the *shema'* liturgy is relevant to the earliest legal agendum associated with Eleazar.

The issues of tithing, the discharge of a woman, and the *shema'* relate to previous traditions in the earlier strata of the corpus. The two remaining pericopae do not. The following Tannaitic material also appears in b. and y.:

First appearing in M.-T.: b.: 3, 4, 11, 13, 30, 36, 38, 44, 48, 49, 50, 67, 68, 74, 93. y.: 4, 6, 10, 26, 30, 36, 74.

First appearing in Mekh.: 18, 20.

First appearing in Sifra: 21, 46, 95.

First appearing in Sifré Deut.: 31, 94, 95.

First appearing in Sifré Num.: 51.

We proceed to the Amoraic stratum. It adds five more new legal pericopae (two of which we consider along with the exegetical material as well). Two items report new issues. One relates back to a Tannaitic statement given in a *beraita*:

Legal Traditions in b. and y. not designated as Tannaitic

12. *Tithes to the priest.* As above (Tannaitic materials) and y. M.S. 5:5.

25. *b. M.Q. 24b. Funeral of an infant.* The issue is new on the agendum. Eleazar rules that if a child "is recognized" outside the house, a public funeral is conducted for him. No link can be found to connect this ruling to previous pericopae. M. Sem. has Judah

as the tradent of a similar tradition. The eulogy is reserved for a child that was old enough to venture forth from the house in public.

41. *b. Mak. 23a. The strap for lashes.* Sheshet is the tradent of the ruling that the strap be made from calfskin. The exegetical basis for the ruling derives from the proximity of two verses. M. Mak. 3:12 specifies a calfskin strap for lashes but gives no exegetical basis and no attribution for the ruling.

42. *b. Yeb. 4a. The levir afflicted with boils.* A *yebamah* may not be forced to marry the brother-in-law if he is so afflicted. Proximity of verses serves again as the hermeneutical principle used to "derive" the exegesis. The legal issue is new on the agendum.

43. *b. Shabuot 35b. The Divine names.* The word *'dny* must be considered holy as if it were a divine name. The issue is unique in the tradition. There is no exegesis *per se* in the pericope, merely a reference to the "name" in question.

The *gemarot* in sum contain three new traditions which may relate to items first appearing in M.-T. (5, 12, 63). The remaining traditions are not at all consistent with the picture of Eleazar's concerns developed in the earliest stratum of legal rulings.

c. *Later Compilations*

The later midrashim and other rabbinic compilations show almost no interest in legal rulings. Two items are listed below, the second relating to familiar material.

The later compilations

35. *M. Kallah 1:3. Kallah.* One should not drink from the hand of a bride. No relation can be discerned between this and previous legal or non-legal issues.

55. *ARN A 25. The shoelast.* Two previous traditions are conflated here. One attributed the issue of the uncleanness of the shoelast to Eleazar (54). The second

has Eleazar visit the sick Eliezer (93). ARN A combines the two traditions and thus assigns the ruling concerning the shoe and the list of five items, which may be immersed as they are, to Eliezer.

d. *Summary: The Later Legal Traditions*

Except for two *beraitot* in b., and three items in the midrashim, the new material examined above does not follow the outlines set out by the agendum of issues in M.-T. At best, the fresh traditions bear a tangential relationship to the legal corpus of M.-T. If the midrashim, for example, had been our only source of information about Eleazar's legal thought and agendum, we would have had a totally different picture of the man. The editors of b. and y., of course, have M. before them. Our *beraita* editors give us refined versions of many pericopae in M.-T. (as we have shown, see Chapter II). The new materials introduced in the *gemarot*, however, in the majority of cases, share no common roots with traditions first appearing in M.-T.

Thus the new legal materials in the later sources remain a problem. They are for the most part not spun out of or closely related to items in M.-T. Accordingly, we cannot argue that internal consistency of the legal tradition attests the authenticity of the attribution of these traditions to Eleazar. There is clearly little correlation and consistency between the agenda of issues in M.-T. and those of the midrashim, b. and y., and later compilations. This factor renders problematic the use of the latter group as data for filling in gaps in the reconstruction of the larger picture of Eleazar's legal thought.

NOTES

CHAPTER VII

[1]See Neusner, *HMLP*, Vol. III, Chapter 35, "The Weaving of the Law."

[2]I do not believe that a detailed comparison of the rulings of the several masters for which thorough analyses are available would be helpful at this point. Outlines of the issues of the traditions of Eliezer, the Houses, Ishmael, and Joshua are readily available. A catalogue would only reveal that, for example, Joshua and Eliezer deal at length with Heave-offering, Eleazar does not. Ishmael rules on Jewish-gentile relations and on *dema'i*, Eleazar does not. Eliezer deals with the issue of the *ʿeruv* at length, Eleazar does not. Eleazar deals with tithes in a significant percentage of traditions, Eliezer and Ishmael do not, and so on. The list could go on down to the last details of the traditions. We would learn little more than we already know now.

[3]Kanter, *op. cit.*, Conclusions.

[4]Neusner, *Eliezer*, Vol. I, based on my count of the traditions.

[5]Porten, *op. cit.*, Chapter 11.

[6]Data cited by Kanter, *op. cit.*

[7]The figures do not include Eleazar's percentages in arriving at the mean. If Gamaliel's traditions are ignored the deviations are a bit smaller: 1,1,4,0,1,3,4% respectively. Some preliminary figures for Aqiva's legal rulings in M. have been provided for me by Spencer Ackerman. He has found the distribution of the legal rulings to be as follows:

Agricultural laws	17%	(46)
Purity	29%	(81)
Liturgy	2%	(5)
Sabbath and festival	15%	(43)
Civil	12%	(32)
Family	7%	(19)
Temple, vows	17%	(48)
Other	1%	(4)
Total		(278)

Though these figures do not take Toseftan pericopae into account, there seems to be no marked deviation from the pattern of distribution which we observe in the traditions of other major Yavneans. The spread of Aqiva's rulings throughout M. is most remarkably close to Eliezer's.

[8]Many of the pericopae examined above do not assign a specific ruling on a given matter to Eleazar. They may report a story about his actions (1,4,11,15,17,38) or represent him as a commentator on a previous ruling or dispute (6,13,30). In such cases we may associate Eleazar with the issue of the pericope but cannot assign to him any role in the formulation of a ruling. Similarly, in the case of disputes, the presence of other Yavneans, ruling on the same issue along with Eleazar, obviates any attempt on our part to trace the inception of that issue to Eleazar (7,67,19,29,50,28,36,52,57,62). We, however, do consider the attitude of subsequent rulings to Eleazar's opinion expressed in a dispute or story, to determine his influence on the course of the law. In no case does Eleazar's ruling set the agendum for the contrary conception of a tractate. If one did we would consider that an important central ruling. See Neusner, *HMLP*, VIII, on Aqiva in Nega'im, pp. 197-200.

[9]The second major characteristic of the rulings is their interest in concrete or practical matters. Curiously, those few that address seemingly abstract, theoretical issues are found mainly in seder *Ṭohorot* (five of six: 56, 57,58,59,60. Nineteen deals with the Sabbath Limit.) Perhaps the nature of the issues in *Ṭohorot* calls for a more theoretical approach to the law.

[10]Moreover, the agendum of issues of the unrelated items does not fit the pattern of distribution established by the items in the M.-T. stratum, as the following chart shows. (The chart lists the number of pericopae appearing in each midrashic compilation in each of seven general legal categories and then gives the total percentage of the legal traditions in the midrashim for those categories.)

	Mekh. Ishmael	Mekh. Simeon	Sifré Deut.	Sifré Num.	Sifra	Total items	Total %
Sabbath	1				1	2	10%
Purity	1	1			2	4	20%
Liturgy			2			2	10%
Civil, Criminal	2	2				4	20%
Agricultural						0	0%
Family			2		1	3	15%
Temple, Vows		1		2	2	5	25%
TOTALS	4	4	4	2	6	20	100%

Though the chart shows a sizeable portion of the tradition is concerned with purity, no item deals with agricultural laws. Moreover, Temple laws and Family rules occupy a disproportionately high percentage of the corpus.

CHAPTER VIII

THE EXEGETICAL AND THEOLOGICAL TRADITIONS
THE STORIES

i. *The Exegetical and Theological Traditions: The Problem*

The exegetical and theological traditions attributed to Eleazar in the various compilations of rabbinic literature do not seem to stem from a collection of materials which may be traced back to a single group of tradents. The editor of each compilation appears to assign to Eleazar (or perhaps, selects) statements dealing with themes and concerns relating to his, the editor's, central thesis, *Tendenz*, or polemic. We cannot, however, prove this assertion until the study of each compilation (e.g., the books of the Tannaitic Midrashim) has been completed. Only then will we perhaps be able to show a close correspondence or divergence between themes of a compilation and those assigned to individual masters in that document.

At this point, however, we may show the consistency, or lack thereof, among the theological traditions assigned to Eleazar in the various compilations. Accordingly, we review all the non-legal items in the corpus. Most themes occur in only one tradition or compilation. A few quite general issues recur in several places. We thus suggest that the editor of one compilation knew little or nothing of traditions appearing in a second document.

This insight conforms to what we have shown in Chapter IV (pp. 211-37). A careful look at the listing of all the sources of the tradition as a whole reveals that thirty-one non-legal traditions appear first in either the Tannaitic Midrashim or in b. and y. Of course, sixteen appear in b. and y. but not in the midrashim, Nos. 77-92. Twelve are given in the midrashim but not in b. and y., Nos. 96-107. Only three appear both in a midrash and in b. or y., Nos. 93-95. Only two appear in two midrashic compilations, Nos. 95 and 107 (in both Sifré Deut. and Sifra). These figures imply that the traditions known in the midrashim were, by and large, unknown to (or, at least, not repeated by) editors of b. and y. and *vice-versa*. Only four items, 13% of the total, appear in more than one compilation. The figures for the legal traditions, however, are strikingly different. Of the fourteen items first appearing in b. and y. or in the Tannaitic Midrashim, 43% (6 items of 14) appear in two or more compilations. Five turn up in b. alone, three in the midrashim. We may draw no probative conclusion on the basis of the lack of parallels. However, the figures do suggest that the b., y., and midrash-editors drew legal materials from fully formulated tradental pericopae. The same cannot be said for the non-legal traditions.

Thus, in the present chapter we consider the themes of the theological pericopae in each compilation. In addition, we note the hermeneutical principle used in each exegetical item, where one is distinguishable. Throughout we return to the question, are the concerns and/or exegetical methods of Eleazar's traditions in one compilation in any way consistent with those found in others?

ii. *The Stories: The Problem*

Our problem in assessing the stories about Eleazar is much simpler. Our basic assumption is that M.-T. serves as a source for data integrated into later stories by Amoraic editors. Where no reference can be found in M.-T. that might have generated a later statement, we assume that statement is based on an independent tradition. We cannot say, however, how early or late that tradition is. Accordingly, it may go back to Tannaitic sources or it may have been imaginatively generated by a late editor. We now review first the exegetical and theological tradition. Then we turn to the stories and biographical materials. Each compilation is considered separately, M.-T., of course, first.

iii. *The Exegetical and Theological Traditions: The Data*

a. *Mishnah-Tosefta*

Nine exegetical and theological traditions attributed to Eleazar appear in M.-T.[1] Most of the pericopae are both exegetical and theological. Thus, as we said, we consider them together. Only two are legal traditions already listed above (30, 50). The remainder are aggadic, non-legal, and include wisdom sayings, theological statements and straightforward exegeses. We can trace no particular hermeneutical principle which runs through the tradition nor any encompassing aggadic theme. We list the traditions below. For each we summarize its issue and describe the exegetical method employed therein where it is unusual. We also note the theological principle which serves as the basis of the tradition.

47. M. Arak. 8:4, T. Arak. 4:23. *Dedication of property*. Eleazar says that God will not permit man to bequeath his entire estate to the Temple. The lesson of the pericope is: One should not needlessly squander his possessions for vain purposes. The saying is a wisdom aphorism.
48. T. Arak. 4:26. *Eating meat*. Eleazar's rulings here are based on appropriate verses. He says, (1) that one should eat meat only when one craves it. (2) A person may not eat meat until he has his own flock. (3) One may slaughter or sacrifice part, but not all of one's herd.
49. T. Arak. 4:27. *Daily diet*. The lemma continues the former pericope's concerns. It spells out the correlation to be expected between one's economic status and his daily diet.

The three preceding pericopae seem to constitute a small unit of wisdom sayings on proper conduct especially relevant at the time after the cessation of the cult and the destruction of the Temple.

75. T. Soṭ. 11:2-3. *Manna*. Eleazar presents a parable to interpret a verse. It is: A king wished wine mixed with warm water, but settled for cold since that was the only water available. So too, the Israelites settled for food since there was no manna available. The pericope relates in theme to the preceding items (47-49) whose concern is the sustenance and diet of man.

69. M. Yoma' 8:9. *Atonement*. Eleazar defines the effects of the Day of Atonement. All sins are not mechanically absolved. An apology between the parties must precede the atonement for sins between two parties. Then the Day of Atonement has an effect. The teaching is given an exegetical basis. The problem of sin and atonement was crucial in first and second century Palestine. The early Christians and several mystery religions presented one mode of atonement through personal mystical union with the divinity. Rabbinic myth provided another mode of redemption from sin, through remembrance of the cult. After the destruction of the Temple cultic center, the mechanics of the system for atonement had to be reformulated as we perhaps see in this pericope.

70. M. Ned. 3:11. *Circumcision*. Another important issue in the first and second centuries was circumcision. The Pauline letters, for example, illustrate a repeated interest in the matter. Eleazar's comment precedes a series of six others extolling the greatness of circumcision. He condemns the uncircumcised with an appropriate verse appended as proof. The statement reflects the kind of xenophobia associated with other Yavnean masters. Eleazar thus may share this particular popular xenophobic view. His legal agendum as a whole to this stage does not reflect such an attitude, though. In fact, there is no other reference to gentiles in his traditions in M.-T.

76. M. Abot. 3:17. *Wisdom.* Eleazar is associated with the ideas of Torah, wisdom, seemly behaviour, fear, knowledge, and understanding. The sayings attributed to him are balanced "wisdom sayings." A query as to which is greater, wisdom or deeds, follows. Deeds is judged superior through appropriate exegeses.

74. T. Soṭ. 7:9-10. *What new teaching*? The exegeses of *Qoheleth*, Chapter 12, provide propaganda for the study house and for the oral Torah. References are made to the role of children in Torah study, the growth of the tradition, the procedure for study, and the content of the legal literature.

40. M. Mak. 1:10. *The Sanhedrin.* Eleazar clearly glosses the anonymous ruling. He says, "A Sanhedrin that executes once in seven years is called destructive." He extends the description to a court which executes even once in 70 years. The tradition seems to be a clear statement opposing the death penalty. Though we have previously categorized this item as a legal issue, at present it seems more appropriate to the theological corpus of materials.

Summary: Our pericopae in M.-T. clearly show no sustained interest in either exegesis or theological issues (with the possible exception of 74, a long dialectical exegesis). We have several wisdom-sayings, a brief anti-gentile lemma, an oral-Torah-polemic, a statement on capital punishment, and a reference to atonement. There are few outstanding exegetical traits. One pericope uses a parable to explain a verse (75). One gives a sustained dialectical exegesis. The other exegeses are routine, giving verses as simple proof texts.

b. *The Tannaitic Midrashim*

The exegetical and theological traditions in the M.-T. stratum form only a small portion of that corpus of items, about 15%. In sharp contrast, but not surprisingly, the midrashim are comprised mainly of exegetical pericopae.

Of the thirty-nine items appearing in the midrashim, 26 have no parallels in M.-T. We have discussed all the exegetical traditions dealing with legal issues in the preceding chapter. They are: Nos. 18, 32, 20, 34, 37, 31, 51, 46. Only 21 given above is not.

The fourteen remaining items develop several theological themes. Atonement appears as an issue in M. as well as our present sources. Sin, merit, reproof, and punishment are new issues developed in the midrashim. These theological themes are not a prominent facet of the corpus of Eleazar's traditions elsewhere. We recall that the midrashim seem to impose their own formal traits on the traditions (see Chapter V). That is, we found that the forms familiar to us from M.-T., the dispute, gloss, story were absent in the traditions introduced in the midrashim. Those items were given in the standard attributive form common to the contexts of each. Curiously, the themes which the midrashim develop in traditions assigned to Eleazar seem closer to the concerns of the individual compilations than to those associated elsewhere with our master. As we said, the evidence at this point suggests that the redactors of the midrashim rather than the transmitters of the tradition relate these themes to Eleazar's name in the pericopae in the various compilations before us.

Below we list the exegetical and theological traditions in the midrashim. As above, we note the issue of each, any outstanding hermeneutical principle, and prominent interrelationships with other pericopae.

Mekhilta de R. Ishmael

96. Mekh. *Pisḥa*. 16. *The merit of Abraham.* The Exodus from Egypt and the miracle of the splitting of the Red Sea are associated with the merit of Abraham. The pericope provides an answer to the question "on what basis is the nation to be saved"? The merit of Abraham, Eleazar tells us, assisted the Israelites at the sea and will (implicitly) save the current

generation as well. The pericope is especially relevant to the generations following the destruction of the Temple.

70. *Uncircumcision.* (See M.)

74. *What new teaching?* (See M.)

Mekhilta de R. Simeon

97. *Great is labor.* No connection can be made between this and other Eleazar traditions.

Sifré Deuteronomy

93. Sifré Deut. 32. *Eliezer sick.* Eleazar clearly has no personal role in this pericope. He and three other rabbis visit the ailing Eliezer. Ṭarfon, Joshua, and Aqiva appear along with Eleazar in the "conditional-divorce" pericope where the elders reply to Eliezer's opinions after his death (30). We surmise that to be the source for the names included in this item.

94. Sifré Deut. 43. *The din of Rome.* A second list of masters is utilized here. The names which appear in M. M.S. 5:9 (the four rabbis travelling on a ship) appear together here as well. The content of the pericope is surely not personally relevant to Eleazar. He is just one of the three rabbis who serve as a foil for Aqiva, as above.

95. Sifré Deut. 1. *Reproof.* Ṭarfon and Eleazar appear together commenting on the issue of administering/receiving reproof.

106. Sifré Deut. 50. *Israelites feared beasts because of sin.* Eleazar suggests that the Israelites were not righteous since they feared wild beasts would multiply against them if the nations were speedily driven from the land. The decree making gradual and difficult the process of the conquest of Canaan was issued because of the sins of the people. This Deuteronomic interpretation of history would be appropriate for the

second century. The Jews had witnessed one destruction after another without relief first in 70, then in 115, and finally perhaps in 135 after the Bar Kokhba episode.

Sin and atonement do appear often as issues on the earlier agendum of Eleazar's traditions. (But see No. 69 on atonement.)

107. Sifré Deut. 252, 283. *Intention for merit*. A *qal veḥomer* is here applied to two different issues (and a third in Sifra). The Egyptians were rewarded even though they never intended to do good. They accepted the Israelites into their land; *qal veḥomer*: One who has good intentions from the start will be rewarded. If a poorman finds a lost coin, the former owner receives reward in spite of the unintentional nature of the act of charity. Sifra *Vayiqra*, par. 12:13, connects the lemma with the law of the forgotten sheave. The previous owner is blessed even though he performed a good deed without knowing it. The linkup of intention with sin and atonement seems to be a common theme in several traditions. Here the link is made between intention and merit. Below in Sifra (101) we shall see the connection between one's thoughts and sin. Atonement was alluded to also in M. (69) and sin, in the preceding pericope.

48. *Eating meat*. (See M.)

Sifré Numbers

102. Sifré Num. 103. *Recite a man's praise*. In a man's presence, one does not recite all of his praise. For support, Eleazar alludes to verses concerning Noah.

103. Sifré Num. 105, 138. *Moses made four requests*. Eleazar singles out the word *l'mr* as significant in four verses.

104. Sifré Num. 157. *Moses made three errors*. Because of his anger, Moses erred. In all three instances, Eleazar cites two verses.

105. Sifré Num. 140. *The attributes of mercy and punishment.* These attributes are attached to the specific case of the manslayer who has fled to the city of refuge. A major theme of Eleazar's traditions in the midrashim is sin and its punishment as we have shown. Merit also figures prominently in several traditions.

Sifra

98. Sifra *Šemini, pereq* 1:2. *Nadab and Abihu: Precedence in honor.* The tradition about the incident of the two errant sons of Aaron may be appropriately attributed to Eleazar. It is an excellent example of an incident involving the usurpation of legitimate rights of succession and the consequences of such an act. Moreover, the statement assigned to Eleazar that "all those who take precedence in inheritance take precedence in honor," implies that traditionally, leadership is hereditary. Our analysis of the pericope suggests a further analogy to the deposition incident might be made (see below, No. 77).

99. Sifra *Aḥare, par.* 1:2. *The sons of Aaron.* Concern with the consequences of hunger for power continues in this pericope.

100. Sifra *Aḥare, par.* 1:3. *Parable of the physician.* The lesson of the unsuccessful attempt to seize power is spelled out.

101. Sifra *Qedošim, pereq* 11:22. *Should not say, I do not wish to sin.* Man's inner consciousness regarding both intention to sin and to atone are consistent themes in the corpus of traditions. The issues of guilt and the right attitudes of man are powerful themes in the aftermath of the destruction of the Temple and subsequent hardships.

69. *Atonement.* (See M.)

95. *Reproof.* (See Sifré Deut.)

107. *Intention for merit.* (See Sifré Deut.)

To review the main theological themes in the midrashim:

Sifré Deut. has significant new theological themes. Reproof and punishment for the nation, two Deuteronomic themes, appear there for the first time. Intention is not seen as a necessity for reward. A man's merit automatically brings the rewards. Sifré Num. introduces the question of the proper procedure for praising a fellowman. Moses is the subject of two further pericopae. The attributes of Mercy and Punishment appear in an exegesis concerning the city of refuge. Sifra give us a third separate tradition about sin and intention. References to the succession of legitimate authority may be the hidden agendum of other exegeses about Nadab and Abihu, the sons of Aaron. After considering the traditions in b. and y., we shall return to the exegetical traits of this stratum as well.

c. *Babli and Yerushalmi*

There are few if any links between the exegetical and theological traditions in b. and y. and the items in either M.-T. or in the midrashim. The theological issues of the stratum are for the most part new: procreation, man's sustenance, man's bodily functions, the miracle at the sea, mocking the festivals. Only one familiar theme recurs--judgment of the world. The stratum gives us a good number of exegeses, as the list below shows. We have, though, for the first time, the repeated use of one hermeneutical principle. Eleazar derives teachings by referring to two verses in close proximity which seem ostensibly unrelated. As we have noted above, neither the midrashim nor the M.-T. traditions show any preference for any single hermeneutical tool. Lastly, we reiterate that there are no significant correlations between the theological and exegetical traditions of b. and y. and any of the legal material that precedes in the earlier strata or in the b. and y. stratum itself. These traditions seem entirely separate from what we have elsewhere. The list which follows details the conclusions we have outlined above. Again, for each entry we summarize the content, exegetical principle where relevant, correlation with other traditions, and problems of attribution.

Designated as Tannaitic:

85. b. M.Q. 28b. *Consoles Ishmael*. Four rabbis, Eleazar and Aqiva, Tarfon and Yosé the Galilean, console Ishmael after the death of his sons. Eleazar is just a name on a list.

88. b. Yeb. 63b. *Procreation*. Based on the proximity of two verses, Eleazar reasons that one who neglects the commandment of procreation diminishes God's image. B.R.'s version of the pericope assigns to Eleazar the same position. T., however, omits mention of his name. The exegetical principle used here will recur in the b. traditions.

92. b. San. 99a. *Days of the messiah*. Eliezer and Eleazar dispute the duration of the messianic age which Eleazar says will last 70 years. Each cites an appropriate verse. The idea of the messiah does not occur in the earlier strata of Eleazar's corpus. Eleazar also refers to the 70 year time period in No. 40, the Sanhedrin which executes.

Not designated Tannaitic:

80. b. Erub. 54b. *Exegesis of Proverbs*. Eleazar provides an Aramaic proverb to explain a biblical one.

81. b. Erub. 64b-65a. *Free the world from judgment*. Eleazar says he can deter fate by employing an appropriate excuse to account for the behavior of the Jews. The issue of judgment as central to the concerns of the nation after the destruction of the Temple. Eleazar's traditions in the midrashim show a Deuteronomic conception of divine justice. Sin brings down the judgment of the Lord. Only behavior for which man is not responsible, such as the actions of an intoxicated person, can be excused and thus avoid the acts of

divine judgment. The tradition clearly fits the pattern of Eleazar's conception of man's fate spelled out in earlier attested sources.

82. b. Pes. 117a. *Hallel*. The pericope is an artificial composite. Eleazar plays no distinctive role in it.

83. b. Pes. 118a. *Four exegeses*. All four exegeses are based on the proximity of two verses--a common hermeneutical principle in the b. stratum of the corpus. The issues of the exegeses are the splitting of the sea, the sustenance of man, man's bodily functions, mocking the festivals, idolatry, and speaking maliciously. Idolatry has appeared earlier as an issue in No. 51.

86. b. Ḥag. 14a. *God's throne*. Eleazar attacks Aqiva's exegesis, suggesting that he expound the laws of Negaim and Ohalot instead of Scripture. The verses have a mystical connotation. Eleazar interprets a verse in Daniel by making reference to one in Isaiah.

87. b. San. 67b. *Frog*. The form of the pericope is the same as the previous. Eleazar belittles Aqiva's exegesis and proposes his own.

90. y. Soṭ. 5:6. *Exegesis of Job*. Aqiva identifies Elihu with Balaam. Eleazar shows that Elihu was Isaac. The book of Job and the suffering of Israel were probably central themes in the post-destruction era.

Also consider: 3, 41, 42, 51, legal exegeses mentioned above.

d. *The Later Compilations*

Before turning to the exegetical traditions *per se* we review the later compilations. They contain mostly exegetical traditions. A few are related, in a general way, to preceding pericopae. There is, however, no apparent attempt to develop or continue the themes set out in the earlier strata.

Bereshit Rabbah

108. *The creation*, and not the Exodus, was God's greatest act in history.

109. *Three wonders* occurred on the day that Cain was born.

110. *Isaac's eyes were dim* so that he could not see the wicked Esau.

111. *Joseph's robe causes jealousy.* Joseph's actions later lead to the splitting of the sea for the Israelites. The latter exegesis makes use of a play on words, the only example of such an exegesis in the corpus of traditions. Splitting the sea is a common motif in the non-legal agendum of issues.

112. *The judgment of God* is compared to the judgment of Joseph *vis a vis* the brothers. Reproof and judgment are common themes of the traditions.

Abot de Rabbi Nathan A

113. *Moses broke the tablets* because God told him to do so.

Pesikta deRav Kahana

116. *Jerusalem will expand* to accommodate the ingathered exiles in the messianic era.

Tanḥuma

117. Messianic interpretation of Jacob's dream of the ladder.

118. Eleazar gives a parable to explain the holiness of the Song of Songs. See above, tradition 65. Eleazar's name is associated with a ruling about the canonicity of the Song of Songs.

Exodus Rabbah

119. *The ways of God* are not like the ways of man.

Numbers Rabbah

120. Before the Exodus from Egypt, Israel despoiled the Egyptians.

[*Midrash Mishlei*]

The master should serve the slave (ed. Buber, pp. 62-63).

[*Pesikta Rab. 23. Golem*]

In sum, we have seen that the exegetical and theological traditions bear little relation to the legal traditions. They could easily constitute a separate corpus of materials. We have differentiated among the compilations and strata of the traditions. The exegetical and theological interests of the midrashim vary but they in turn do not interrelate with the traditions in b. and y. b. has assigned to Eleazar both its own set of concerns and its own hermeneutical principle.

iv. *The Exegeses: Conclusions*

The exegeses attributed to Eleazar bear few prominent traits. Most serve as simple proof texts for his lemmas. No attempt is made in most items to portray his lemma in each as having been generated by the verses. That is to say, the verse is not an integral part of the pericope, but seems to be tacked on to the tradition. (Cf. 70, 76, 81, 85, 92, 96, 97, 98, 101, 102, 105, 107, 108, 111, 112, 113, 116, 117, 120.) In several other instances the teaching of the pericope seems to be derived from an exegesis of the text cited. A difficult verse or phrase, unusual or ambiguous syntax, or superfluous words render interpretation of the verse necessary (cf. 69, 86, 87, 90, 99, 103, 104, 106, 109, 110). There are single examples of several exegetical methods: 111 employs a play on words; 90 gives an etymology, 103 and 104 expound an extra word in several verses; 74, a lengthy pericope, uses dialectical exegetical style; 51 employs a proverb to explain a verse.

As we have said, b. consistently introduces the principle of referring to the proximity of two verses to derive a teaching (*semikhut*). b. gives seven examples which make use of that hermeneutical principle (cf. 41, 42, 83, 88). This is the only clearly distinctive trait of the exegetical corpus of traditions. As we saw, the remainder of the exegeses are routine. No single approach to Scripture can be discerned in the traditions attributed to Eleazar.

v. *The Stories: Data*

a. *Mishnah-Tosefta*

Biographical or incidental references to Eleazar, and historical stories or accounts are of little interest to M.-T. A few references which might be taken as biographical notes about our master are preserved in M.-T. In the chart which follows, we detail the biographical information supplied in the traditions. Where possible, we suggest links between various references. We also show that sources in earlier strata did generate developments in later compilations. The first chart below clearly shows that biographical data in M.-T. is, at best, sketchy, episodic, and often cryptic.

Incidental references to Eleazar and biographical materials: M.-T.

44. T. A.Z. 4:1. *Dealer in wine and oil.* This statement about Eleazar is reported as a support for the anonymous ruling that one may deal in wine and oil in Israel. It alleges Eleazar's involvement in commerce and perhaps implies that he was a man of wealth. Thus it may serve as the origin for all of the subsequent traditions describing Eleazar as a wealthy man.

53. T. Kel. B.B. 2:2. *The elders in the store of Eleazar.* The elders are alleged to have asked a question about the purity of an object while in the store of Eleazar b. Azariah. The rabbis mentioned are not associated with Eleazar in other traditions. Thus it is unlikely that they were his disciples. The reference to a 'store' recalls the previous tradition ascribing wine and oil dealership to Eleazar (44).

65-66. M. Yad. 3:5, M. Yad. 4:2. *On that day.* These two traditions are supposed to have been rendered on the day that "they seated Eleazar in the Academy." One rules on sacrifices that were slaughtered not for their own sake. The other alludes to the decision that Song of Songs and Ecclesiastes render the hands unclean. Neither of these issues figures in any way in the agendum of Eleazar's legal pericope in M.-T. Thus Eleazar had no role in the rulings. The "on that day" phrase serves merely as a formalized framework for the introduction of these rulings. M. Yad. 4:3 associates Eleazar with a third issue "on that day" in which he is directly involved as a disputant. b. and y. fill in their picture of the events of that day. On that day they allege Gamaliel was deposed as patriarch and Eleazar installed in his stead. This tradition in M., however, does not mention accession to the patriarchate. Indeed we have no way of determining what the reference to being seated in the academy actually means (see Goodblatt, p. 65).

71. M. Soṭ. 9:15. *Riches.* As we have mentioned, the tradition concerning Eleazar's riches may stem from other references in M.-T. (i.e., his dealing in wine and oil or his store). The first explicit mention of Eleazar as a symbol of wealth is in the latter part of M.-T. Soṭ. b. picks up the reference and expands the tradition. It makes Eleazar the "dream-symbol" for wealth and asserts that he had large herds of livestock (72, 73).

Also consider references in Nos.

1: "Behold I am as a seventy year old."
26: "expounded before the sages at *Kerem be Yavneh*."
74: "whose week was it"?
11: Rabbis on a ship
30: Rabbis answer Eliezer after his death.

b. *The Tannaitic Midrashim, Babli and Yerushalmi*

Biographical data are almost totally absent from the midrashim. Only incidental reference is made to Eleazar travelling (94, 21) or visiting the sick Eliezer (93)--all standard formulaic traditions. It is in the stratum of b. and y., to which we turn next, that we first find a sustained interest in biographical or historical stories. It seems likely, though, as we shall see, that the traditions are the work of Amoraic editors who have made use of the passing remarks in M.-T. and interpreted them historically. The themes first appearing in M.-T., such as Eleazar's riches and his early aging, are used creatively to develop the details of later accounts. Several new themes appear for the first time. The list below spells out the details of the Amoraic legends. For each item we list the relation, if any, to traditions or references in M.-T. We also specify the clearly new data first supplied by this stratum of materials.

72. b. Ber. 57b. *Eleazar in a dream.* The appearance of our master in a dream signifies wealth. Clearly this pericope is based on M. (71).

73. b. Shab. 54b. *12,000 calves.* Eleazar was the owner of a large herd. The pericope relates back to 71, 22, and 15 in M.

77. y. Ber. 4:1, b. Ber. 27b-28a. *The deposition.* The account is a classic piece of Amoraic "history." We focus our concern on the references to Eleazar in the narrative. The account of Eleazar's appointment to the patriarchate seems to be based mainly on shreds of literary evidence in M.-T., and only secondarily on a separate tradition. Knowledge of the deposition incident itself may be based on recollections of an important historical event.

    Eleazar's appointment to the academy is clearly referred to in Nos. 65 and 66. The story of his gray hair surely recalls his statement in No. 1. The tradition that he was tenth in descent from Ezra is a fact that cannot be derived from any extant source in M.-T. Accordingly, this tradition that he was of a distinguished priestly family is new datum, first reported in this stratum. Reference is made to the vineyard at Yavneh of No. 26. The last story of Aqiva's debate with Eleazar over hereditary authority recalls references to authority in previous strata. The argument is appropriate for the situation. Eleazar is told that just as the priesthood is based on a hereditary system, so too the patriarchate, by implication, can be occupied legitimately only by members of the appropriate family.

b. alone adds other data from elsewhere in Eleazar's tradition to the deposition account. He was rich (71). He shared the patriarchate after his submission to Gamaliel (explaining the "week" of 74).[2]

78. y. Pes. 6:1. *Eleazar relinquished the crown.* The pericope is our only source outside of the deposition narrative itself which alludes to the incident. Clearly Rabbi, the Patriarch, tradent of the pericope, might have a record or recollection of important events in the history of the Patriarchate. His allusion to a "conditional deposition" may explain why Eleazar is alleged by y. to have served as *ab bet din* after relinquishing his position back to Gamaliel.

The pericope itself provides a powerful, albeit simple, polemic for the institution of patriarch. Three central events are singled out in the mythic-history of the office: Saul's replacement by David; Eleazar's resignation; the Sons of Batyra's demurral to Hillel. The inclusion of a reference to the incident involving Eleazar suggests an event of tremendous impact, at least in the estimation of Rabbi, tradent of the pericope.

79. y. Yeb. 1:6, b. Yeb. 16a. *Tenth to Ezra.* Eleazar's priestly lineage is recalled.

84. y. Suk. 2:4. *The sukkah on a ship.* The *m'śh* has Eleazar ask Aqiva rhetorically where the *sukkah* is which he built on the bow of the ship. No mention of *sukkah* appears elsewhere in Eleazar's pericopae, though Aqiva and Eleazar appear together frequently. b.'s version of the item substitutes Gamaliel for Eleazar (see b. Suk. 23a).

89. y. Ket. 11:3. *Story about Yosé the Galilean's wife.* It appears that this tradition is a development of the pericopae attributing wealth to Eleazar. There is no *prima facie* reason to group Yosé and Eleazar together. In the earlier strata of the tradition they do not frequently coincide. It seems that Eleazar appears here because he was assumed to be wealthy and had several rulings on divorce and the divorce settlement. He thus fit the literary needs of the pericope.

91. b. Giṭ. 67a. *Eleazar: a spice peddler's basket.* Isi b. Judah gives a catalogue of the praise of the sages. ARN A expands on the praise: Eleazar was like a salesman's basket. Asked about any aspect of rabbinic law and lore, he could respond and fill the inquirer with good and blessing.

Conclusions: Several pericopae make use again of the standard formulaics and include Eleazar (84, 85, 91). The two strikingly new themes in the *gemarot* are the references to the deposition and to the priestly lineage of Eleazar. The redactor of the deposition story in b. includes all of the off-hand biographical remarks of M.-T. in the narrative. Accordingly, we see that the path of the development of the stories about Eleazar goes directly from M.-T. to b.-y.

c. *Later Compilations*

Later compilations have almost no interest in the Eleazar-stories. Two items, one questionably attributed to our master and the second a standard formulaic, may be cited as the sum and substance of this stratum's contribution to this side of the Eleazar-tradition.

Kallah Rabbati

114. We are told that Eleazar made a public proclamation but not informed of its content. (See T. Demai' 2:17.)
115. The standard four rabbis journey to visit a philosopher.

vi. *Summary*

The value of all the non-legal traditions for data about Eleazar, the historical figure, is minimal. Accordingly, we have not addressed the issue above. However, our data has proved useful in considering the process of the development of traditions about Eleazar. Among the theological traditions, for example, we have found some consistency of theme and subject matter. For the most part, though, the consistency is limited to general concerns and themes which recur frequently in rabbinic literature.

It is only in b. that we find Eleazar's exegetical traditions return to one hermeneutical principle several times. The remaining exegeses are routine. Nothing marks them as having been generated from one circle or group of tradents. Thus we have shown that, in the main, both the exegetical and theological traditions focus around not one, but several issues. Each compilation contains traditions attributed to Eleazar dealing with a different set of issues.

We have, on the other hand, shown remarkable consistency in the development of the stories. In our centerpiece, the deposition story, the editor draws heavily on references in M.-T., interpreting them to fit the purposes of the narrative. Other traditions in M.-T. clearly generate later legends in one form or another. New themes introduced in the stories such as the relationship between Eleazar and Gamaliel (and the Patriarchate), are not reflected in our earliest and best evident, M.-T.[3]

NOTES

CHAPTER VIII

[1]Several traditions which we considered in Chapter II are included here. They are on the borderline between legal and theological traditions. For the purposes of this chapter, they fall with the theological items.

[2]The opposition of parties in the pericope is interesting. Gamaliel is first opposed by Joshua. Eleazar replaces Gamaliel as patriarch, presumably as a willing cohort of Joshua. Aqiva serves as Gamaliel's messenger, sent to appease Eleazar, though the insertion of his name seems to be a gloss, not integral to the story. At least one other tradition gives us a picture of Joshua as a friend of Eleazar (74). Many instances find Aqiva and Eleazar at odds, thus accounting perhaps for the work of the glossator. Elsewhere, however, we do not find Gamaliel in dispute with Eleazar. If indeed the facts of this account (the deposition) are accurately represented, all references to discord between Eleazar and Gamaliel have been carefully avoided in M.-T. and other Tannaitic sources. It is more likely, however, that the event referred to in our deposition account never took place. It may be just the reconstruction of a rabbinic historian far removed from the times he describes. Gamaliel's specific concerns in M.-T. rarely coincide with Eleazar's:

(a) *Sabbath laws and Festival laws*: The ʿ*erub* for private dwellings; Sabbath limit for a town; shipboard travel (*); contact with gentiles; laundry before the Sabbath; Passover: Preparation of *maṣṣah*, burning the *ḥameṣ*, burning the *ḥameṣ* on the Sabbath, the elements of the Passover *seder*, studied laws of Passover after the *seder*; The *lulav* (*); New Year liturgy; agent of congregation for the prayers; prerogative to set calendar; (b) *Purity*: Ovens, utensils; water of purification and serpent; Levitical purity and immersion of himself; (c) *Liturgy*: *Seder* liturgy (*); *lulav* during Hallel; time for the *shema*ʿ (*); leader of service; blessings for foods; text for prayer; *tefillin* thrice daily; (d) *Civil law*: Definition of interest (*)-loan of seed grain; oath for debtor; (e) *Agriculture*: Tithing carob; designating tithes (*); giving *demai* to workers; forgotten sheaf (*); *Peah*; Syria; (f) *Family law*: Levirite marriage; rights of woman for inheritance; rules of evidence for determining marital status; (g) *Temple and vows*: Sacrifices, three rules; Nazirite vow of a minor; (h) *Miscellaneous*: Gentiles, Sadducees, Samaritans and proselytes; gentile bathhouse at Akko; gentile merchant's bench; Ammonite cannot become proselyte; Sadducee restricts ʿ*erub*.

[Those traditions marked with an asterisk are related to, or identical with, Eleazar's rulings.]

The points of contact between Gamaliel's and Eleazar's specific agenda are not many. No pattern emerges from the schedule of issues in either corpus that would call to mind a patriarchal agendum. For instance, there is no overwhelming interest in court procedure in either Gamaliel's or Eleazar's traditions. Nor is there an emphasis on decrees or public utterances in either corpus. Except perhaps for the interest in the setting of the calendar and in Jewish-non-Jewish relations, Gamaliel's materials contain little which might lead one to suspect that he was patriarch. It is most striking to note, as we said, that there is *no* hint whatsoever of any strife between Eleazar and Gamaliel. Nothing in our legal sources backs up the claim that Gamaliel was succeeded by Eleazar after the deposition of the former. The closest we come to a reference to the incident as we see are the two mentions of Eleazar being seated in the academy. Gamaliel, however, is not tied to those traditions in any way.

[3]The chart below schematizes the traditions as they have been presented in Chapters VII and VIII.

Stratum	*Law*	*Exegetical/ Theological*	*Stories*
M.-T.	Total: 42	Total: 8 Exegetical: 5 [Legal exegeses: 1 (Possibly also Nos. 26,30)]	Total: 5 References in legal pericopae: 3
Midrashim	Total: 20 New: 11	Total: 19 New: 15 [Legal: 8]	0
b. and y.	Total: 41 New (Tannaitic): 5 New (Amoriac): 5	Total: 13 New (Tannaitic): 3 New (Amoriac): 7	8 (including the lengthy deposition narrative)
Later compilations	New: 2	New: 11 exegeses	New: 2

CHAPTER IX

CONCLUSIONS

The conclusions we have reached reveal some aspects of the history of Judaism in four distinct eras. First, information about Eleazar b. Azariah, the historical personality, tells us something about rabbinic Judaism at Yavneh. Second, our theories about the transmission of the traditions draw some conclusions about tradental processes over the span of time between Yavneh and the redaction of Mishnah and Tosefta, from about 100 to 200 C.E. Third, the result of our study of the role of Eleazar's traditions in M.-T. reveals something of the nature of those compilations and the period of their redaction. Finally, from the items which appear in the midrashim, b. and y., and subsequent compilations, we learn about how and whether later rabbinic Judaism uses and develops the earlier legal and non-legal traditions.

i. *Biographical Data. Yavneh.*

We separate the data which may tell us something about the historical Eleazar b. Azariah into two general categories, the explicit biographical references and the legal rulings. We consider here only the earliest traditions, those attested by their appearance in M.-T. Few explicit references to Eleazar contain biographical information, as we have shown. In all cases the data supplied is a secondary concern of the pericope. Its primary interest usually is to give a legal ruling or story which teaches a law of proper conduct. Accordingly, information appears in four types of settings. It may be given in the protasis of an item which is then followed by a ruling in which Eleazar plays no role (53,65,66). In five instances biographical information in a protasis is followed by a ruling in Eleazar's name (1,26,74,11,30). The data are used in one instance to serve as a precedent to prove a legal point (44). Finally, one bit of datum appears in a long list of lemmas which detail the single prominent characteristic of a number of the sages (71). Of these few traditions most provide nothing of historical value both because of their cryptic nature (71) and because they serve in many instances as integral parts of the literary framework of the pericope (74,11,30), thus giving us no information distinctive to Eleazar.

The remaining biographical references tell us that wealth is attributed to Eleazar (44,53,71) as a merchant. In one pericope he is portrayed as standing outside the group of sages at Yavneh (26), but in two others we see that the event of his admission to the rabbinical academy served later as an important or pivotal reference point in rabbinic history (65,66). But no other traditions in M.-T., either legal or non-legal, reflect the biographical data or develop a theme in any way related to it. Nothing of value about Eleazar can therefore be learned from the direct historical references in M.-T.

Turning next to the agendum of legal rulings preserved in M.-T., we see that they closely follow the pattern of general areas of concern exhibited by the preserved traditions of other contemporary Pharisaic-rabbinic masters. Agricultural and purity laws are the two most common issues followed in descending order of frequency by Sabbath and festival law, family law, liturgical rules, Temple laws and rulings concerning vows, and finally, civil law. The agendum of issues defined by the range of rulings of the Houses and Eliezer is closely adhered to by Eleazar's materials. The specific issues, however, coincide in only a few instances. How do the individual lemmas of Eleazar relate to those of Houses and Eliezer? The rulings preserved in his name do not duplicate or consistently refine or develop the specific issues raised by either the Houses or Eliezer. They deal rather with new, albeit generally related issues. For instance while all the corpora deal with certain agricultural rulings, Eleazar's interests bear no relation to the specific rulings of the others. Accordingly, we may conclude only that Eleazar shared the general concerns of a Pharisee at Yavneh.

No single issue predominates in the preserved traditions. Though four rulings, for instance, deal with agricultural tithes, no definitive position *vis a vis* tithes emerges from these rulings, nor can we draw any conclusions about the historical activity of our master based on single legal rulings or sayings which may or may not have been enforced or reflect social and economic conditions of Eleazar's era. Moreover, no consistent approach to a legal philosophy, theological, or exegetical method is inherent in the best traditions, those in M.-T. They rest on diverse principles. Accordingly, we cannot reconstruct a biographical picture of Eleazar in any significant fashion. But this is not surprising since M.-T. itself shows little concern for history or biography of individual masters.

ii. *Transmission and Preservation of Traditions. Yavneh to Bet Shearim.*

When we turn to the question of the tradental and redactional processes which preserved and influenced Eleazar's traditions, we are on firmer ground. The forms of approximately 2/3 of the traditions in Mishnah do not follow the literary pattern of the chapter in which they appear. Those same items adhere most closely to the standard forms characteristically associated with traditions attributed to other Yavneans, the standard attributive form, the dispute, and the story. The remaining one third, which are most at variance in form from tight dispute-forms of Yavneh, show evidence of having been reworked by the redactor of their respective chapters.

A sizable segment of the materials was not tightly linked to Aqivan lemmas in the early stages of transmission. In several specific instances our literary analyses show that Eleazar's lemmas were appended to completed Aqivan units. Thus at least a portion of Eleazar's traditions were initially transmitted through separate channels before being taken over by post-Aqivan tradents or editors and combined with existing units of Aqivan tradition. Strikingly, in five instances which join Eleazar's lemma to an Aqivan dictum (7,36,50,56,62), the influence on them of the redactional style of their contexts is detectible in the pericopae. That is to say they closely adhere to the formal preferences of their respective chapters or tractates. Some of Eleazar's traditions circulated independently of Aqivan materials up until the redaction of his lemmas with appropriate corresponding rulings transmitted by Aqivan tradents, perhaps at the last stages of the redaction of M.

iii. *Eleazar's Rulings in M.-T.*

Mishnah is comprised of tightly redacted chapters and tractates. The editor has seen to it that each pericope contained therein serves a distinct purpose. From the perspective of the redactor, we can easily account for the appearance of a great number of our traditions in the literature though, Eleazar's rulings do not consistently serve as the generative basis for further law, as we have shown above in Chapter VII.[1]

How so? A ruling, legal story, or comment may serve one of at least three purposes in its context in the structure of M.-T. It may either generate further rulings, or directly present alternative opinions to the prevailing generative ruling or play another role in its context by introducing a related, though peripheral, issue. At most six items in Eleazar's corpus bear only a casual relationship to the development and spinning out of the law of their respective areas of concern.

To review, twelve traditions give generative rulings,[2] thirteen give alternative views.[3] Four are stories illustrative of central issues,[4] one of an alternative ruling.[5] One story reflects an unsettled disputed matter.[6] Two have Eleazar comment on Yavnean/Houses' dispute.[7] In one he repeats the Aqivan view.[8] In all instances it is clear that the redactor uses the pericope as a needed thread in the weaving of his larger fabric. Two others are ambiguous in nature.[9] Of the six remaining, two contain completely alternative conceptions of an area of law.[10] Four are surely appropriate to their respective contexts but are neither generative of further rulings nor alternative to other existing laws.[11] Clearly Eleazar's individual rulings and the pericopae in which he appears are integral to their literary and legal contexts in a number of different ways. That is, they fit the agenda of the chapters in which they appear. Eleazar, however, is not represented as a central authority in the formulation of the larger conceptions which underlie the law, nor do his traditions set the agenda of the law of M.-T. A thorough and systematic study of all the tractates in which the pericopae appear will provide more definitive explanations of the role of each item in its context. But even that will explain only what role the traditions serve in their final redactional contexts. We cannot ascertain the reasons for their preservation up to the time of the redaction of M.-T. on the basis of the present evidence. What we know of Eleazar thus is limited to the data that a few editors chose to preserve for the direct needs of their compilations. We have only brief glimpses of the whole tradition and the man. The thought and life of Eleazar remains as we said for the most part unknowable.

iv. *Eleazar in Later Rabbinic Judaism*

Several patterns in b. and y. illustrate the development of Eleazar's tradition from early to later sources. The forms of the pericopae first appearing in b. closely resemble those in M.-T., both in their nature and distribution. The legal issues in the traditions in b. relate in several instances to those appearing in Eleazar's materials in M.-T. Most striking is b.'s tendency to develop and give some interpretation of the scant biographical data present in M.-T. Last, only b. evinces there any consistency in the type of exegetical material which it attributes to our master.[12]

By contrast, the midrashim assign to Eleazar new laws which are completely unrelated to his agendum in M.-T. The forms of the traditions in the midrashim likewise vary markedly from the pattern established in M.-T. The exegeses seem random and relate neither to those few in M.-T. nor to those in b., y., and other compilations. The midrashim omit all stories and develop no biographical data. The later compilations make no attempt to adhere to the forms or content of the legal and non-legal traditions in other sources. Only b. makes a clear, systematic effort to develop upon other traditions relating to Eleazar. Other Yavnean masters such as Aqiva, Eliezer, and Yohanan b. Zakkai captured the imagination of later rabbinic Judaism. Stories about them were developed, refined, and preserved, and generated traditions in later compilations. The same is not true for Eleazar b. Azariah. His tradition survived, preserved as part of the larger literature. But it never took on a life of its own. In the eyes of later rabbinism, Eleazar remained an interesting but minor figure.

v. *Conclusion*

Joshua, a contemporary of Eleazar, describes him as the father of his generation. "The generation in whose midst is R. Eleazar b. Azariah is not an orphan," he said (T. Soṭ. 7:10). Eleazar's corpus does not reflect this assessment. A more apt description of the tradition and perhaps the man behind it is given in the name of Judah the Patriarch. "R. Eleazar b. Azariah he called a spice peddler's basket (ARN A 18)." The traditions concerning Eleazar in rabbinic literature form an interesting but diverse set of materials. They comprise a "sample case" of disparate phenomena rather than a legacy representing a powerful and influential leader of the generation of Yavneh.[13]

NOTES

CHAPTER IX

[1]We limit our discussion to the forty legal rulings considered in Chapter VII. We exclude therefore Nos. 40, 44, 47, 48, 49, 53, 65, 66--items we initially considered legal. For the purposes of the present discussion, they are best seen as primarily theological or biographical traditions in the Eleazar-corpus.

[2]Nos. 2, 22, 23, 28, 52, 54, 58, 59, 60, 61, 62, 68.

[3]Nos. 7, 9, 10, 14, 22, 24, 30, 36, 38, 45, 60, 64, 67.

[4]Nos. 1, 3, 4, 11.

[5]No. 15.

[6]No. 19.

[7]Nos. 6, 13.

[8]No. 50.

[9]Nos. 17, 29.

[10]Nos. 56, 57.

[11]Nos. 6, 16, 26 (which may be an alternative to T.), 27.

[12]Inconsistency may be a positive factor in judging the relative worth of the traditions in, for example, the midrashim. For when there is no apparent reason for associating an issue or lemma with Eleazar, it may be that the origin of the attribution goes back to Eleazar or his circle. To be sure, Eleazar's name may have been arbitrarily attached to the teachings at a later date.

[13]Jack Lightstone raises an interesting question at the conclusion of his analysis of Yosé the Galilean's traditions in M.-T. The same issue applies to our results. I cite several paragraphs from the concluding section of *Traditions of Yosé the Galilean in Mishnah-Tosefta*, Missoula, 1977:

> Given our results, one might ask, Why should anything at all of Yose's tradition have been preserved in Mishnah-Tosefta? But this question moves beyond the capabilities of the data and methods of such a study as this. We have been able to lay

bare traits and a general history of the transmission of a sample body of Rabbinic data. The query, however, presupposes knowledge of the characteristics and development of Mishnah-Tosefta itself. We must know in detail what types of materials are likely to be found in these highly complex compilations. We have need of specific notions regarding the diverse redactional and tradental circles through which materials in Mishnah-Tosefta reached penultimate and ultimate redactors. What theory of historical interaction among these groups suffices to explain the preservation of all data in Mishnah-Tosefta? Were all circles operating with similar criteria of what should be transmitted? There are, admittedly, rather general questions. But it is difficult to be more specific about what information we should require to solve our enigma. More detailed queries presuppose more detailed knowledge than is as yet available to us.

The larger literary and historical issues regarding Mishnah-Tosefta cannot be solved by the study of materials about one or any number of named masters. Studies like our own may, as we have seen, inform us about the nature and history of individual corpora of data. But they will not tell us how Mishnah came to be, and they do not deal with the vast amount of anonymous traditions in the documents. Analyses taking Mishnah's own divisions, the tractates, as their point of departure must complement works such as this volume. Our highly selective batch of data has been pushed to its limit; it has yielded interesting and unequivocal results. But our findings also invite inquiries beyond the potential of our analysis of the traditions about Yose.

BIBLIOGRAPHY

MANUSCRIPTS AND SCHOLARLY EDITIONS OF TEXTS

Babylonian Talmud: Codex Florence. Introduction by David Rosenthal. Jerusalem, 1972.

Babylonian Talmud: Codex Munich. Jerusalem, 1971.

Manuscripts of the Babylonian Talmud from the Collection of the Vatican Library. Jerusalem, 1972.

Mishnah Codex Parma deRossi 138. Jerusalem, 1970.

Mishnah 'Im Perush HaRambam, Defus Rishon: Napoli. Introduction by A. M. Haberman. Jerusalem, 1970.

The Palestinian Talmud: Leiden M.S. Cod. Scal. 3: A Facsimile of the original manuscript. Introduction by Saul Lieberman. Jerusalem, 1970.

Talmud Babli. Defus Rishon: Venezia 5280. Jerusalem, 1968.

Talmud Yerushalmi According to the Venice Text.

Talmud Yerushalmi: Codex Vatican: Vet. Ebr. 133. Introduction by Saul Lieberman. Jerusalem, 1971.

Beer, Georg (ed.). *Faksimile-Ausgabe des Mischna Codex Kaufman A50.* Jerusalem, 1968.

Epstein, Jacob N. and Melamed, E. Z. (eds.). *Mekhilta d'Rabbi Sime'on b. Yoḥai.* Jerusalem, 1956.

Finkelstein, Louis (ed.). *Sifra or Torat Kohanim According to Codex Assemani.* New York, 1956.

________. *Siphré ad Deteronomium.* New York, 1969.

Higger, Michael. *Masekhtot Ze'irot.* New York, 1929.

________. *Masekhtot Derekh Ereṣ.* New York, 1935.

________. *Masekhtot Kallah.* Jerusalem, 1970.

________. *Masekhet Semaḥot.* New York, 1931.

________. *Masekhet Soferim.* New York, 1937.

Horovitz, H. S. (ed.). *Siphré D'bé Rab.* Jerusalem, 1966.

________ and Rabin, I. A. (eds.). *Mekhilta d'Rabbi Ishmael.* Jerusalem, 1960.

Lieberman, Saul (ed.). *The Tosefta: Mo'ed.* New York, 1962.

________. *The Tosefta: Nashim.* New York, 1967.

________. *The Tosefta: Zera'im.* New York, 1955.

Lowe, W. H. (ed.). *The Mishnah on which the Palestinian Talmud Rests.* Jerusalem, 1966.

Margulies, Mordecai (ed.). *Midrash Wayyikra Rabbah.* Jerusalem, 1966.

Schechter, Solomon. *Aboth de Rabbi Nathan.* Reprinted New York, 1945.

Theodor, J. and Albeck, Hanok (eds.). *Midrash Bereshit Rabbah.* Jerusalem, 1965.

Weiss, Isaac H. (ed.). *Torat Kohanim.* New York, 1946.

Zuckermandel, M. S. (ed.). *Tosephta.* Jerusalem, 1963.

TRANSLATIONS, COMMENTARIES, AND SECONDARY WORKS

Allon, Gedalyahu. *Meḥqarim beToledot Yisrael.* Tel Aviv, 1957.

Albeck, Hanok. *Shishah Sidré Mishnah: Seder Mo'ed.* Jerusalem, 1952.

________. *Shishah Sidré Mishnah: Seder Nashim.* Jerusalem, 1959.

________. *Shishah Sidré Mishnah: Seder Neziqin.* Jerusalem, 1953.

________. *Shishah Sidré Mishnah: Seder Qodoshim.* Jerusalem, 1958.

________. *Shishah Sidré Mishnah: Seder Ṭohorot.* Jerusalem, 1959.

________. *Shishah Sidré Mishnah: Seder Zera'im.* Jerusalem, 1957.

Bacher, Wilhelm, *'Aggadot HaTannaim.* Trans. to Hebrew by A. Z. Rabbinowitz. Jaffa, 1920.

Braude, William G. (trans.). *Pesikta Rabbati: Discourses for Feasts, Fasts and Special Sabbaths.* New Haven, 1968.

Danby, Herbert O. (trans.). *The Mishnah.* Oxford, 1933.

Epstein, Jacob N. *Introduction to Amoraic Literature.* Hebrew. Jerusalem, 1962.

________. *Introduction to Tannaitic Literature.* Hebrew. Jerusalem, 1957.

________. *Introduction to the Text of the Mishnah.* Hebrew. Jerusalem, 1964.

Feliks, Yehoshua. *Agriculture in Palestine in the Period of the Mishnah and the Talmud.* Hebrew. Jerusalem, 1963.

Goldenberg, Robert. "The Deposition of Rabban Gamaliel II: An Examination of the Sources." *Journal of Jewish Studies*, Vol. 23, no. 2, 1972, pp. 167-90.

Goodblatt, David M. *Rabbinic Instruction in Sassanian Babylonia.* Leiden, 1975.

Gorelik, Morris. *Legal Traditions of Eleazar b. Azaryah.* Ph.D. dissertation. Brandeis University, 1973.

Green, William Scott. *The Legal Traditions of Joshua ben Hananiah in Mishnah-Tosefta and Related Materials.* Ph.D. dissertation, Brown University, 1974.

Halevi, Y. I. *Dorot Harishonim.* Trans. to Hebrew from German, ed. Berlin-Vienna, 1923.

Halivni, David. *Meqorot UMesorot.* Tel Aviv, 1968.

Jastrow, Marcus. *A Dictionary of the Targumin, the Talmud Babli and Yerushalmi and Midrashic Literature.* New York, 1971.

Josephus (complete works). Vols. i-iv, ed. by H. St. John Thackeray. Vol. v, ed. by H. St. J. Thackeray and R. Marcus. Vols. vi-vii, ed. by R. Marcus. Vol. viii, ed. by R. Marcus and Allen Wikgren. Vol. ix, ed. by L. H. Feldman. Cambridge, Mass., 1926-1965.

Kanter, Shammai. *Legal Traditions of Gamaliel II.* Ph.D. dissertation. Brown University, 1974.

Lauterbach, J. Z. (trans.). *Mekhilta de Rabbi Ishmael.* Philadelphia, 1933.

Levi, Jacob. *Wörterbuch über die Talmudim und Midraschim.* Darmstadt, 1963.

Lieberman, Saul. *Tosefta Ki-fshutah: A Comprehensive Commentary on the Tosefta.* Parts i-vii. Hebrew. New York, 1955-67.

Lieberman, Saul. *Tosefeth Rishonim: A Commentary*. Hebrew. Jerusalem, 1937-1939.

Löew, I. *Die Flora der Juden* I-IV. Vienna, 1924-1934.

Mendelsohn, S. "Eleazar b. Azariah." *The Jewish Encyclopedia*. I. Singer, ed. New York, 1970, Vol. 5, pp. 97-98.

Neusner, Jacob. *Development of a Legend*. Leiden, 1970.

________. *Eliezer b. Hyrcanus: The Tradition and the Man*. Leiden, 1973.

________. *A History of the Jews in Babylonia*. Leiden, 1965-1970.

________. *A History of the Mishnaic Law of Purities*. Leiden, 1974-1977.

________. *The Idea of Purity in Ancient Judaism*. Leiden, 1973.

________. *The Rabbinic Traditions About the Pharisees Before 70*. Leiden, 1971.

Porton, G. G. *Legal Traditions of Rabbi Ishmael: A Form-Critical and Literary-Critical Approach*. Ph.D. Dissertation. Brown University, 1973.

Philo (complete works). Vols. i-v, ed. F. H. Colson and G. H. Whitaker. Vols. vi-x, ed. F. H. Colson. Cambridge, Mass., 1929-1962.

Rabbinovicz, R. *Variae Lectiones in Mischnam et in Talmud Babylonicum*. Hebrew. New York, n.d.

Ratner, B. *Sefer Ahavat Ṣiyyon VeYerushalayim*. Vilna, 1901-1917.

Safrai, S. "Eleazar b. Azariah." *Encyclopedia Judaica*, Cecil Roth and Geoffrey Wigoder, eds. Jerusalem, 1971, Vol. vi, pp. 586-588.

Schürer, Emil. *A History of the Jewish People in the Age of Jesus Christ*. Rev. and ed. by G. Vermes and F. Millar. Edinburgh, 1973.

Schwab, M. (trans.). *Le Talmud de Jérusalem*. Paris, 1932-1933.

Smith, Morton. *Tannaitic Parallels to the Gospels*. Rep. Philadelphia, 1968.

Strack, Herman L. *Introduction to the Talmud and Midrash*. Rep. New York, 1959.

Urbach, E. E. *The Sages: Their Concepts and Beliefs.* Trans. from the Hebrew. Jerusalem, 1975.

Weiss, I. H. *Dor Dor VeDorshav.* Jerusalem, n.d.

Wright, G. E. and Freedman, D. N. (eds.). *The Biblical Archaeologist Reader.* New York, 1961.

INDEXES

I. Bible

II. Mishnah

III. Tosefta

IV. Mekhilta De R. Ishmael

IX. Babli

X. Other Compilations

XI. Names of Rabbis

This index contains only the names of rabbis. For abstract terms and concepts the reader should consult the analytical Table of Contents. The charts and lists in Chapters IV, VII, and VIII provide keys to the issue of each pericope.